D1566128

This study explores the egalitarian policies pursued in the provinces during the radical phase of the French Revolution, but moves away from the habit of looking at such issues in terms of the Terror alone. It challenges revisionist readings of Jacobinism that dwell on its totalitarian potential or portray it as dangerously utopian.

The mainstream Jacobin agenda held out the promise of 'fair shares' and equal opportunities for all in a private-ownership market economy. It sought to achieve social justice without jeopardising human rights and tended thus to complement, rather than undermine, the liberal, individualist programme of the Revolution. The book stresses the relevance of the 'Enlightenment legacy', the close affinities between Girondins and Montagnards, the key role played by many lesser-known figures and the moral ascendancy of Robespierre. It reassesses the basic social and economic issues at stake in the Revolution, which cannot be adequately understood solely in terms of political discourse.

Past and Present Publications

Fair shares for all

Past and Present Publications

General Editor: JOANNA INNES, *Somerville College, Oxford*

Past and Present Publications comprise books similar in character to the articles in the journal *Past and Present*. Whether the volumes in the series are collections of essays – some previously published, others new studies – or monographs, they encompass a wide variety of scholarly and original works primarily concerned with social, economic and cultural changes, and their causes and consequences. They will appeal to both specialists and non-specialists and will endeavour to communicate the results of historical and allied research in readable and lively form.

For a list of titles in Past and Present Publications, see end of book.

Fair shares for all

Jacobin egalitarianism in practice

JEAN-PIERRE GROSS

CAMBRIDGE
UNIVERSITY PRESS

Published by the Press Syndicate of the University of Cambridge
The Pitt Building, Trumpington Street, Cambridge CB2 1RP
40 West 20th Street, New York, NY 10011-4211, USA
10 Stamford Road, Oakleigh, Melbourne 3166, Australia

First published 1997

Printed in Great Britain at the University Press, Cambridge

A catalogue record for this book is available from the British Library

Library of Congress cataloguing in publication data
Gross, Jean-Pierre.
Fair shares for all: Jacobin egalitarianism in practice / Jean-Pierre Gross.
      p.   cm. – (Past and present publications)
Includes bibliographical references and index.
ISBN 0 521 56318 6 (hardcover)
1. Income distribution – France – History – 18th century.
2. Equality – France – History – 18th century.
3. France – Economic conditions – 18th century.
4. France – History – Revolution, 1789–1799.
I. Title.   II. Series.
HC280.I5G76   1996
339.2'0944'09033 – dc20   96–13021   CIP

ISBN 0 521 56318 6 hardback

CE

In memory of Marcel Reinhard

Contents

Tables

Acknowledgements

I wish to record my debt to Michel Vovelle for his advice and encouragement during the early stages of this research project, to Claude Mazauric for sharing with me his thoughts on graduated taxation and sustained economic growth, to Marcel Dorigny for his insights on the close affinities between Girondin and Montagnard economic thinking, and especially to Florence Gauthier for patiently reading through the original version of my manuscript. Her unstinting support and sound critical judgement over several years are in no small way responsible for this project finally coming to fruition. I am also very grateful to Ruth Harris for her invaluable suggestions on the text before the final version went to print.

My thanks are due to the Société des Etudes Robespierristes and to Jean-Paul Bertaud in his capacity as chairman of the editorial board of the *Annales historiques de la Révolution française* in whose pages much of my research work has previously appeared; and to Jean Valette, the curator of the Aquitaine Archives and director of the Archives of the Gironde, who as organiser of the annual colloquium on the history of social security first enabled me to float some of my ideas on Jacobin social welfare. Last but not least, I wish to express my deep gratitude to Joanna Innes for allowing me to reproduce part of my article on 'Progressive Taxation and Social Justice in Eighteenth-Century France', published in the August 1993 issue of *Past and Present*, and who as general editor of Past and Present Publications kindly agreed to sponsor the present volume.

The revolutionary calendar

CONCORDANCE FOR THE YEAR II (1793–1794)

Vendémiaire:	1 = 22 September 1793	10 = 1 October 1793	20 = 11 October 1793
Brumaire:	1 = 22 October 1793	10 = 31 October 1793	20 = 10 November 1793
Frimaire:	1 = 21 November 1793	10 = 30 November 1793	20 = 10 December 1793
Nivôse:	1 = 21 December 1793	10 = 30 December 1793	20 = 9 January 1794
Pluviôse:	1 = 20 January 1794	10 = 29 January 1794	20 = 8 February 1794
Ventôse:	1 = 19 February 1794	10 = 28 February 1794	20 = 10 March 1794
Germinal:	1 = 21 March 1794	10 = 30 March 1794	20 = 9 April 1794
Floréal:	1 = 20 April 1794	10 = 29 April 1794	20 = 9 May 1794
Prairial:	1 = 20 May 1794	10 = 29 May 1794	20 = 8 June 1794
Messidor:	1 = 19 June 1794	10 = 28 June 1794	20 = 8 July 1794
Thermidor:	1 = 19 July 1794	10 = 28 July 1794	20 = 7 August 1794
Fructidor:	1 = 18 August 1794	10 = 27 August 1794	20 = 6 September 1794
Complementary days:		1 = 17 September 1794	5 = 21 September 1794

Abbreviations

Annales ESC [Annales HSS]	*Annales: Economies, Sociétés, Civilisations [Annales: Histoire, Sciences Sociales]*
Annales hist. Révol. fr.	*Annales historiques de la Révolution française*
Annales révol.	*Annales révolutionnaires*
Arch. dép.	Archives départementales
Arch. Guerre	Archives du Service historique de l'Armée
Arch. mun.	Archives municipales
Arch. Nat.	Archives Nationales
Arch. parl.	*Archives parlementaires des Chambres françaises*
Aulard, *Jacobins*	F. A. Aulard, ed., *La Société des Jacobins: recueil de documents pour l'histoire du club des Jacobins de Paris*
Aulard, *Recueil*	F. A. Aulard, *et al.*, eds., *Recueil des actes du Comité de salut public*
Bibl. Nat.	Bibliothèque Nationale de France
La Révol. fr.	*La Révolution française*
Revue d'hist. mod. et cont.	*Revue d'histoire moderne et contemporaine*
Revue hist. Révol. fr.	*Revue historique de la Révolution française*

Introduction

> If we try to establish exactly what the greatest good for all consists in, which must be the true end of any system of legislation, we find it comes down to these two main objects: *liberty* and *equality*.
>
> Rousseau, *Du contrat social*, 1762[1]

The social and economic history of the French Revolution has been receiving a poor press in recent years and it may appear foolhardy to propose a new interpretation of Jacobin egalitarianism at a time when it has come under fire as extremist, dangerously utopian and inherently violent. Yet the central question at issue has been left unanswered by historians for whom intolerance and terror appear integral to the entire revolutionary project. How, in practice as well as in the legislative texts, were the egalitarian principles proclaimed by the Jacobins put into effect? What, in the context of a Revolution dedicated to liberalism and to individualism, could be achieved by democrats whose prime purpose was not to impose equality, but to reduce inequality?

While the language of redistribution has several registers, some quite threatening, the prevailing one is altogether less strident and seems to indicate that the various tendencies at play in mainstream Jacobinism favoured the emergence of a broad-based consensus where matters of fundamental principle were involved. Commitment to social justice did not necessarily entail adherence to a single rigid ideology, or imply a willingness to resort to force. It grew out of the liberal critique of aristocracy, privilege and wealth heard in

[1] J.-J. Rousseau, 'Du contrat social', book II, chapter 11 ('Des divers systèmes de législation'), *Œuvres complètes*, ed. by J. Fabre and M. Launay, 3 vols. (Paris, 1967–71), vol. II, p. 538.

the early days of the Revolution and voiced in many of the *cahiers de doléance*, the widely felt sense of grievance at the enduring nature of economic inequalities, reinforced by a shared awareness of what was legitimate or illegitimate, right or wrong in the pattern of social relations. Respect for the material needs of others was bound up with perceptions of the common good. A set of moral assumptions inherited from the past helped fashion this deep-seated notion of natural justice, justice as fairness in the Rawlsian sense,[2] dedicated to the welfare of society as a whole, but implying a vision of honourable decency and equal opportunities for all its members: fair shares, rather than equal shares, for all.

If this reading is correct, the Jacobin egalitarian agenda has much to tell us about the Revolution and deserves critical analysis. By choosing to focus on the policies pursued away from the centre, in the depths of the French provinces, I have sought to achieve two things: firstly, to move away from the ingrained habit of discussing such issues in terms of the Terror alone; and secondly, to use the opportunity this distance affords to take into account not just the theoretical discourse of the Revolution, but also the practical measures which gave it substance, the words *and* the deeds. One of the virtues of examining Jacobinism in the field is that the researcher does not feel obliged at the outset to question the politics of men whose bold claims to radical reform may at times sound hollow or even appear, to some sceptical observers, as little more than empty posturing. As Alan Forrest points out in a recent work, if the language of the Revolution is unfailingly political, much of the action of the revolutionary assemblies was aimed at ending social wrongs.[3] That serious attempts were made to carry this action through at the local level is apparent from archival sources, which are very rich in this regard and provide a sound empirical base from which to mount a balanced assessment.[4] Moreover, the fact that the policies implemented seldom produced spectacular or

---

[2] See John Rawls's 'two principles of justice': in short, that each person has an equal right to liberty and that inequalities must work out for everyone's advantage: J. Rawls, 'Justice as Fairness', *Philosophical Review* 67 (April 1958), pp. 164–94, and further expanded in *A Theory of Justice* (Oxford, 1972), p. 60, and *Political Liberalism* (New York, 1993), pp. 6–7.

[3] A. Forrest, *The French Revolution* (Oxford, 1995), p. 10.

[4] On the desirability of maintaining the empiricist foundations to historiography, see G. Noiriel, 'Foucault and History: The Lessons of a Disillusion' (review article), *Journal of Modern History* 66 (September 1994), p. 567.

substantial results, or that such as there were proved ephemeral, should not detract from the need for an objective review of their content.

No historian of political discourse would deny the existence of a strong egalitarian component to revolutionary ideology, nor fail to recognise in the promise of civic equality the implicit prospect of greater economic equality. The evils of oppression and subjugation, and the resulting extremes of wealth and poverty, were subjects which engaged the minds of Montesquieu, Rousseau and Mably, and remained an important consideration in the awakening of the revolutionary conscience during the second half of the eighteenth century. Mably, for example, indulged in day-dreaming about a golden age of social equality which depended upon the community of goods, but concluded that it was an unrealisable ideal in a society irreversibly marked by property, commerce and luxury, an ideal against which, in the words of Keith Baker, 'the achievement of liberty would not be mortgaged'.[5] Hence Mably's dream did not induce him to propose a radical programme for social transformation. The logic of this pragmatic conclusion was not lost on the Jacobins, faced as they were with the practical problems of policy-making and policy implementation. But this is not to say that Mably's utopian vision did not stir their consciences or have a profound impact on their project. Conversely, recognition of the undoubted influence of Mably's visionary thinking on revolutionary egalitarianism does not oblige us to adopt a linear interpretation of the history of doctrines, such as that put forward by J. L. Talmon in the early 1950s, seeking to show that Mably's idea of egalitarian happiness directly inspired Jacobin attempts to enthrone virtue and thus accounts for the perceived drift of the French Revolution into totalitarianism.[6]

The tendency during the Jacobin phase of the Revolution to move away from an overriding interest in the abolition of privilege and the achievement of equal rights, as in 1789, to a deeper concern with issues of ownership and the reduction of real inequalities, in keeping with the intellectual legacy handed down by the Enlightenment, is clearly reflected in the legislation of the years 1793 and

[5] K. M. Baker, *Inventing the French Revolution: Essays on French Political Culture in the Eighteenth Century* (Cambridge, 1990), p. 104.
[6] J. L. Talmon, *The Origins of Totalitarian Democracy* (London, 1952), pp. 52–65; Baker, *Inventing the French Revolution*, p. 19.

1794. It is evident that this development occurred in parallel with a
gradual radicalisation of the Revolution and with the emergence of
a radical theory of revolutionary violence, that it coincided with the
apparent drive to fashion a 'new man' and forge a 'new society'
based on a single and indivisible republican identity.[7] To acknowledge these various trends together with their ideological ante-
cedents, however, is not to endorse the view, inherited from
Talmon, that they were one and the same, or that the reactions and
interactions which they bred made the Terror inevitable, and that
consequently efforts to achieve greater equality were tantamount to
'regenerating' society from above, by checking people's arbitrary
selfish urges and attempting to make them equal and identical by
constraint.[8]

No doubt the earliest acts of economic levelling in which
François Furet identifies a 'frumentarious' version of the 'terrorist
idea' at work[9] are ominous indeed. Thus, the spectre of forcible
redistribution is already perceptible in July 1789, when the heads of
Foullon and Bertier de Sauvigny, the 'starvers of the people', were
carried around Paris impaled on pikes; or in Marat's call on the
famished to throttle the well-fed and 'devour their palpitating
flesh';[10] or when, in October, Carlyle's avenging furies took hostage
the 'baker, the baker's wife and the little baker's boy' and marched
them under duress from Versailles to Paris; or when, as Furet
suggests, 'the psychological and political mechanism of the Terror'
was put to the test during the September massacres of 1792; or
when finally a year later the spectre came home to roost, with the
Convention bowing to plebeian threats, instituting the guillotine as
an instrument of economic leverage and sending forth firebrand

[7] Colin Lucas refers in this context to 'the remapping of absolutism onto an
indivisible sovereign people': C. Lucas, 'Revolutionary Violence, the People and
the Terror', in K. M. Baker (ed.), *The Terror*, vol. IV in K. M. Baker, C. Lucas,
Fr. Furet and M. Ozouf (eds.), *The French Revolution and the Creation of Modern
Political Culture*, 4 vols. (Oxford, 1987–94), p. 58.
[8] Fr. Furet, 'Terreur', in Fr. Furet and M. Ozouf (eds.), *Dictionnaire critique de la
Révolution française*, 2nd rev. edn, 4 vols. (Paris, 1992), vol. I, *Evénements*,
pp. 293–314, and M. Ozouf, 'Egalité', *ibid.*, vol. IV, *Idées*, pp. 139–63; this view
stems from Talmon, *Origins of Totalitarian Democracy*, p. 143; see also Lucas,
'Revolutionary Violence', p. 58.
[9] Furet, 'Terreur', pp. 294–6.
[10] J.-P. Marat, 'Projet de déclaration des droits de l'homme et du citoyen', in *Œuvres
politiques, 1789–1793*, ed. by J. de Cock and C. Goëtz, 10 vols. (Brussels,
1989–95), vol. I, p. 74.

revolutionaries into the countryside to extract grain from the forestallers at bayonet-point.

While it is undeniable that a punitive brand of egalitarianism was present in the Revolution from its beginnings and contributed to the spiral of violence characteristic of the Terror, a more measured version of distributive justice made its appearance in the speeches delivered to the Constituent Assembly by members of the third estate and the enlightened nobility. Robespierre, the self-appointed champion of the underdog, was forever lambasting the excessive self-indulgence of the very rich, but stopped short of incitement to violence.[11] Mirabeau was sensitive to extreme inequalities of fortune but confined himself to seeking a more equitable distribution of the tax burden, based on proportionality and the ability to pay.[12] The duc de La Rochefoucauld d'Enville, the rapporteur of the tax committee, alert to the arguments of his friend, the marquis de Condorcet, in favour of graduated taxation, acknowledged that it was only fair 'to relieve the less well-off by making slightly greater demands on the rich'.[13] And his cousin La Rochefoucauld-Liancourt, the noted philanthropist and influential chairman of the welfare committee, pointed to a significant omission in the recently adopted Declaration of the Rights of Man, namely the 'right to subsistence'.[14] No one doubted these men's sincerity. The philanthropists of the Comité de mendicité were only too keenly aware of the incidence of poverty and were determined to do something about it. Olwen Hufton estimates that in 1789 more than a third, 'perhaps as much as half', of the total population were 'poor' and comprised working men and their families, whose main economic feature was vulnerability: they were chronically undernourished

[11] 'Mémoire pour François Deteuf' (Arras, 1783), 'Adresse à la nation artésienne' (early 1789), speeches of 22 October 1789, 25 January, 26 March and 23 October 1790, and April 1791: C. Mazauric (ed.), *Robespierre, écrits* (Paris, 1989), pp. 20–1, 67–9, 78–80, 96–100.

[12] Ozouf, 'Egalité', p. 149.

[13] L. A. de La Rochefoucauld, 'Idées générales sur le mode constitutionnel de l'impôt', 18 August 1790, in *Archives parlementaires des Chambres françaises: première série, 1787 à 1797*, 98 vols. (Paris, 1862–1995), *Assemblée constituante*, vol. XVIII, pp. 143–6.

[14] January 1790, in Ch. Rist, 'Les rapports du Comité de mendicité de l'Assemblée constituante', *La Révol. fr.* 29 (1895), p. 267; O. H. Hufton, *The Poor of Eighteenth-Century France, 1750–1789* (Oxford, 1974), pp. 167–8; J. D. de La Rochefoucauld, C. Wolikow and G. R. Ikni, *Le duc de La Rochefoucauld-Liancourt, 1747–1827, de Louis XV à Charles X, un grand seigneur patriote et le mouvement populaire* (Paris, 1980), pp. 182–98.

and liable to fall into indigence at the slightest mishap.[15] The sheer scale of poverty made the reduction of inequality an issue the first revolutionary Assembly could not circumvent, let alone ignore.

It is of course true that some Constituents used formal equality as a smokescreen to preserve material *in*equality, but their concern with the latter was very real, and even the opponents to further egalitarian concessions, such as the comte de Clermont-Tonnerre, feared the potential or even imminent extension of civic equality into the economic arena. Abbé Sieyès's concern with equal rights as a precondition to liberty and Jérôme Pétion's desire to see the principle of equal shares enacted in inheritance law reform bear out Aléxis de Tocqueville's claim that the Constituent Assembly was obsessed with equality in all its forms from a very early stage, and that 'equality' was far from being a Jacobin invention.[16] Indeed, as Isser Woloch reminds us, in Tocqueville's view the gradual movement of French society toward an increasing 'equality of condition' had already begun under the old regime and straddled the great divide of 1789.[17]

The ongoing discourse on equality, pursued against a background of recurring food riots, was nonetheless to find its natural home in the Jacobin Club, attuned to the pressing demands of the Parisian sans-culottes, yet always at one remove from extremist intimidation. As the Revolution entered its radical phase after the fall of the monarchy in August 1792, the National Convention rose to the occasion in its long-drawn-out economic debate on the corn trade, to which I shall of necessity return; so that when the crisis point was reached in the spring of 1793, there was a general awareness among deputies of all persuasions that the time had come to 'terminate the Revolution' by making urgent concessions to the poor and giving them at last a fair deal. Georges Lefebvre and Albert Soboul both held the view that the measures which ensued were imposed by 'popular pressure' from below rather than resolute conviction from above, though their case was far from conclusive.[18] It is at all events worthy of note that the period

---

[15] Hufton, *The Poor*, pp. 19–24.

[16] Ozouf, 'Egalité', pp. 148, 152–5; Fr. Furet, *Penser la Révolution française*, 2nd rev. edn (Paris, 1983), p. 81; E. H. Lemay, *Dictionnaire des Constituants, 1789–1791*, 2 vols. (Oxford, 1991), vol. I, pp. 220–3, and vol. II, pp. 748, 863.

[17] I. Woloch, *The New Regime: Transformations of the French Civic Order, 1789–1820s* (New York, 1994), p. 13.

[18] G. Lefebvre was of the opinion that the Montagnards 'yielded' in April 1793, but

between the first *maximum* of 4 May 1793, which established price ceilings for grain and flour, and the imposition of the death penalty on hoarders on 26 July was one of intense social legislation which saw the enactment by the Montagne of a wide range of radical reforms. It is not without significance that this reform programme reached the statute book well before the September timeframe and the official declaration of the Terror, and coincided with Robespierre's first serious confrontation with extremist lobbies and a refusal on his part to allow his radical pre-eminence to be subverted and his image as popular leader to be appropriated by Jean-François Varlet, Jacques Roux and the Enragés.[19] It can therefore be argued that social justice pre-empted the Terror, if only by a short head.

Admittedly, the two appeared to merge in the autumn of 1793, when Joseph Fouché's 'bread of equality' served as a prelude to a sort of class war waged against the well-to-do, and Claude Javogue's melodramatic attempts at social rectification walked roughshod over sacrosanct property rights.[20] Likewise, the 'official' Terror, as implemented by members of the governing Committee of Public Safety, at times seemed bent on systematic levelling, with the institution of a 'reign of equality' in the hapless city of Lyons by Collot-d'Herbois, and Saint-Just's ruthless economic clampdown on the city of Strasburg, where the wealthy merchant Mayno was exposed on the scaffold for trying to evade exorbitant revolutionary taxes, and citizen Schauer saw his house dismantled brick by brick for having speculated on the public purse and circumvented price regulations.[21]

that their 'reluctance persisted', and faced with the *maximum*, 'the Committee [of Public Safety] and the Convention, clinging desperately to the principles of a liberal economy, only backed down step by step': *La Révolution française*, 3rd rev. edn (Paris, 1963), pp. 344, 367; Albert Soboul likewise considered that 'the Montagnards were so attached to economic liberty that it required the extreme peril of the summer of 1793 and the popular pressure which ensued for them to consent in adopting, against their will and under constraint, the law of 29 September 1793': Saint-Just, *Discours et rapports*, ed. by A. Soboul, 2nd edn (Paris, 1970), p. 86.

[19] Lefebvre, *La Révolution française*, 3rd rev. edn, pp. 360–1, 368.

[20] E. Liris, 'On rougit ici d'être riche', *Annales hist. Révol. fr.* 300 (April–June 1995), pp. 295–301; and C. Lucas, *The Structure of the Terror: The Example of Javogues and the Loire* (Oxford, 1973), pp. 61–95, 156–256, 282–4.

[21] Instruction of 26 Brumaire II, in M. Biard, *Jean-Marie Collot-d'Herbois, homme de théâtre et homme de pouvoir (1749–1796)* (Lyons, 1995), part III, chapter 4; and J.-P. Gross, *Saint-Just: sa politique et ses missions* (Paris, 1976), pp. 291, 298.

Is it fair, however, to imply, as does Mona Ozouf, that the desire to achieve greater equality and the consent to the use of force went hand in hand? That the combination of these two urges in revolutionary practice represents a watershed, the true dividing line between Girondins and Montagnards, the point of no return at which democratic politics gave way to a moral crusade, when Robespierre and his followers threw in their lot with the militant sans-culottes and demonstrated their conviction that equality could and should be imposed by coercion? That the only way to correct the anti-social inclinations of the recalcitrant rich was to 'force them to be good'?[22]

There is an understandable tendency among historians to equate 'the Terror' with the radical phase of revolution as such, an assimilation which has obvious implications for the nature of Jacobin egalitarianism and which results from the lack of any commonly agreed definition of the term. To what extent in particular are we justified in referring to the Terror as an 'economic and social programme'?[23] There is, for example, a marked difference, which is more than semantic, between price controls brought about by bread riots or the violent rhetoric of subsistence[24] and a consciously elaborated and coherently executed programme of food rationing. Crisis management of vital supplies necessitated by wartime mobilisation relied heavily not on the Terror, but on the power of requisition exercised by the revolutionary government for the duration of the emergency. Arms production and full employment in the defence industries were governed by the war effort, not by the Terror, even if at times fear of political reprisals prompted workshop managers to yield to workers' demands.[25] The degree to which the Terror actually coincided with agrarian policy has taxed specialists of land reform without any consistent correlation emerging from their investigations.[26] Again, the fact that a number of democratic practices were initiated 'during the period of the Terror' does not make the Terror synonymous with civic egalitarianism; it rather invites reflection on the symbiosis of the two.[27] The basic

[22] Ozouf, 'Egalité', pp. 157–8.   [23] Baker, Introduction, *The Terror*, p. xxiv.
[24] W. H. Sewell Jr, 'The Sans-Culotte Rhetoric of Subsistence', *ibid.*, pp. 249–69.
[25] H. Burstin, 'Problems of Work During the Terror', *ibid.*, p. 288.
[26] J.-P. Hirsch, 'Terror and Property', and J.-P. Jessenne, 'The Land: Redefinition of the Rural Community', *ibid.*, pp. 211–22, 223, 235, 238–9.
[27] I. Woloch, 'The Contraction and Expansion of Democratic Space During the Period of the Terror', *ibid.*, p. 310.

problem, which is one of philosophy rather than terminology, would appear to lie in the inadequacy of any generalisation linking the Terror, or more broadly revolutionary violence, with the determination to reduce inequality and achieve greater fairness, which implies at the outset a deeply rooted concern for the individual.

In what way do 'fair shares' differ from 'equal shares'? The policies on offer in Year II reveal interesting variations in this respect and the chapters which follow endeavour to elucidate and illustrate the uneasy relationship between 'equality' and 'equity'. The latter is clearly relevant to the kind of liberal community posited by the French Revolution as a replacement for the *ancien régime*. Montesquieu, who was anxious to avoid both too much inequality *and* too much equality, had argued that freedom was more desirable than equality, and inequality a lesser evil than despotism.[28] *Liberté* was consequently the single most cherished value proclaimed by the Revolution. *Egalité* came second in the hierarchy of priorities established in 1789, although this sequence was to be reversed in 1793. Some modern thinkers continue to share Montesquieu's view that the two really are incompatible. Thus, Jean Baechler is of the opinion that you cannot maximise liberty and equality simultaneously: the more liberty you allow, the more inequality tends to thrive; and conversely, the harder you push equality, the more you encroach on people's freedom, by redistributing assets, power or prestige. There is, claims Baechler, 'no solution to this very profound contradiction'.[29]

Rousseau, for his part, would have disagreed, one of the arguments of his *Social Contract* being that liberty cannot exist without equality and it is therefore essential to give the same weight to each. Sieyès in turn predicated his conception of citizenship upon this duality.[30] Historical dictionaries, which separate the two, tend to gloss over contemporary perceptions of their complementary

[28] Montesquieu, *De l'esprit des lois*, ed. by R. Derathé, 2 vols. (Paris, 1973), vol. I, pp. iv–v, 234–8, and vol. II, pp. 4–8; see also R. Shackleton, *Montesquieu: une biographie critique*, trans. by J. Loiseau (Grenoble, 1977), pp. 208–16.
[29] Interview with J. Baechler in *Le Monde* of 4 October 1985; see also J. Baechler, *Démocraties* (Paris, 1985).
[30] Rousseau, 'Du contrat social', book II, chapter 11, *Œuvres complètes*, vol. II, p. 538; E. J. Sieyès, *Essai sur les privilèges* (Paris, 1788) and *Qu'est-ce que le Tiers Etat?* (Paris, 1789); see J.-D. Bredin, *Sieyès, la clé de la Révolution française* (Paris, 1988).

role.[31] The 'hidden' egalitarian foundation that another modern philosopher and economist detects in utilitarianism is not without relevance to the passionate discussions which took place not only in the Jacobin Club, but also in the Cercle Social, and which hinged on domestic free trade, equal property rights, freedom of enterprise and the capability of self-fulfilment. As Amartya Sen points out, not only is equality an essential feature of liberal theories of social arrangement (equal liberty for all, equal consideration for all), but the opposition between liberty and equality is faulty and inaccurate: liberty being among the possible fields of application of equality, and equality among the possible patterns of distribution of liberty.[32] The deceptive Manichaean antinomy between equality and freedom, collective rights versus possessive individualism, Montagnard egalitarians at loggerheads with liberal Girondins, tends to obfuscate the main issues at stake during the crisis years of the Revolution – namely, the right to existence, fair distribution of vital commodities, fair shares in property ownership, a fair division of tenancies and other economic resources and social benefits – all of which imply a shared vision of the equal right to freedom.

The powerful eighteenth-century rhetoric surrounding the 'equality of man' ('all men are born equal', and so on) should be seen in this light. The revolutionary focus, as from late 1792 onward, came to rest on the central issue of poverty, or rather on the threshold between abject and decent poverty, the threshold at which equality becomes meaningful, at which individual rights can begin to flourish. Inasmuch as poverty is 'lack of freedom', as Sen contends,[33] then well-being in Jacobin perception was understood as the ability to enjoy freedom ('honourable poverty' in Robespierre's parlance).[34]

Hence the close affinity between Girondins and Montagnards and the difficulty authors have had in differentiating between their

---

[31] Furet and M. Ozouf in their *Dictionnaire critique*, while Soboul's *Dictionnaire historique* leaves out liberty altogether: P. Goujard, 'Egalité', in A. Soboul, *Dictionnaire historique de la Révolution française*, ed. by J.-R. Suratteau and Fr. Gendron (Paris, 1989), pp. 403–4.

[32] A. Sen, *Inequality Reexamined* (New York and Oxford, 1992), pp. 13, 16–17, 21–3.

[33] *Ibid.*, pp. 110, 152.

[34] Speeches of April 1791 and 24 April 1793, in *Œuvres de Maximilien Robespierre*, ed. by M. Bouloiseau, J. Dautry, E. Déprez, G. Laurent, G. Lefebvre, E. Lesueur, G. Michon, and A. Soboul, 10 vols. (Paris, Nancy and Gap, 1910–67), vol. VII, p. 165, and vol. IX, p. 459.

brands of political culture.[35] You can be a bourgeois liberal like Pétion or an enlightened nobleman like Condorcet and feel strongly about equal rights to a loaf of bread or a fair distribution of the burden of taxation. And as André Delaporte aptly puts it in the case of Sylvain Maréchal, you can be a confirmed egalitarian and yet staunchly defend the sacred right of individual ownership.[36] The French Revolution was cast simultaneously in a liberal bourgeois mould and an egalitarian 'petit-bourgeois' or sans-culotte mould, as the Declarations of the Rights of Man make clear: that of 1789, but especially the amended Girondin–Montagnard version of 1793,[37] which puts equality before liberty. Babeuf was fond of paying lip-service to this text, and he according to Barrie Rose was not a precursor of Bolshevism, but of a 'widely based and even libertarian democracy'.[38] Herein lies a paradox that deserves further exploration.

The hybrid 1793 Declaration of Rights assumes that once the means of subsistence are assured and the threshold of equal opportunity has been reached, human beings, on account of the deep diversity of their abilities, talents and weaknesses, will be prepared to accept a fair arrangement of social and economic inequalities; that once society has enabled the underprivileged to overcome the disadvantages which prevent them from enjoying their individual rights, freedom will truly begin to flourish, and be allowed to do so. Such is the thrust of article 1 which describes the goal of society as the pursuit of the 'common happiness', but adds the rider that the first task of government is to 'guarantee the enjoyment' of the rights of man.[39]

Although the concept of fair shares is essentially a moral one, it obviously has far-reaching economic implications viewed as

---

[35] See P. Higonnet, *Sister Republics: The Origins of French and American Republicanism* (Cambridge, Mass., 1988), pp. 244–53; M. Dorigny, 'Violence et Révolution: les Girondins et les massacres de septembre', in A. Soboul (ed.), *Actes du Colloque Girondins et Montagnards, Sorbonne, 14 décembre 1975* (Paris, 1980), p. 104; M. Dorigny, 'Gironde/Girondins', in Soboul, *Dictionnaire historique*, pp. 503–7.

[36] A. Delaporte, *L'idée d'égalité en France au XVIIIe siècle* (Paris, 1987), p. 331.

[37] Drafted mainly by Condorcet and Robespierre: see *Les Déclarations des droits de l'homme (du débat 1789–1793 au préambule de 1946)*, ed. by L. Jaume (Paris, 1989), pp. 220, 254, 299.

[38] R. B. Rose, *Gracchus Babeuf, the First Revolutionary Communist* (Stanford, 1978), p. 342.

[39] *Les Déclarations*, ed. by Jaume, p. 299.

'entitlement', that is the ability of people to command the basic commodities required for their survival, and ultimately their prosperity, through the legal means available in a private-ownership market economy.[40] The most relevant parameters in the revolutionary context are, firstly, the protection of the citizen's endowment, in which the ownership of food stands out as one of the most primitive property rights; and secondly, the development of the exchange entitlement, for example enabling citizens to produce a bundle of food from their smallholdings, or grow cash crops and sell them in exchange for other commodities, or sell their labour power for a decent wage or make use of their skills as craftsmen to buy commodities, or exploit to the full the opportunities offered by the family economy in a mixed agrarian/cottage industry system.[41] To this set of commodity bundles the Jacobin perception of welfare added some quite innovative notions: social security, not just in the form of provision of work by the state, but in the right to unemployment benefit if one failed to find a job; the extension of minimum property rights to ensure the means of achieving sustainable self-sufficiency; and self-promotion and self-reliance brought within reach through education.

All this suggests that the period of Jacobin rule was not, as is commonly held, a 'hiatus' during which the new civic order went adrift, liberal principles were systematically violated and the seeds sown in 1789 and before withered and died, but rather a period of continuity when the turbulent tide of events did not prevent significant institutional developments taking place, and one in which commitment to social justice in theory did not automatically entail in practice, as Furet contends, a 'necessary curtailment of human rights'.[42] With the overthrow of the monarchy, the reopening of the conceptual space between revolution and constitution may well have led, as Baker suggests, to the supremacy of political will over 'government limited by the rights of man',[43] but it would be hasty to infer from this that the injection of equality into the ideological equation fatally implied a terrorist outcome. Yet the view continues to prevail among political scientists such as Luc Ferry and Alain Renaut, whose thesis flows from Fichte's

[40] A. Sen, *Poverty and Famines: An Essay on Entitlement and Deprivation* (Oxford, 1982), p. 45.
[41] *Ibid.*, p. 46; Hufton, *The Poor*, pp. 33–8.   [42] Furet, 'Terreur', p. 295.
[43] Baker, *Inventing the French Revolution*, pp. 304–5.

contemporary analysis of the Revolution, that belief in the power of human intervention to transform reality in the name of a universal moral ideal, be it one finding its expression in a bill of rights, carries with it the 'inherent and historically verifiable risk' of the Terror.[44] And because of the 'proven link' between the ethical, voluntaristic view of humanity's progress implicit in Jacobinism and the emergence of the totalitarian state, no serious philosopher or historian, apart from the credulous or naive, would call on the Jacobin legacy as testimony in the defence of human rights.

[44] L. Ferry and A. Renaut, *Philosophie politique 3: des droits de l'homme à l'idée républicaine* (Paris, 1985), p. 37; see also L. Ferry, 'Fichte', in Furet and M. Ozouf, *Dictionnaire critique*, 1st edn (Paris, 1988), pp. 962–3.

1. The Jacobin mainstream and the Robespierrist ascendancy

Believe me, Sir, those who attempt to level, never equalise ... The levellers therefore only change and pervert the natural order of things; they load the edifice of society, by setting up in the air what the solidity of the structure requires to be on the ground.

Edmund Burke, *Reflections on the Revolution in France*, 1790[1]

WHO'S WHO AMONG THE JACOBINS AND THE GEOGRAPHY OF MODERATION

Before attempting to elucidate further the ideological under-pinnings of Jacobin egalitarianism, it may be helpful to introduce the principal protagonists of this study, many of whom belong to the amorphous body of rank-and-file Montagnards not often the subject of historiographical scrutiny. The reader is entitled to ask who they were and why the regional centres in which they operated, often far from the capital, are of specific interest to our topic. The short answer is that they represent the mainstream, though by no means the silent majority, that they put into practice what they preached and that their activities were largely concentrated in areas free from terrorist excess.

While none were major revolutionaries of the stature of a Danton or a Robespierre, it would be equally misleading to suggest that they were merely practitioners imposing the will of the legislature in the depths of the French countryside. A few were men of exceptional ability directly involved in fashioning government

[1] *The Works of the Right Hon. Edmund Burke*, ed. by H. Rogers, 2 vols. (London, 1837), vol. I, p. 399.

14

policy, who commanded the respect of their peers in the Paris Jacobin Club and were considered key figures in the Assembly and its standing committees. Among these Montagnards of distinction, five stand out as men of considerable intellect: Jeanbon Saint-André, Joseph Lakanal, Gilbert Romme, Jean-Baptiste Bo and Pierre Roux-Fazillac. Highly cultured and articulate, at home in the cut and thrust of parliamentary debate, they also made their mark on local public opinion during their journeys to the provinces by combining a strong commitment to radical reform, a gift for leadership and an understanding of politics as the art of the possible. In this, their example was followed by others engaged as they were in the difficult task of promoting the new republican lifestyle. Collectively, they injected into revolutionary practice some uncommon qualities which were to prove indispensable during the critical months of the Terror: sound judgement, realism and equanimity. The ability to exercise such qualities under pressure may explain, at least in part, why these five and the trend which they represented have tended to remain out of the historical limelight. The problem essentially lies in the fact that their mainstream status has been usurped by others.

The 'Jacobin mainstream' is certainly not easy to pin down, notwithstanding ready sources of factual information on the deputies such as Auguste Kuscinski's dictionary, Alison Patrick's tables of political affiliations, and for those who also sat in the first Assembly, Edna Lemay's two-volume reference work on the Constituents.[2] A recent spate of biographical studies has given prominence to a number of major Jacobin figures closely associated with the Terror who had until now remained shadowy, suspect or distorted by legend. Thus, under the aegis of Michel Vovelle[3] at the Institut d'histoire de la Révolution at the Sorbonne, authoritative reappraisals have appeared of Saint-Just by Bernard Vinot, Marat by Olivier Coquard, Billaud-Varenne by Françoise Brunel and

---

[2] A. Kuscinski, *Dictionnaire des conventionnels* (Paris, 1916; facs. reprint, Brueil-en-Vexin, 1973); A. Patrick, *The Men of the First French Republic: Political Alignments in the National Convention of 1792* (Baltimore, 1972), appendices i–v; Lemay, *Dictionnaire des Constituants*.

[3] On the complex task of biographical 'reconstruction', see M. Vovelle, 'De la biographie à l'étude de cas: Théodore Désorgues', in M. Vovelle (ed.), *Problèmes et méthodes de la biographie: actes du colloque, Sorbonne, 3–4 mai 1985* (Paris, 1985), pp. 191–8; and the same author's introduction to Fouché's *Mémoires*, ed. by M. Vovelle (Paris, 1993).

Collot-d'Herbois by Michel Biard. Work is under way on other representative terrorists such as Fouché (Elisabeth Liris) and Maignet (Jacques Guilhaumou and Martine Lapied). The snag is that this research, commendable as it is, has had the effect of turning the spotlight onto the hardliners, or the revolutionary 'maximalists' as Brunel and Guilhaumou call Billaud, Collot and Maignet,[4] those whose activism attracted much publicity at the time and won them the dubious reputation of bloodthirsty extremists, who vigorously pursued government policy, who did not shy from brutal tactics in their interpretation of that policy or who were unable to resist the corrupting influence of absolute power.

This tendency is by no means new. Colourful extremists have traditionally provided good copy for a gripping yarn. Already during the Third Republic Louis Madelin's biography of Fouché had gained notoriety at the expense of Louis Lévy-Schneider's life of Jeanbon Saint-André; and Gaston Martin's harrowing account of Carrier's crimes at Nantes had naturally overshadowed Henri Labroue's staid thesis devoted to Lakanal's proconsulship in Périgord. More recently, when Alessandro Galante Garrone's penetrating study of the democrat Gilbert Romme was winning deserved acclaim, Colin Lucas published his striking psychological analysis of unbridled terrorism let loose in the person of Claude Javogues, the epitome of the instinctively violent and callous ultra-revolutionary.

Collective narratives of the provincial Terror in action have tended to have the same effect. In the last century, Henri Wallon's work of reference on the missions was in fact devoted to 'revolutionary justice in the departments' and the incidence of the death penalty,[5] while modern evaluations – such as Richard Cobb's spellbinding history of the people's armies and the hardline deputies who spurred them on (Carrier, Chasles, Baudot, Taillefer and others),[6] or Vovelle's descriptions of the anarchical activism of

---

[4] J. Guilhaumou and M. Lapied, 'La mission Maignet', *Annales hist. Révol. fr.* 300 (April–June 1995), p. 283.

[5] Wallon's five-volume work on the *représentants* in fact began life as a history of revolutionary tribunals: see H. Wallon, *La Révolution du 31 mai et le fédéralisme en 1793, ou la France vaincue par la Commune de Paris*, 2 vols. (Paris, 1886), vol. II, pp. 425–38, and H. Wallon, *Les représentants du peuple en mission et la justice révolutionnaire dans les départements en l'an II (1793–1794)*, 5 vols. (Paris, 1889–90).

[6] R. C. Cobb, *Les armées révolutionnaires, instrument de la Terreur dans les départements, avril 1793–floréal an II*, 2 vols. (Paris and The Hague, 1961–3).

outstanding dechristianisers in the Massif and the south-east (Fouché in Nivernais, Javogues in Forez, Albitte in Dauphiné, Chateauneuf-Randon in Auvergne)[7] – have, through scholarly treatment of their subjects, greatly reinforced the compelling image of rampant intolerance and the gratuitous use of force, or 'energetic action' as Cobb euphemistically calls it. In the process, we are given a vivid but one-sided picture of 'Jacobinism' as a strictly terrorist and inherently violent phenomenon.

Jacques Godechot was of the opinion that, among the deputies-on-mission, 'some demonstrated revolutionary intolerance and were the artisans of Terror, while the others, and they were the majority, were moderates who endeavoured to establish a reign of justice'.[8] A rough calculation shows that some 20 per cent belonged to the first category, while the remaining 80 per cent represent what I have called the Jacobin mainstream. While it would be over-simplistic to portray complex individuals in black and white, it is undeniable that a handful of forceful activists have tended to eclipse a substantial number of thoughtful radicals, such as the five mentioned above, and with them many middle-of-the-road Montagnards who followed in their wake, moderates who adhered loosely to the Jacobin fold, or those on the outer fringe sympathetic to the Gironde who sided with the Montagne for reasons of political expediency; these activists thus, quite involuntarily, project an incomplete and unbalanced image of the Jacobin family. It is hardly surprising in these circumstances that the very Jacobin programme of social and economic reform which would one day give rise to innovative notions, such as those of a property-owning democracy, free and universal elementary schooling and the welfare state, should be branded by many authors as reckless in the extreme.[9] Conversely, the presence on the ground of reasonable Montagnards endeavouring to implement this programme – un-successfully, as it turned out, because of the new regime's chaotic management of public finances,[10] but patiently and conscientiously

---

[7] M. Vovelle, *Religion et Révolution: la déchristianisation de l'an II (dans le Sud-Est)*, (Paris, 1976); and M. Vovelle, *La Révolution contre l'Eglise: de la Raison à l'Etre Suprême* (Brussels, 1988).

[8] J. Godechot, *Les institutions de la France sous la Révolution et l'Empire* (Paris, 1951), p. 308.

[9] One notable exception is Isser Woloch's recent work on the institutions of the new regime: Woloch, *New Regime*.

[10] F. Aftalion, *The French Revolution: An Economic Interpretation* (Cambridge,

– may well go some way toward explaining the meaning of the Revolution for ordinary French people and may in parts of France at least, such as the centre and the south-west, help explain the positive memory of the Revolution which lingered on through the nineteenth century.

It is, of course, a singular case of bad timing that the Jacobin blueprint of a just and fair society should have reached maturity at a time when France was engaged in a full-scale European war and torn apart by civil strife, when democracy was replaced by dictatorship and human relations were distinguished more often by fratricide than by fraternity. Its incidence is therefore best detected away from the hotbeds of tension, in those areas where relative tranquillity prevailed, where the Terror was contained or coercion applied with discrimination. Thus, the former archivist of the Yonne department claimed there were 'few towns and few regions where the Revolution was as moderate and free from bloodshed as Auxerre and the Auxerrois',[11] a fact that Wallon also recognised and attributed to the amenable nature and leftish inclinations of the natives, although a resistant strain of Catholic republicanism may also have been involved.[12] Similarly at Agen and in the surrounding Agenais, there prevailed after the quenching of the Federalist uprising what Cobb describes as a 'gentle terror';[13] in Montauban and the Montalbanais, Protestant ethics and Jacobin politics coexisted peacefully and fairly amicably;[14] and the Dordogne was a department where, according to Alphonse Aulard, 'nothing extraordinary happened, where the new regime operated without dramatic incidents, without civil war, in an almost peaceful, almost normal manner';[15] so too, the Creuse department was a 'forgotten' part of central France where provincial anarchy reigned until an

1990), p. 157; first published in French as *L'économie de la Révolution française* (Paris, 1987).

[11] H. Forrestier, cited by Cobb, *Les armées révolutionnaires*, p. 664, n. 80.

[12] S. Desan, *Reclaiming the Sacred: Lay Religion and Popular Politics in Revolutionary France* (Ithaca, 1990); S. Desan, 'The Family as Cultural Battleground: Religion vs. Republic Under the Terror', in Baker, *The Terror*, pp. 180, 183–4, 188.

[13] Cobb, *Les armées révolutionnaires*, p. 453.

[14] D. Ligou, 'L'épuration des administrations montalbanaises par Baudot', *Annales hist. Révol. fr.* 26 (1954), pp. 60–1.

[15] F. A. Aulard, review of H. Labroue, *La mission du conventionnel Lakanal dans la Dordogne en l'an II (octobre 1793–août 1794)* (Paris, 1912), in *La Révol. fr.* 69 (1916), p. 236.

intelligent mainstream volunteer was prevailed upon to republican-ise the region.[16] It must be stressed that these were no sleepy outbacks but areas of sporadic peasant unrest, some of which had been in the forefront of insurrectionary action during the *guerre aux châteaux* of the years 1790–2.[17]

Indeed, the principal contributory factor to the temperate climate which prevailed here during the Terror was the presence, for relatively long spells or at regular intervals, of a moderate or careful Montagnard, not infrequently operating on home ground or in familiar surroundings: Maure at Auxerre, Paganel at Agen, Saint-André at Montauban, Lakanal at Bergerac, Romme at Angoulême, Brival at Limoges, Vernerey at Guéret. After all, Nevers and Moulins were quite peaceful communities until the arrival of Fouché, as was Saint-Etienne until the arrival of Javogues, or Orange until the belated terrorist intervention of Maignet. Clearly, it would be tilting the balance the other way to confine oneself to the safe havens just described. I have therefore cast the net more generously and tried to survey in some depth a larger number of missions to a wider range of essentially rural departments, stretching from the southern Auvergne through Gascony and the Périgord to the outer limits of Limousin, availing myself of published research findings for other parts of France, in the hope that the picture which emerges is fairly representative.

Our five leading protagonists escape Edmund Burke's stricture that revolutionary assemblies were predominantly made up of 'obscure provincial advocates, of stewards of petty local jurisdictions, county attorneys, notaries and the whole train of the ministers of municipal litigation, the fomenters and conductors of the petty war of village vexation'.[18] Indeed, the professional catchment of the Jacobin mainstream, while symptomatic of the social levelling process under way and the rise of many *gens à talents* with

---

[16] Rapport de Chauvin, Germinal III, Bibl. Nat., 8° Le[39] 245, pp. 56, 77; J. L. Broilliard, 'Diagoras Boscovir [J.-Fr. de l'Etang]: un homme, un style, un tempérament', in *Pages sostraniennes* (La Souterraine and Guéret, 1982), p. 81.

[17] Peasant unrest during the Revolution was endemic to south-western France and centred on the departments of Corrèze, Dordogne, Lot, Aveyron, Cantal, Lot-et-Garonne, Tarn and present-day Tarn-et-Garonne: see A. Ado, *Paysans en Révolution: terre, pouvoir et jacquerie, 1789–1794* (Paris, 1996), pp. 159–88, 261–73; cf. the uprisings of the old regime described by Y.-M. Bercé, *Histoire des Croquants: etude des soulèvements populaires au XVIIe siècle dans le Sud-Ouest de la France*, 2 vols. (Paris and Geneva, 1974).

[18] Burke, 'Reflections', vol. I, p. 397.

a legal background, extended also to a significant number of erstwhile clerics belonging to both the Catholic and Protestant confessions and a fair sprinkling of doctors, soldiers, businessmen and shopkeepers.

Thus, Jeanbon Saint-André was a former Protestant pastor from Montauban and the son of a wealthy textile manufacturer, whose progressive radicalism led him to trade his Girondin sympathies for closer allegiance to the Montagne; his election to the governing Committee of Twelve projected him to centre stage and led him to acquire renown as the moderniser of the French navy. Joseph Lakanal, a high-ranking constitutional cleric, professor of rhetoric and educationalist, was the close associate and spokesman of abbé Sieyès at the Convention, and one of the leading members of the Comité d'instruction publique. Gilbert Romme, likewise a distinguished member of the education committee, was a mathematician, latter-day philosophe and social reformer who had mixed with Parisian high society under the *ancien régime*, befriended d'Alembert and Condorcet and been appointed roving tutor to the cosmopolitan Stroganov family; his main claim to celebrity at the Convention was his defence of learning and his contribution to the design of the new republican calendar. Jean-Baptiste Bo was a provincial physician from a worthy Rouergat family influential in local politics, who specialised in social welfare, won the confidence and support of Robespierre and became the dynamic spokesman of the Comité des secours publics, inheriting in the process the prestigious mantle of the philanthropist La Rochefoucauld-Liancourt. And Pierre Roux-Fazillac, a former cavalry officer from the petty Périgourdin nobility newly promoted to the rank of brigadier-general, was not only an expert in military matters, but also an active member of the education committee, devoted to the cause of the rural poor and a proponent of radical land reform, who was nevertheless by temperament more of a Cromwellian ironside than a Winstanleyan communist.

The fairly wide political spectrum represented by these leading figures is reflected further down the scale, encompassing men who were temperamentally right of centre, such as Jean-Baptiste Harmand, a justice of the peace from Bar-le-Duc with Girondin leanings, or François Ingrand, Protestant advocate and provincial administrator from Poitiers; those who in general acted with exemplary restraint such as Nicolas Maure, the humanitarian grocer from Auxerre, Pierre Paganel, the former country priest from Villeneuve-sur-Lot, or Jacques Brival, the Tulle attorney and procurator of the Corrèze; those who, like Bo, consistently toed the government line, such as Jean-Baptiste Monestier (du Puy-de-Dôme), former canon and episcopal vicar at Clermont, a friend and supporter of Couthon; judicious left-of-centre radicals in the manner of Saint-André and Romme, such as Pierre Monestier (de la Lozère), the egalitarian attorney from the *causses*; and wistful levellers bent on agrarian reform in the manner of Roux-Fazillac, but tending to the far left, such as Pierre Dartigoeyte, the advocate son of a country notary from the Landes, and Antoine Lanot, another lawyer from Tulle who was styled the 'new Cincinnatus' of Limousin.[19]

It is invidious to attempt to pin labels onto men who often reconciled in their persons divergent tendencies or conflicting urges. Thus, Charles Vernerey, a quiet lawyer from Franche-Comté, was successful as an outsider in pacifying the troubled Creuse and Allier departments, but his impartiality was accompanied by a strong commitment to distributive justice. Brival, whose towering height and athletic build belied his gentle disposition, was both the staunch defender of the manufacturing and business community of Tulle, Limoges and Poitiers and the advocate of the unemployed, who regularly set aside part of his deputy's salary for the poor (as did Romme) and lent an ear to Marat's incantations. Paganel was a Girondin at heart, a partisan of free enterprise, a man of order 'fearful of the excesses of anarchy';[20] yet he was also for a while one of the most prolific organisers of 'people's armies' in the south-west, a confirmed if circumspect requisitionist and interventionist. Fringe activists like the former Capuchin friar and Cordelier François Chabot who, disguised as 'a bird of paradise' (the tricolour plume on his broad-brimmed hat),[21] solemnly announced

[19] Cf. Coupé de l'Oise, Isoré, Duquesnoy and Fayau: G. R. Ikni, 'Jacques-Michel Coupé, curé jacobin (1737–1809)', in Fl. Gauthier and G. R. Ikni (eds.), *La guerre du blé au XVIIIe siècle: la critique populaire contre le libéralisme économique* (Montreuil, 1988), pp. 159–63; and P. M. Jones, 'The "Agrarian Law": Schemes for Land Redistribution During the French Revolution', *Past and Present* 133 (November 1991), pp. 131–3.

[20] Cobb, *Les armées révolutionnaires*, pp. 238–40.

[21] From an anonymous lampoon published at Castres in the summer of 1793: M. de Vissac, *Camboules* (Riom, 1893), p. 143; cited by A. Mathiez in 'Glanes', *Annales hist. Révol. fr.* 7 (1930), p. 77.

the advent of the 'era of equality' to his native Aveyron in 1793, or the idiosyncratic episcopal vicar Jacques Laplanche, who had himself proclaimed 'father of the people' and 'public benefactor' at Bourges, were men whose credibility rested on shaky foundations and who, when the dust had settled, were found to have enhanced their reputations as mavericks, but made little lasting impact.

Romme, the philosophe, whose temperament according to Georges Lefebvre was 'hardly that of a man of action',[22] organised a highly effective if short-lived programme of food rationing and put into motion the most original social security project of his century. Maure, the moderate Auxerrois, leapt to the defence of Marat and personally carried the invalid Couthon to the rostrum to enable him to propose the proscription of the Girondins.[23] The 'Dantonist' Pierre Philippeaux also considered himself a radical 'Maratist', before circumstances brought about his exclusion from the Jacobin Club. Lakanal, the highbrow educationalist, promised to come to the aid of his 'plebeian brothers' of Bergerac by 'selling the last shirt off the rich man's back', and to that end introduced progressive taxation to Périgord. Albert Mathiez, who was unsparing in his criticism of Labroue's book on Lakanal, partly because his subject was a supporter of the 'mole' Sieyès, but mainly because the author himself was a pupil of Aulard's, finished his diatribe with the surprising conclusion that 'the priest Lakanal', that 'deceitful and self-promoting Gascon weather-vane', in fact shared Robespierre's opinion on all important issues of the day, including social and economic policy: 'He was de facto a Robespierrist.'[24] Inasmuch as Robespierre stood for social justice and many now looked to him for guidance and inspiration, Mathiez's description may well be applicable to others besides Lakanal, and I shall perforce return to the Robespierrist ascendancy at the end of this chapter.

Not all were so outspoken. Harmand, who had drafted a radical new declaration of rights, confined himself while on mission to levying horses for the cavalry at Angoulême and his policy state-

---

[22] G. Lefebvre, preface to A. Galante Garrone, *Gilbert Romme: histoire d'un révolutionnaire (1750–1795)*, trans. by A. Manceron and C. Manceron (Paris, 1971), p. 7.

[23] O. Coquard, *Jean-Paul Marat* (Paris, 1993), pp. 372, 404, 412.

[24] A. Mathiez, review of Labroue, *La mission du conventionnel Lakanal dans la Dordogne en l'an II (octobre 1793–août 1794)* (Paris, 1912), *Annales révol.* 8 (1916), pp. 438–41.

ments never strayed beyond oats and saddlebags. Ingrand, in charge of recruitment in Poitou and Limousin, refused to raise any taxes or detain any suspects, though he delivered plenty of patriotic speeches. But this does not necessarily place these deputies among the 'renegades of 1789', to use Aulard's fond distinction between the loyal 'men of 1789' and the deserters who betrayed the 'rational ideal of social justice and solidarity proclaimed by the eighteenth century'.[25] Only too well aware of the gravity of the issues at stake, they were mindful of the constraints imposed by human relations and quite sensibly preferred not to rush things. James Guillaume once wrote that, apart from a few exceptions, 'the men of the Revolution, faced with the fundamental problems of politics and philosophy, generally tackled them in a spirit of scrupulous restraint'.[26]

Their ideological prudence, which often stands in marked contrast to the boldness of their language, is closer to tolerance than persecution. It is not without significance in this regard that, while many of the confirmed terrorists were militant atheists, who took naturally to blasphemy and adhered to the dechristianisation movement in the autumn and winter of 1793,[27] the moderates were often deists who shared Robespierre's and Tom Paine's belief in the usefulness of religion.[28] Lakanal's brand of deism was Voltairian in inspiration, the distinction between good and evil being inseparable in his view from belief in the Great Clockmaker, the Creator, the Author of nature.[29] Bo continued to hold the gospel in veneration and referred at Aurillac to the 'sublime morality' of this 'divine book'. Chabot, preaching at Saint-Etienne's in Toulouse, stated that the true evangelical message was to bring about celestial bliss on earth and expressed admiration for Jesus, the carpenter's son, 'Jésus-Christ sans-culotte', an *honnête homme* whose poverty and modesty were lessons in equality and fraternity. Jean-Baptiste Monestier called the gospel 'the most sublime of books where you

[25] F. A. Aulard, 'La journée du 4 septembre 1870', *La Révol. fr.* 31 (1896), p. 394; F. A. Aulard, *Histoire politique de la Révolution française: origines et développement de la Démocratie et de la République (1789–1804)* (Paris, 1901), p. 46.

[26] J. Guillaume, 'La liberté des cultes et le Comité d'instruction publique', *La Révol. fr.* 31 (1896), p. 53.

[27] For example, Lequinio, who used the Terror at Rochefort as an instrument of religious persecution.

[28] J. Keane, *Tom Paine: A Political Life* (London, 1995), pp. 391–6.

[29] Resolutions of Prairial and Messidor II, Sarlat, in Labroue, *La mission de Lakanal*, pp. 34, 231, 252–3.

find the true principles of liberty and equality', while Jacques Brival in Tulle cathedral pointed out that it was Rousseau who had first used the adjective 'sublime' to describe the scriptures in his *Contrat social.*[30]

Christian charity and republican *bienfaisance* clearly have much in common. But more important still, the Christian ideal of brotherly conduct ('love thy neighbour') was not lost on men who were making a virtue of justice understood as fairness. Roux-Fazillac was a confirmed sceptic and quite an enthusiastic icono-clast, yet he instructed his philosophical spokesman Charles Foulhioux to make it clear to the citizens of Périgueux assembled in Saint-Front cathedral that the 'first moral truth' was to be found in the gospels according to St Matthew and St Luke, in Rousseau's second *Discourse* on the origins of inequality and in the amended Declaration of the Rights of Man: 'And as ye would that men should do to you, do ye also to them likewise.'[31]

RADICAL DRIFT, CLASS ANTAGONISM AND THE 'DEMOCRATIC MAXIMUM'

Radicalisation is an ambiguous process. Gilbert Romme expressed his regret after Thermidor that the Revolution should have abandoned its 'majestic course'.[32] In contrast, his colleague Pierre Paganel, writing at the time of the Empire, was of the opinion that the struggles of the Jacobin period had changed 'a reforming revolution into a devastating torrent ... Absolute equality was for

[30] Bo's speech delivered at Aurillac on 13 Pluviôse, Montauban on 17 Ventôse and Castres 8 Floréal II: *Discours prononcé aux sociétés populaires d'Aurillac, de Montauban et de Castres*, Castres, Year II, Bibl. Nat., 8° Lb40 2504; Chabot in March 1793, Arch. dép. Tarn, L 130, missions, and A. Mathiez, review of Vissac, *Camboules*, p. 77; Monestier at the *société populaire* of Guéret: Arch. dép. Creuse, L 733, f° 13, Jacobin Club of Guéret (30 March 1793); Brival's speech of 10 Nivôse II, Arch. Nat., AF$_{II}$ 171, Western Bureau, pl. 1407, p. 19; J.-J. Rousseau, 'Du contrat social', book IV, chapter 8 ('De la religion civile'), *Œuvres complètes*, vol. II, p. 576; R. Schnerb, 'Notes sur les débuts politiques de Couthon et des Monestier dans le département du Puy-de-Dôme', *Annales hist. Révol. fr.* 7 (1930), pp. 323–8.

[31] Ch. Foulhioux, 'Instruction morale et civique', 10 Nivôse II, Arch. Nat., AF$_{II}$ 171, Western Bureau, pl. 1406, p. 20; the references are to St Matthew, vii. 12 and St Luke, vi. 31, to a passage in part I of Rousseau's second *Discourse*, in *Œuvres complètes*, vol. II, p. 225, and to article 6 of the 1793 Declaration; see also P. Caron, 'Recherches biographiques: Foulhioux', *La Révol. fr.* 84 (1931), pp. 255–60.

[32] Galante Garrone, *Gilbert Romme*, pp. 267–70, 367.

a short while, in 1793, a trap laid by ambition to the impetuous fanaticism of the multitude.'[33] The fashion was in the 1970s to talk of *dérapage*, a 'veering off-course', which later turned to *dérive* or 'drift',[34] both of which correspond roughly to the radical shift lamented long after the event by the second of the two protagonists.

A majestic course to one, a devastating torrent to the other – yet both Romme and Paganel were liberals who chose to take part on their own terms in the egalitarian adventure. Both displayed fairness and prudence, those pre-eminent bourgeois values which Adam Smith built into his doctrine of commutative justice.[35] According to his biographer, Romme's itinerary was dictated by circumstance, taking him from bourgeois detachment to revolutionary involvement, from an independent reformist stance to ever more daring social commitment, until the fateful insurrection of Prairial Year III, when, together with Soubrany, Duquesnoy, Goujon and their radical companions, he was prepared to accept ultimate martyrdom in the defence of social justice:[36] a tragic destiny, but an exemplary *revolutionary* trajectory.

Romme was not alone in submitting thus to the process of 'rational' radicalisation. It was commonly felt in March 1793 that the point of no return had been reached. Jeanbon Saint-André, who before his election had mingled with the Girondin shipowners of Bordeaux, briefly returned to his home town of Montauban and shared his concerns about the plight of the country with Barère in Paris:

> The time has now come, Citizen Colleague, to sound the depths of the abyss into which we are rapidly being drawn ... The Revolution is not accomplished ... We are bound in the most intimate manner to the fate of the Revolution ... Everywhere people are wearied with the Revolution, the rich detest it, the poor lack bread and they are persuaded that we are to blame ...

---

[33] P. Paganel, *Essai historique et critique sur la Révolution française*, 3 vols. (Paris, 1815), vol. I, p. 307.

[34] On François Furet's choice of epithets, see S. L. Kaplan, *Farewell Revolution: The Historians' Feud, France, 1789/1989* (Ithaca, 1995), pp. 140–1.

[35] A. Smith, *The Theory of Moral Sentiments* (1759); see in this regard Patricia Werhane's elegant solution to 'the Adam Smith problem': P. Werhane, *Adam Smith and His Legacy for Modern Capitalism* (New York and Oxford, 1995).

[36] Galante Garrone, *Gilbert Romme*, p. 345.

It is imperative that we enable the poor to live, if we want him to help us complete the Revolution.[37]

The sense of urgency was echoed from Toulouse by Jean-Baptiste Bo and François Chabot: 'At this time, we dare say the most critical moment of the Revolution, it can be terminated, if we are able to take the vigorous measures that the circumstances dictate; we are on our way to Castres and Rodez with the firm intention of determining once and for all the fate of a revolution which has not yet benefited the poor.' And three days later, Bo and Chabot were the first to raise a graduated tax on 'affluence and surplus wealth' on the 'suspect citizens' of the Tarn and Aveyron departments.[38]

To complete the Revolution, determine its fate, terminate it 'to the benefit of the people', as Robespierre noted in his diary,[39] is another way of placing the blame for inaction squarely on the shoulders of the Girondins, the party of cautious liberals who failed to stand up to the egalitarian challenge and were therefore deservedly heading for defeat. Indeed, the tangible proof of a new departure in policy was the first slice of important social legislation enacted between May and August 1793: price controls on grain and flour (*premier maximum*), the forced loan of 1,000 million livres, poor relief for servicemen's families, agrarian reform, including the sale of émigré properties in small lots, division of the commons and final abolition of seigneurial dues, the pooling of corn supplies in public grain-stores (*greniers d'abondance*), the establishment of primary schools.[40]

These measures heralded what Patrice Higonnet considers to have been an economic 'about-face' (possessive individualism set aside, the Bourse closed down, the death penalty decreed for hoarding),[41] and it is certain that the 'levelling' exercise was to gain

[37] Letter from Moissac, 26 March 1793, Arch. Nat., AF$_{II}$ 167, Western Bureau, pl. 1369, p. 42; F. A. Aulard *et al.* (eds.), *Recueil des actes du Comité de salut public, avec la correspondance officielle des représentants en mission et le registre du Conseil exécutif provisoire*, 27 vols. (Paris, 1889–1933), vol. II, p. 532.

[38] Letter of 23 March 1793 and resolution of 26 March 1793: Arch. dép. Tarn, L 135, Missions, p. 1; and Arch. dép. Aveyron, I L 354, Bo's correspondence.

[39] A. Mathiez, 'Le carnet de Robespierre: essai d'édition critique', *Annales révol.* 10 (1918), p. 15.

[40] Decrees of 4, 5, 7, 20 and 30 May, 3, 4, 8 and 10 June, 13 and 17 July, 9 August 1793: Ph. Sagnac, *La législation civile de la Révolution française (1789–1804): essai d'histoire sociale* (Paris, 1898), pp. 154–243; Lefebvre, *La Révolution française*, pp. 408–13.

[41] Higonnet, *Sister Republics*, p. 251.

in pace and intensity during the months which followed. It was the considered opinion of Saint-André that 'more violent and more dangerous crises' were inevitable;[42] indeed the September crisis generated the *maximum général*, while the crisis of the following winter triggered what Bo called the 'awakening of the people' and the 'implementing of social virtues', the time having come 'for the Revolution to begin an independent and rapid advance'.[43] This theme was echoed by Saint-Just, who referred to the 'force of circumstances' which 'may lead us to results we had not expected', namely the Ventôse decrees.[44]

Rather than accomplishing an about-turn, however, let alone willingly embarking on a process of rational social reform, some of the protagonists appear either to be drifting dangerously with the tide, or to have committed themselves to a reckless venture which was rapidly getting out of hand. But any explanation of the process, as that offered by Albert Soboul, based on compulsion (popular demands coupled with pressure from the Hébertists resulting in a progressive swing to the left) fails to take into account the necessarily anti-liberal slant of any egalitarian commitment, and, conversely, the democratic scruples which tend to restrain the action of even the most committed radicals. Marat, for example, whose threatening utterances in the *Ami du peuple* were interpreted as proclaiming the wholesale redistribution of land and the imminent end to private property, was in fact assuming a frequently misunderstood role, which was that of a safety valve. 'His fits of madness', wrote Levasseur de la Sarthe, 'were not dangerous, yet at the same time, they were a sort of *democratic maximum* [my italics] beyond which it was not possible to venture.'[45] Indeed, Marat's incendiary tone frequently masks a rational philosophical message, such as that the fruits of the earth were for all to enjoy,[46] or each citizen had the right to be fed, clothed and housed and to raise and establish his children decently, which did not imply an abandon-

[42] Letter to Jean Filsac, 18 June 1793, published by A. Lods in *La Révol. fr.* 24 (1893), p. 156.

[43] Aurillac, 13 Pluviôse II.

[44] Report of 8 Ventôse II, in Saint-Just, *Discours et rapports*, p. 145.

[45] A. Mathiez, 'Le manifeste des Enragés du 23 juin 1793', *Annales révol.* 7 (1914), 547–60; *Marat, textes choisis*, ed. by M. Vovelle, (Paris, 1963), pp. 28–9.

[46] Cf. Rousseau, 'De l'inégalité', part 2, *Œuvres complètes*, vol. II, p. 228; Rousseau, 'Projet de constitution pour la Corse', *ibid.*, vol. III, p. 510; Mably, *Des droits et des devoirs du citoyen*, ed. by J.-L. Lecercle (Paris, 1972), p. 111.

ment of human rights and should not have raised many eyebrows among the revolutionary élite. This point is well made by Olivier Coquard, Jacques de Cock and Michael Sonenscher.[47]

Nevertheless, in the eyes of the citizens of Bordeaux in June 1793, Marat remained a bugbear. The pacificatory mission of the moderate deputies Jean-Baptiste Treilhard and Jean-Baptiste Mathieu was interpreted as a 'Maratist' intrusion aimed at 'putting the rich to ransom' and 'oppressing persons', an incitement 'to murder and the violation of property', at a time when the flower of the nation's youth were marching to battle 'out of love for liberty and in defence of their properties'. Treilhard attributed the Federalist revolt in south-western France to the rumour that Marat had just been appointed mayor of Paris and the fall of the Gironde was understood by the provinces as signifying the victory of extremism and a call to social confrontation.[48] The assassination of Marat and his transformation into a 'martyr of liberty' contributed to this myth of militant Maratism, inasmuch as several radical representatives set about achieving social justice in his name in flagrant disregard of the 'democratic maximum'.

It is not always easy to differentiate between radical rhetoric and radical purpose. On the one hand, we have Marat's Cordelier companion Chabot declaring his intent to 'level' the citizens of Loir-et-Cher into 'a people of equals' until there are no more 'opponents to equality' left, or Laplanche declaring 'open war' on the rich and propertied classes of the Cher, but resigning themselves in effect to marginal redistribution.[49] On the other, there are men apparently determined to tip the scales and who run into legal obstacles. Thus, Marc-Antoine Baudot, the 'consummate Héber-

---

[47] Coquard, *Jean-Paul Marat*, pp. 408–9; J. de Cock, 'Marat prophète de la Terreur?', *Annales hist. Révol. fr.* 300 (April–June 1995), pp. 261–9; M. Sonenscher, 'A Limitless Love of Self: Marat's Grim View of Human Nature', *The Times Literary Supplement* 4827 (6 October 1995), p. 3.

[48] *Récit exact de Treilhard et Mathieu*, Bordeaux, 24–8 June 1793, Bibl. Nat., 8° Lb⁴¹ 3132; A. M. Cocula, 'Les représentants de la Convention à Bordeaux en juin 1793: une mission impossible', in Fr. Furet and M. Ozouf (eds.), *La Gironde et les Girondins* (Paris, 1991), pp. 207–18.

[49] On Chabot, see his letter to Rochejean, 14 December 1792, published by J. Gallerand in 'Quelques lettres de Chabot à Rochejean', *Annales hist. Révol. fr.* 7 (1930), p. 367, and N. Hampson, 'François Chabot and His Plot', *Transactions of the Royal Historical Society* 5-26 (London, 1976), pp. 1–14; on Laplanche, see E. Campagnac, 'Les débuts de la déchristianisation dans le Cher, septembre 1793–frimaire an II', *Annales révol.* 4 (1911), pp. 626–37 and 5 (1912), pp. 41–9, 206–11.

tist' according to Ernest Hamel, clearly meant business when he proposed to expropriate the captains of the Tarn textile industry, nationalise the mills and hand the workshops over to the mill-workers; as did Joseph Fouché, who not only vowed to dispossess the 'rich egoists' of the Nièvre and Allier, but embarked upon an active programme of spoliation;[50] or Claude Javogues, whose economic terrorism and extravagant self-indulgence provoked dismay in the Loire;[51] or Jean-Guillaume Taillefer, who secured the active support of the physician Félix Lagasquié, the colleague and friend of Marat, in weeding out 'the aristocrats, usurers, hoarders, monopolists, speculators, egoists and free-wheelers' of the Lot and Aveyron.[52]

Whatever the final results, precious little fraternity emerges from this theatrical brand of class warfare. The agents of Fouché, Laplanche, Baudot and Taillefer were ruthless henchmen, some of whom armed themselves with swords and whips to intimidate their victims. They practised widespread extortion and their example was followed by local tinpot dictators such as the 'omnipotent' Jean-François de l'Etang, self-styled 'Diagoras Boscovir', at La Souter-raine (Creuse), or the Hébertist Charles Jumel, nicknamed 'Le Père Duchesne', at Tulle and Ussel (Corrèze).[53] Such flagrant abuse of power gave rise to numerous accusations of tyranny and dictator-ship which spilled over on to all the economic measures taken in the French provinces during Year II, as if the Terror itself was conceived of as an instrument of egalitarian retribution and redis-tribution, the poor claiming their due from the rich in shrill confrontation, a levelling of society by force, as it were. It reveals

50 On Baudot's activity at Montauban, see L. Lévy-Schneider, 'Le socialisme et la Révolution française (à propos du livre de ce titre de A. Lichtenberger, Paris, 1898)', *La Révol. fr.* 36 (1899), pp. 131–2, and Ligou, 'L'épuration', p. 60; at Moulins, Fouché relied for his extortion campaign on the Cordelier Boissay, a close friend of Momoro, Hébert and Vincent: Cobb, *Les armées révolutionnaires*, pp. 141, 239–42, 268–9, 622–8, 764–5; Liris, 'On rougit ici d'être riche'.
51 Lucas, *Structure of the Terror*, pp. 75–88.
52 P. Caron, 'La Commission civile révolutionnaire et de surveillance de l'Aveyron', *La Révol. fr.* 84 (1931), pp. 345–8; and J. Godechot, review of C. Petit, 'La terreur à Saint-Geniez d'Olt', Ph.D dissertation, University of Toulouse (1976), *Annales hist. Révol. fr.* 49 (1977), pp. 133–4.
53 Report by Chauvin, Germinal Year III, Bibl. Nat., 8° Le[39] 245, pp. 49, 57 and 86; J. Michelet, *Histoire de la Révolution française*, ed. by G. Walter, 2 vols. (Paris, 1939), vol. II, p. 995; Broilliard, 'Diagoras Boscovir', p. 81; F. Arsac, 'Une émeute contre-révolutionnaire à Meymac (Corrèze)', *Annales hist. Révol. fr.* 13 (1936), pp. 151–6.

an alarming readiness to overstep the 'democratic maximum' and is a far cry indeed from just and fair government.

Some of the hardliners were transferred, though most were summoned back to Paris and called to account: 'Casse-Fer' Taillefer from Aveyron and 'Pioche-Fer' Bernard from Besançon, Carrier from Nantes, Barras and Fréron from Toulon and Marseilles, Javogues from Montbrison and Fouché from Lyons. Cobb considers this to have been a demonstration of remarkable hypocrisy by the Robespierrists in government, those whom the terrorist Chasles in Lille called the 'appropriators of virtue' and the 'monopolisers of good conscience'.[54] Indeed, the arbitrariness of anarchical terror was soon to be overshadowed by the official Terror, orchestrated by the police bureau of the Committee of Public Safety and centred on the main revolutionary tribunal in Paris, and whose extension into the provinces was often supervised by members of the ruling committees themselves, Saint-Just and Le Bas in Alsace and the northern marches, Collot-d'Herbois in Lyons, or by trusted colleagues such as Le Bon in the Nord and Pas-de-Calais or Maignet in the Bouches-du-Rhône and Vaucluse.[55] The moral responsibility for the death sentences passed by the revolutionary commissions of Arras, Cambrai and Orange and the mass executions by firing squad on the Brotteaux plain at Lyons clearly devolves onto Robespierre and his close associates.

As he was caught up in the spiral of revolutionary terror, Robespierre's position gradually became untenable. His claim to represent the rigorous middle road between hardliners like Hébert and indulgents like Danton resembled a perilous tightrope walking act, which others, such as his brother Augustin, found themselves emulating: 'Yes indeed, I am a *moderate*', declared the younger Robespierre to the Convention on 3 Thermidor, 'provided we understand by that word a citizen who is not content with proclaiming the principles of morality and justice, but wants them to be applied.'[56] The younger Robespierre had just returned from a

---

[54] Cobb, *Les armées révolutionnaires*, pp. 689, 765.

[55] L. Madelin, *Fouché, 1759–1820* (Paris, 1900); G. Martin, *Carrier et sa mission à Nantes* (Paris, 1924); P. Gaffarel, 'La mission de Maignet dans les Bouches-du-Rhône et en Vaucluse (1794)', *Annales de la Faculté des Lettres d'Aix* 6 (1912), pp. 12–26, 57–73, 73–85; Cobb, *Les armées révolutionnaires*, pp. 239–42, 536–41, 627–9, 684, 764; Lucas, *Structure of the Terror*; Gross, *Saint-Just*, pp. 180, 246, 496; Guilhaumou and Lapied, 'La mission Maignet'.

[56] *Histoire parlementaire de la Révolution française, ou Journal des Assemblées*

mission to the Haute-Saône, on the tracks of the hardliner 'Pioche-Fer' Bernard, whose measures he had countermanded, only to realise he had shown too much leniency. He now demonstrated his strict impartiality by actually *re*-incarcerating suspects whose freedom he had previously secured.

Nothing gives a better illustration of the uncertain course of revolutionary 'justice' than the differing reactions of two deputies, one in Vaucluse, the other in Lot-et-Garonne, faced with incidents involving the uprooting of liberty trees. While Maignet gave orders for the small Comtat town of Bédoin to be delivered to the flames and razed to the ground, Pierre Monestier de la Lozère committed the accused to the revolutionary tribunal and invited the citizens of Nérac to plant a new tree, gather around it and swear to 'live free or die'.[57]

The tightrope dilemma inherent in revolutionary justice is also reflected in the economic and fiscal policies announced by those at the highest level of government. The image of an enemy class had become part of the Jacobin catechism by the middle of Year II, with the Committee of Public Safety vilifying the capitalist and commercial bourgeoisie in no uncertain terms: 'hidden in the obscurity of its business dealings, mercantilism cannot support the strong and burning air of liberty', declared Barère, appearing to acknowledge quite openly that government policy consisted in 'milking rich commerce' and 'demolishing large fortunes'.[58] Placed in the context of the merchant city of Bordeaux, the Girondin connotation carries with it a distorted implication, that of a defeated opposition party assimilated with an enemy class, the upper bourgeoisie, while studies conducted into their social origins show that the typical Girondin was in fact no richer than his Montagnard counterpart.[59] The citizens of Bergerac, in the

---

nationales depuis 1789 jusqu'en 1815, ed. by B.-J. Buchez and P.-C. Roux, 40 vols. (Paris, 1834–8), *Convention*, vol. XXXIII, pp. 379–80; A. Mathiez, *Autour de Robespierre*, 2nd edn (Paris, 1957), pp. 25–8, 167–8.

[57] Agen, 4–5 Floréal; Mont-Adour, 11 Prairial II: Aulard, *Recueil*, vol. XIII, p. 37; Gaffarel, 'La mission de Maignet', pp. 59–72; M. Ozouf, *La fête révolutionnaire, 1789–1799* (Paris, 1976), pp. 281–94, 300–2; Guilhaumou and Lapied, 'La mission Maignet'.

[58] *Arch. parl.*, vol. XC, *Convention*, p. 246; Aulard, *Recueil*, vol. X, p. 325.

[59] A. Forrest, 'Bordeaux au temps de la Gironde', in Furet and M. Ozouf, *La Gironde et les Girondins*, pp. 25–43; J. Boutier, 'Elie Guadet', *ibid.*, pp. 389, 408; M. Dorigny, 'Soutenance de thèse sur travaux', *Annales hist. Révol. fr.* 290 (October–December 1992), p. 600.

Aquitaine hinterland, were subjected to a similar discourse from the moderate democrat Lakanal who used language worthy of Fouché (or Proudhon *avant la lettre*) in promising to discharge society's 'sacred debt' to the poor by stripping the rich and obliging them to 'return to my plebeian brothers the money which has been stolen from them'; and Lanot labelled the rich 'the enemy of the people', a formula similar to the 'open war' which Taillefer declared against the new 'aristocracy of wealth'.[60]

The converse is self-evident, with the Montagnards of Year II identifying themselves in their discursive practice with the 'working-class' (Saint-André), with 'everyone who is sans-culotte, everyone who is poor, who tills the soil' (Brival). Louis Beffroy, who belonged to the Plain, had in the economic debate of November 1792 coined the phrase 'the most interesting portion of the people', and when Lakanal speaks of *le peuple*, he likewise refers to the 'purest, the most interesting part' of the people, the poor, the 'elder sons of the Republic'.[61]

However, class distinctions between 'rich' and 'poor' are deceptive, since the Jacobin ideal looks forward to a society reconciled with itself, a *grande famille* in which the children of all classes would be merged by education, in which the extremes of wealth and deprivation would be eroded, in which all would gain access to property and live in 'mediocrity' or 'decent poverty' from the fruits of their labour. The social challenge of Year II was best sum-marised by Paganel, a friend of the Gironde, who invited the rich to join the cause of the people by 'transforming themselves into sans-culottes', by which he understood a 'renunciation of egoism', a readiness to 'popularise wealth'. By detaching themselves from their surplus assets to the benefit of the suffering poor, the rich would be divesting themselves of the vices 'which make them odious to all the friends of equality' and investing in the people, becoming a 'portion of the people', the 'adoptive brothers of the sans-culottes'.[62]

[60] Aulard, *Recueil*, vol. VI, p. 122, and vol. X, p. 325; Labroue, *La mission de Lakanal*, pp. 299, 304, 308, 330.

[61] Beffroy, 16 November 1792, *Arch. parl.*, vol. LIII, p. 438; Saint-André, 15 May 1793, Aulard, *Recueil*, vol. IV, p. 180; Lakanal, Bergerac, 21–4 October 1793, in Labroue, *La mission de Lakanal*, pp. 219–21; Brival, 18 Pluviôse II, Arch. dép. Haute-Vienne, L 820, Jacobin club of Limoges.

[62] Toulouse, 12 Brumaire II, Arch. dép. Dordogne, 1L 231, mission of Paganel, and Lot-et-Garonne, L 152 and 300, mission of Paganel.

By no stretch of the imagination can the rich man's consent to reach out to his adoptive brethren be understood as an acquiescence to an absolute levelling; 'equality of ownership', stated Robespierre, 'is a chimera', and Bo amplified this idea in his speech to the citizens of Aurillac, in which he reproduced word for word a passage from Rousseau's *Social Contract*: 'By equality, one must not understand that the degrees of power and wealth are absolutely the same; but that, as for power, it can only be exercised in virtue of the laws and short of any violence; and as for wealth, that no citizen should be opulent enough to be able to buy another, nor any poor enough to be obliged to sell himself.'[63] Egalitarianism in a property-owning democracy where the rights of man are fostered can only be a relative affair. This view prompts us to study further the content of the 'moral equality' or 'fraternal equality' which Bo and Romme consider to be the cornerstone of republican democracy.

Appearances have an important role to play in a polemical exercise which lends to the bourgeoisie both the trappings and the mentality of the *ancien régime* nobility, calling it a 'new aristocracy', *l'aristocratie de la richesse*. Baudot the hardliner thus refused to enter into dialogue with the merchants, shipowners and former members of the *parlement* of Bordeaux on the pretext that their dress and lifestyle excluded them from his version of society: 'these Gentlemen in their fine robes, with their broad cravats, their fastidious apparel'. The Dantonist Philippeaux was shocked by the haughtiness and insolence with which regular army officers treated the country conscripts, the 'gentlemen's unbearable arrogance' bringing aristocracy 'into the common tent'. At the civic banquet he organised in Toulouse, Paganel was dismayed to see the bourgeois and the sans-culottes sitting at separate tables. Dartigoeyte in the Gers expressed his disgust at the 'gentlemen' who still 'have the impudence to say *bourgeois* and *petit peuple*', while Lakanal at Bergerac denounced 'the tyranny of the aristocratic breed known as *bourgeois vivant noblement*'. When Pierre Garrau was accused by Girondin sympathisers of having 'insulted the people' by aping the financiers and driving around in a gilt coach

---

[63] Robespierre, 24 April 1793, *Œuvres*, vol. IX, p. 459; Bo, Aurillac, 13 Pluviôse II, Bibl. Nat., 8° Lb⁴⁰ 2504; the passage from Rousseau is taken from 'Du contrat social', book II, chapter 11 ('Des divers systèmes de législation'), *Œuvres*, vol. II, p. 538.

drawn by ten chargers 'with the pomp of a king', he retorted that he travelled in a 'poor worm-eaten carriage' drawn by four rented nags.[64]

Accustomed as people were to the inequalities of the old regime, and given the 'brotherhood of man' anticipated in the new, language, dress and behaviour were of the essence in the egalitarian challenge, especially since the superiority of the rich was matched by the habitual deference of the poor. Lanot was kept busy in the Corrèze eradicating from the countryside 'that sort of servility which keeps the farmer out of habit subservient to the bourgeois aristocracy' who buy up the nationalised lands and monopolise all the benefits of the Revolution. 'Monsieur le Citoyen' was a form of address encountered by Lakanal among the Sarladais peasantry victimised by 'servile usage': how can they rid themselves, he asked, of the obstructions which hinder their economic and social promotion? There can be no moral equality, claimed Bo, while the poor working man is still encumbered with 'this ridiculous respect which is but the fruit of ignorance: the lower classes must no longer ingenuously think of themselves as less worthy than the wealthy classes'.[65] 'Moral levelling' entails a learning process which needs to accompany or precede the redistribution of social goods and which cuts both ways: the rich man's acquired taste for mediocrity[66] and his readiness to renounce his surplus wealth must be matched by the working man's own awareness of his equal status, enabling him to rise to the full height of his dignity.

When Bo and Chabot introduced progressive taxation to the provincial cities of southern France, or when Romme introduced food rationing, prescribing a 'bread of equality' made from the whole grain of the rich man mixed with the poor man's siftings and baked in the communal oven, they were expecting moral and

---

[64] Baudot, La Réole, 26 August 1793, Aulard, *Recueil*, vol. VI, p. 122; Philippeaux, Limoges, 11 July 1793, *ibid.*, vol. V, p. 237; Paganel, Toulouse, 5 Brumaire II, *ibid.*, vol. VIII, p. 49; Lakanal, Monségur, Thermidor II, in Labroue, *La mission de Lakanal*, p. 325; Garrau, Belchenéa, 19 August 1793, Aulard, *Recueil*, vol. VI, p. 33.

[65] Lanot, Meymac, 12 Nivôse II, Arch. Nat., AF$_{II}$ 171, pl. 1405, p. 30; Lakanal, writing in the *Journal d'instruction populaire* of Messidor Year II, Labroue, *La mission de Lakanal*, p. 252; Bo, Aurillac, 13 Pluviôse II, Bibl. Nat., 8° Lb^{40} 2504.

[66] Mediocrity is of course an important leitmotiv of French Enlightenment thought: R. Mauzi, *L'idée du bonheur au XVIIIe siècle* (Paris, 1969), pp. 175–9; and J. Ehrard, *L'idée de nature en France au XVIIIe siècle*, 2 vols. (Paris, 1963), vol. II, pp. 575–605.

fraternal equality to prevail. Rather than succumbing to the temptations of a class war or, alternatively, projecting the deceptive utopian image of a classless society, they were expressing the hope that the love of frugality and spirit of sacrifice, the willingness to share and share alike, would make it unnecessary to redistribute *everything*, and thus bring the virtues of family life closer to reality.

ROBESPIERRE: THE EMBLEMATIC FIGURE OF EGALITARIANISM

The figure of Robespierre is central to this narrative because, foremost among his contemporaries, he took it upon himself to convey the 'rational ideal of social justice and solidarity' which the Enlightenment, in the words of Aulard, had bequeathed to the Revolution. The fact that he commanded the attention of his political generation in this respect led many Jacobins to rally to his banner or take their cue from him, while others who did not subscribe to his personal cause found much sense in the reforms he proposed, or shared his vision of a fair society with which his name came to be associated by the middle of 1793. Unfortunately for his posthumous reputation, the twelve months that elapsed between then and 9 Thermidor obscured this 'shared vision' to the point of oblivion. The Terror, of which he was the principal architect and proponent, allied to partisan strife, effectively occupied him more and more, and his active personal involvement in all affairs of state, including the establishment of a civil religion, relegated his role as social reformer to the background. Thus, the 'egalitarian' has tended to be eclipsed by the 'advocate of terror' and the 'prophet of virtue', a trend which the prominence given to political discourse by modern historians has only served to reinforce.

Robespierre is indeed considered the most perfect embodiment of revolutionary culture, 'ideology incarnate', as Patrice Gueniffey would have it, a 'living commentary' on the Declaration of Rights and simultaneously terrorist rhetoric at its most consummate.[67] According to Bronislaw Baczko, Robespierre at the height of the Terror fully identified himself with the pure and virtuous republic.[68]

[67] P. Gueniffey, 'Robespierre', in Furet and M. Ozouf, *Dictionnaire critique*, 2nd edn, vol. II, *Acteurs*, pp. 247–9, 251, 258.

[68] B. Baczko, *Ending the Terror: The French Revolution After Robespierre* (Cambridge, 1994), p. 29.

And while François Furet considers Robespierre to have mastered the discourse on equality and incarnated the people, it served him as a means of wielding ideological power, as magisterial communicator and potential manipulator.[69] The majority of participants in the 1993 Arras Symposium on Robespierre continued to see him as a man who spent his career 'inventing the Revolution', constructing in discourse the development of a regenerated society (Colin Lucas); a man of words rather than action, a 'talker', not a 'doer', who let others get on with the doing (Jacques Revel);[70] a man whose discourse is the most perfect manifestation of Jacobin radicalism (Lucien Jaume), implying profound organic change not in the economic sphere, but in the realm of ethics (Jacques Guilhaumou) and in the nature of citizenship (Olivier Le Cour Grandmaison).[71]

Curiously, this ability to prophesy and instigate moral or political change goes hand in hand with a tendency to change with the times, to react to events, to build a theory 'after the event', to 'follow rather than to lead',[72] a form of opportunism which may be attributable not so much to the political manoeuvring of an archstrategist and schemer as to Robespierre's 'singular conception of equality', understood as a virtue to be bred, by his natural inclination to authoritarianism and his readiness to resort to force. Thus, Mona Ozouf interprets Robespierre's acquiescence to the price controls and legalised looting demanded by the sans-culottes not as yielding to pressure, but as a belated yet sincere conversion to economic coercion.[73]

It may however be stretching this line of reasoning to imply, as does Gueniffey, that Robespierre's social convictions lack 'solidity'.[74] On the contrary, as a number of papers presented to the

[69] Fr. Furet, *Penser la Révolution française*, 2nd edn, pp. 81–2.
[70] C. Lucas, 'Robespierre: homme politique et culture politique', pp. 13–17, and J. Revel, 'Robespierre, la politique, la morale et le sacré: table ronde', p. 429 in J.-P. Jessenne, G. Deregnaucourt, J.-P. Hirsch and H. Leuwers (eds.), *Robespierre: de la nation artésienne à la république et aux nations; actes du Colloque d'Arras, 1–2–3 avril 1993* (Villeneuve d'Ascq, 1994); cf. 'Robespierre n'agit pas', 'son rôle n'est pas de faire': Gueniffey, 'Robespierre', pp. 252, 255.
[71] See contributions by L. Jaume and J. Guilhaumou to the round table 'Robespierre, la politique, la morale et le sacré', in Jessenne *et al.*, *Robespierre*, pp. 427–32; Le Cour Grandmaison's paper was not included in the published proceedings, but see his recent work *Les citoyennetés en Révolution (1789–1794)* (Paris, 1992).
[72] Lucas, 'Robespierre', p. 16.   [73] Ozouf, 'Egalité', p. 158.
[74] Gueniffey, 'Robespierre', p. 261.

Arras Symposium indicate, his carefully built charisma as a politician achieved credibility largely on account of his painstaking and untiring devotion to the cause of the poor, the underprivileged and the overtaxed throughout his legal and political career, from 1784 onward. It was because his commitment to equality identified him with the 'people', especially the working people, the cobblers and rope-makers of Artois, and the sans-culottes of the Paris sections, that he came to embody, in the eyes of his many admirers, not the political culture but the social conscience of the French Revolution, not the lust for power but the thirst for justice. This carefully orchestrated image of righter of wrongs, already evident in his speech on the *marc d'argent* of April 1791, gained him resounding acclaim in April 1793 when he submitted his radically amended version of the Declaration of Rights to the Jacobin Club and through the press to the nation at large.[75]

Florence Gauthier has recently offered an explanation of Robespierre's ambivalent notion of property, based on two differing concepts of liberty and on the inherent conflict between acquisitiveness and the desire for greater equality. Whereas life and liberty are gifts of nature and thus inalienable (as Jefferson claimed), Robespierre did not consider the ownership of property a natural right. Basing her argument on E. P. Thompson's account of the 'moral economy' in eighteenth-century England, Gauthier shows that by rejecting the physiocratic notion of free trade where staple foodstuffs were concerned, Robespierre was in effect calling into question the individual right of ownership.[76] The practice of imposing 'martial law' against unlawful assembly in response to food riots and other forms of agrarian revolt (the French version of the Riot Act), as his fellow Constituents did on 21 October 1789 and subsequently by adopting the Le Chapelier law of 14 June 1791, aroused his indignation. Robespierre emerges from Gauthier's analysis as the theoretician of the 'natural right to existence', claiming that all commodities 'essential to the preservation of life are the common property of society as a whole'.[77] His view that

[75] Fl. Gauthier, 'Robespierre, critique de l'économie politique tyrannique et théoricien de l'économie politique populaire', in Jessenne *et al.*, *Robespierre*, pp. 235–43; see also J.-P. Hirsch, 'Terror and Property', p. 216.
[76] Fl. Gauthier, *Triomphe et mort du droit naturel en Révolution, 1789–1795–1802* (Paris, 1992), pp. 66–95.
[77] *Ibid.*, pp. 41–58, 70–3.

curbs must be placed on possessive individualism suggests that economic power too must be circumscribed.

But this is only part of the story. Robespierre's identification with the working man makes him the defender not just of the right to subsistence for those who 'have nothing to lose', as he ironically calls the meanest of the mean in his speech on the *marc d'argent*,[78] but also of the property rights of those who do have something to lose, those whose 'meagre possessions', whose 'modest wage', 'coarse clothes' and 'small savings' endow them with what Robespierre habitually calls a degree of 'honourable poverty'.[79] Olwen Hufton makes the point that passive citizens who were denied the vote, those adult males earning less than 17–20 sols a day in 1790, were potential paupers whose fate hung in the balance: 'Every passive citizen was a vulnerable citizen.'[80] It was this very precariousness which led Robespierre to profess a belief in the right of ownership in no way dissimilar from that of John Locke.[81] As succinctly stated in his speech on the franchise of 11 August 1791, the smaller one's property, the more one is attached to it, the instinct of conservation being 'proportional to one's fortune': 'the closer property is to the basic needs and subsistence necessary to man, the more sacred it becomes'.[82]

One is reminded of Adam Smith's reference to the 'linen shirt' and 'leather shoes' which even the lowest order would not be without, 'the want of which would be supposed to denote that disgraceful degree of poverty which, it is presumed, nobody can well fall into without extreme bad conduct', a reference which Amartya Sen considers basic to any valid definition of poverty.[83] Smith's condition of a 'creditable day-labourer' is closely related to Robespierre's understanding of decent or honourable poverty, but Robespierre believes that the creditable poor, together with the possessions that sustain them, must be protected by law, and that they need to make their voice heard through the ballot-box,

---

[78] Robespierre, *Œuvres*, vol. VII, p. 164.
[79] *Ibid.*, vol. VII, p. 165, and 24 April 1793, *ibid.*, vol. IX, p. 459.
[80] Hufton, *The Poor*, p. 23.
[81] Gauthier, *Triomphe et mort du droit naturel*, pp. 78–9.
[82] Robespierre, *Œuvres*, vol. VII, p. 622.
[83] A. Smith, 'Taxes upon Consumable Commodities', in book V of *An Inquiry into the Nature and the Causes of the Wealth of Nations*, ed. by R. H. Campbell, A. S. Skinner and W. B. Todd, 2 vols. (Oxford, 1976), vol. II (sect. v. ii. j), p. 869; cited by Sen, *Poverty and Famines*, p. 18.

unlike the rich and influential 'whose credit and personal resources are such that they can do without the protection of the laws'.[84]

Robespierre's circumspection on the crucial issue of property together with his evident intellectual affinity with Locke and Smith makes him an awkward liberal of a novel kind: one who simultaneously defends the right of ownership and asks for curbs to be placed on possessive and proprietary individualism;[85] one who is deeply suspicious of the accumulation of wealth and free-wheeling capitalism, yet relies on the autonomy of the economic process; one who tolerates the profit motive and the law of supply and demand but seeks to cushion their ill-effects through social welfare; one who has lingering doubts about the feasibility of reducing inequality (inequality of ownership is 'a necessary and incurable evil', he wrote in 1791; 'equality of ownership is fundamentally impossible in civil society', in 1792; a 'chimera', in 1793),[86] but who is willing to give it a try (through progressive taxation, poor relief, full employment, the enactment of a minimum property right, equality of opportunity through education); but one who remains wedded to individual freedom and the principle of minimum interference by the state, who expressly warns against bureaucratic encroachment by government on the liberties of the governed, who on the very eve of revolutionary dictatorship and terror affirms the right to resist oppression.[87] His is a humanist brand of liberalism based on universal natural right.

But liberalism nonetheless: Robespierre holds out the promise of a fair *and* a free society. In representing the cause of the sans-culottes, he claimed to be serving the interests of the landowners and merchants as well. In a phrase reminiscent of Mably, he expressed the ethical view of social relations and political economy in stating that if only the rich regarded themselves as the 'stewards of society' or as the 'brothers of the poor' (*les économes de la société, les frères du pauvre*), then it might be possible to have 'no

[84] Robespierre, *Œuvres*, vol. VII, p. 622.
[85] See C. B. Mackenzie, *The Political Theory of Political Individualism* (Oxford, 1962), pp. 2–3, 137, 142.
[86] Robespierre, *Œuvres*, vol. IV, pp. 116–19; vol. V, p. 165; vol. IX, pp. 459–71.
[87] Articles 25–31 of his draft Declaration of Rights, Robespierre, *Œuvres*, vol. IX, pp. 463–9.

other law than the most unlimited freedom'.[88] Robespierre's con-
demnation of the unacceptable face of capitalism may not make
him a socialist, but neither should the Marxist view of his
'economic pessimism' lead us to relegate him 'to another age'.[89]
Rather, he stands out as a thoughtful leveller loath to 'pervert the
natural order of things', one whose 'incorruptible' spartan stance is
aimed at winning the confidence of the poor and stirring the
conscience of the rich, a man who seeks not quantum change but a
fair and reasonable redistribution of income, an attenuation of
inequality not by constraint, but by persuasion, 'par des voies
douces'.[90] Robespierre's main contribution to egalitarian Jacobin
discourse was thus to give economic substance to the abstract
political concept of the universal 'brotherhood of man'.

[88] 2 December 1792, Robespierre, *Œuvres*, vol. IX, pp. 109–20; cf. Mably's view of
the elders of the community charged with the management of the common estate,
whom he calls 'les économes de la République' and 'les pères de la patrie': in
Doutes proposés aux philosophes économistes (1768) and *De la législation, ou
Principes des lois* (1776), reproduced in *Sur la théorie du pouvoir politique*, ed.
P. Friedmann (Paris, 1975), pp. 157, 217.

[89] M. Rebérioux, 'Jaurès et Robespierre', in *Actes du Colloque Robespierre: XIIe
Congrès international des sciences historiques (Vienne, 3 septembre 1965)* (Paris,
1967), pp. 199–200.

[90] J.-P. Gross, 'Robespierre et l'impôt progressif', in Jessenne *et al.*, *Robespierre*,
p. 291.

2. The family ethos and the common happiness

> Every evening, at supper, which was the only meal when all the family could be assembled, he would find himself, like a venerable patriarch, at the head of a numerous household; for we were normally twenty-two at table, including the plough-boys and the vine-tenders, who in winter were threshers, the cowherd, the shepherd and two dairymaids.
>
> Restif de la Bretonne, *La vie de mon père*, 1778[1]

THE RIGHTS OF MAN: FROM 1789 TO 1793

The reference to the rights of man is a constant feature of revolutionary egalitarianism and helps underscore its continuity. The abolition of privileges, which introduced civic and political equality into the revolutionary process on the night of 4 August 1789 and heralded the advent of greater material equality, clearly occupied the minds of those who set about drafting the Declaration of Rights that same month. The fact that the Declaration itself gives prominence to the individual liberties enshrined in previous English and American bills of rights should not detract from the recognition that it contains a number of significant egalitarian safeguards as well, and that a basic difference in conception lends it a strong political *and* economic bias.

The comparative analysis offered by Jürgen Habermas shows that the Virginia Declaration of 12 June 1776 and those of the other American colonies, echoed in the Jeffersonian Declaration of Independence defending 'life, liberty and the pursuit of happiness', adopt a 'bottom-up' approach, by assuming that society allows

---

[1] Rétif de la Bretonne, *La vie de mon père*, ed. G. Rouger (Paris, 1970), p. 130.

human rights to flourish spontaneously, provided it is left to itself and the state prevented from interfering. The emphasis is on individual self-determination and self-reliance, and the constitution of a social sphere in which the free play of natural laws allows them to reap their beneficial effects. The French Declaration of 26 August 1789, in contrast, reveals a 'top-down' approach: physiocratic in inspiration, it is strongly Rousseauist in its implication that natural right can only be positively secured through the exercise of political will, by steering an imperfect society toward a moral ideal, and hence by regulating the free competition of private interests and the interplay of market forces.[2]

The projection of the individual into the public sphere does not simply give him a political persona and turn him into a citizen, it also has socio-economic significance. Thus, the preamble of the French Declaration of 1789 refers to rights and obligations, leading to the 'happiness of all'; article 1 refers to 'equal rights'; article 4 to the limits placed on individual freedom by equality and to the equal enjoyment of human rights, here defined as reciprocal rights, the individual being viewed in his social relationship with others;[3] article 6 substantiates the principle of equal opportunity for all, introducing the notion of a meritocracy; article 13 on taxation enshrines both the principle of equal liability and that of fiscal graduation ('from each according to his faculties').[4] All this implies a tacit agreement to the principle of fair apportionment.

Habermas explains the emergence of a public sphere in terms of economic development, active participation by the property-owning bourgeoisie in a liberal market economy leading to individual betterment and the accumulation of capital, which in turn generated the need to defend the right to property and the freedom of enterprise.[5] In eighteenth-century France, the economic discourse inaugurated by the physiocrats and pursued by the Constituents even in areas where the subjects were ostensibly political, as in the case of the franchise, would appear to bear out this

---

[2] J. Habermas, *Theorie und Praxis: sozialphilosophische Studien* (Neuwied and Berlin, 1963), pp. 57–61; Ferry and Renaut, *Philosophie politique 3*, pp. 32–5. See also D. W. Brogan, *The American Political System* (London, 1951), Appendix 1, p. 387.

[3] Gauthier, *Triomphe et mort du droit naturel*, pp. 27–8.

[4] Declaration of 26 August 1789, in *Les Déclarations*, ed. by Jaume, pp. 11–16.

[5] J. Habermas, *Strukturwandel der Öffentlichkeit: Untersuchungen zu einer Kategorie der bürgerlichen Gesellschaft* (Neuwied, 1962), pp. 18–28, 58–65.

interpretation. After all, the main thrust of Robespierre's oft-repeated argument on suffrage and eligibility revolved around the old adage 'no taxation without representation',[6] the *cens* or electoral tax resulting in 'monstrous differences' which made a citizen 'active' or 'passive' on the basis of his position on the income scale and the 'differing degrees of fortune', i.e. in terms of economic inequality.[7] It stems from a liberal view of property rights as voiced by Locke[8] and postulates the desirability of extending these benefits to all without exclusion.

The 'Jacobin' tendencies already discernible in the 1789 Declaration were further developed when the National Convention received the mandate to draft the new republican constitution after the fall of the monarchy. Among the leading members of the drafting committee appointed on 29 September 1792 and chaired by Condorcet were Sieyès, Pétion and Tom Paine, whose two-part *Rights of Man* had secured him notoriety in Britain and America and the status of elder statesman and political philosopher in France. Though the proposed constitution, submitted on 15 February 1793, was a 'flop', as John Keane confirms,[9] the new text of the Declaration of Rights was to prove more enduring.

While several other versions were to be tabled, notably by Gilbert Romme and Jean-Baptiste Harmand on 17 April and Robespierre on 21 April, the so-called 'Girondin' declaration proposed by Barère on 29 May, just before the fall of the Gironde, reproduced most of Condorcet's and Paine's articles, many of which were to be retained in the final 'Montagnard' declaration finally adopted on 24 June. Indeed, out of the thirty-three articles in the final version, twenty-three, or over two-thirds, are either taken wholesale from Condorcet's draft or 'cannibalised', to use Keith Baker's expression,[10] with minor amendments. The remaining ten articles are taken mainly from Robespierre's or Romme's drafts, with some additions from the members of the five-

[6] J.-J. Clamageran, *Histoire de l'impôt en France*, 3 vols. (Paris, 1867–76), vol. II, p. 179.
[7] J.-P. Gross, 'Robespierre et l'impôt progressif', p. 283.
[8] Gauthier, *Triomphe et mort du droit naturel*, pp. 78–9.
[9] Keane, *Tom Paine*, p. 356.
[10] K. M. Baker, *Condorcet: From Natural Philosophy to Social Mathematics* (Chicago and London, 1975), p. 328; on Condorcet's draft, see also E. Badinter and R. Badinter, *Condorcet (1743–1794): un intellectuel en politique*, 2nd edn (Paris, 1988), pp. 574–6, 597–604.

man team appointed to finalise the text: Hérault de Séchelles, Saint-Just, Couthon, Mathieu and Ramel-Nogaret.[11]

The end result, the so-called 'Montagnard' version, is in effect a mixed bag of individual and collective rights, a synthesis of the egalitarian form of liberalism discussed in the introduction. Thus, individual liberties are given a high profile: freedom of opinion, freedom of expression, freedom of conscience, presumption of innocence and due process of law. As for the individual right of ownership, where the text of 1789 affirmed that 'property being an inviolable and sacred right, no one can be deprived of it', the 1793 Declaration spells out 'of the smallest portion' of one's property (article 19). Freedom of enterprise is given full rein: the right of ownership includes that of 'enjoying and disposing of one's property, one's income, the fruit of one's labour and industry', and 'no type of work, cultivation or commerce can be denied a citizen's industry' (articles 16 and 17). Any infringement of a person's liberty or security is roundly condemned, especially if the oppression stems from abuse of power by those in government (article 9).

Significantly, fear of interference by the state is accompanied by a clear emphasis on society's claims. The Declaration of 1793 reinforces the equal nature of civic and economic rights, all adult male citizens without distinction having the right to vote and the right to acquire property, and the abolition of domestic servitude prefiguring the advent of both equal citizenship and universal suffrage (articles 18 and 29). It also introduces a substantial number of new social rights – the right to subsistence, the right to work, the right to social welfare, the right to education – these 'obligations'[12] constituting henceforth a 'sacred debt', not simply a moral duty as in the past. Far from minimising government interference, these provisions, in keeping with Paine's bold proposals to build up social welfare institutions catering to the social rights of citizens, paid for through general taxation and considered 'not of the nature of a charity, but of a right',[13] open up an extensive new vista onto the active and enabling state and ultimately the welfare state.

---

[11] For an analysis of these various contributions, see J.-P. Gross, 'Saint-Just et la déclaration des droits de 1793', in B. Vinot (ed.), *Actes du Colloque Grandes figures de la Révolution française en Picardie, Blérancourt, 17–18 juin 1989* (Chauny, 1990), pp. 171–88.

[12] See Ferry and Renaut, *Philosophie politique 3*, pp. 74–9.

[13] Keane, *Tom Paine*, p. 303.

The fundamental difference between the Declaration of 1789 and that of 1793 resides in this duality: individual liberties and social rights are locked together in an uneasy partnership and held in check. Thus, while liberty in both texts is negatively defined as the power enjoyed by man 'to do everything that does not harm the rights of others', it is preceded by equality in the 1793 version (article 2), yet reinforced by the addition of 'security' and 'property'.[14] It is tempting to conclude in the light of the fierce battle waged by Girondins and Montagnards over constitutional issues[15] that the former contributed the individual rights and the latter the collective rights: indeed, that was the conclusion reached by Albert Mathiez, who thought the final text was the result of an awkward compromise rather than the reflection of a deep-seated consensus.[16] The Condorcet and Girondin texts are already as close as can be to an equal and fair definition of political democracy;[17] both Montagnards and Girondins were wedded to the principle of private ownership, and both Robespierre and Condorcet supported the introduction of progressive taxation and free elementary education, without which the citizens would be unable to take advantage of their equality before the law. The newly proclaimed social rights may have been heavenly music to the ears of Marat, Hébert and the radical sans-culottes, but no true son of the Enlightenment would seriously have repudiated them.

The 1793 Declaration of Rights is both the consecration of 'bourgeois individualism', frowned on by Karl Marx[18] but praised by Aléxis de Tocqueville,[19] and the validation of 'social justice', frowned on by Tocqueville but preached by Jean Jaurès. It implicitly argues that only a combination of the two can lead to the ultimate felicity of society. This combination is already subsumed

---

[14] The four 'natural and imprescriptible' rights of man are, in order: 'l'égalité, la liberté, la sûreté, la propriété', in *Les Déclarations*, ed. by Jaume, p. 299.

[15] Godechot, *Les institutions de la France*, p. 246.

[16] A. Mathiez, 'La Constitution de 1793', *Annales hist. Révol. fr.* 5 (1928), p. 514.

[17] A point made by G. Lefebvre, *La Révolution française*, 1st edn, p. 207.

[18] Marx's critique of human rights as a manifestation of the bourgeois revolution is that citizens free and equal in law are as men at the mercy of the free play of market forces: Habermas, *Theorie und Praxis*, p. 133; Ferry and Renaut, *Philosophie politique 3*, p. 125.

[19] Tocqueville in 1848 voiced the true liberal doctrine on human rights, essentially anti-socialist in nature; ultra neo-liberals such as Hayek concur: F. A. Hayek, *The Fatal Conceit: The Errors of Socialism*, ed. W. W. Bartley III (London, 1988).

in the French republican triad: it was Robespierre who, on 5 December 1790, had asked that the word 'Fraternity' be placed alongside 'Liberty' and 'Equality' on the flags of the national guard.[20] After all, there can be no true democracy, the contrary tendencies of liberty and equality cannot be reconciled and the philosophical contradiction identified by Jean Baechler remains forever unresolved if there is no fraternity between citizens. Jacobin practice suggests that fraternity is not an abstract notion or a decorative afterthought, but an essential ingredient, the lubricant without which liberty and equality reach deadlock and the machinery of government grinds to a halt, and hence a key factor in politics.

FRATERNITY, THE EXTENDED FAMILY AND PATERNALISM

The message of liberty, social justice and solidarity contained in the revised Declaration of Rights was widely circulated and publicised all over France throughout the sombre months of the Terror. While the 1793 Constitution remained locked in a cedarwood 'ark of the covenant', out of sight and out of mind, not so the Declaration, which was deemed to enshrine inalienable and imprescriptible rights, not legal requirements subject to revision, but 'eternal principles' valid for all time. The preamble, drafted by Robespierre,[21] stipulates that the aim of such publicity is to enable the governed to bring their government to book, to prevent free citizens being 'oppressed' and 'degraded by tyranny', to let them see with their own eyes at any time 'the foundations of their liberty and happiness'. And it was Robespierre who insisted that the text of the Declaration should be proclaimed at public ceremonies, posted up in public places, 'on the walls of our houses', and provide 'the first lesson' that children would receive from their fathers.[22] While

[20] M. Robespierre, 'Sur les gardes nationales', 5 December 1790, in *Œuvres*, vol. VI, p. 643; F. A. Aulard, 'La devise "Liberté, Egalité, Fraternité"', *Etudes et leçons sur la Révolution française*, 6th series (Paris, 1910), pp. 1–31; M. Agulhon, *Marianne au combat: l'imagerie ou la symbolique républicaine de 1789 à 1880* (Paris, 1979), pp. 31–3; G. Antoine, *Liberté, Egalité, Fraternité, ou les fluctuations d'une devise* (Paris, 1981); M. David, *Fraternité et Révolution française* (Paris, 1987), pp. 10–11.
[21] *Les Déclarations*, ed. by Jaume, pp. 257 and 299.
[22] Robespierre, speech of 10 May 1793, *Œuvres*, vol. IX, pp. 495–510.

healthy scepticism is of course justifiably aroused at the thought of such a bill of rights on show in town halls, schools and public squares alongside the guillotine, the uncomfortable fact remains that the rights of man were not suspended during the Terror and afforded a visible reminder of a democratic society in the making.[23]

Fraternity as a mainspring of the social contract is a subject which has received scant attention in recent years. Surprisingly, Marcel David, the French historian who has done most to put fraternity on the map (admittedly in the field of the history of ideas), understates its relevance to the Jacobin system of government. Indeed, he denies that fraternity, compared with the principle of 'real equality', came to play any significant role in the policies pursued by those in power: 'Barely any trace of it can be found at the highest level', writes David, 'not that the Convention and its Committee of Public Safety showed no interest in it, or rejected their legal obligation to support it. But apart from measures to reduce discrimination, which fraternity underlies expressly, none of the provisions made in the area of the material living conditions of the population are presented as imbued with a fraternal character.'[24]

It may prove necessary to review this judgement in the light of the measures actually taken, in terms of both their substance and their presentation. What is especially striking is that acts of social and economic solidarity continue unabated during the crisis years 1793–4 and are a natural derivative of the fraternal gatherings which distinguished the Revolution from its very beginnings. The year 1789 bred the habit of the *rassemblement patriotique*, symbolically acted out in the preparations for the National Federation of 14 July 1790, when people from all walks of life, children and

---

[23] Thus, Saint-Just on his way to the scaffold on 10 Thermidor is reputed to have pointed to the Declaration posted on the wall and said to his guard: 'To think it was I who made that!': *Papiers inédits trouvés chez Robespierre, Saint-Just, Payan, etc., supprimés ou omis par Courtois, précédés du rapport de ce député à la Convention Nationale, 16 Nivôse an III*, 3 vols. (Paris, 1828), vol. II, p. 71; E. Dard, *Un épicurien sous la Terreur: Hérault de Séchelles (1759–1794)* (Paris, 1907), pp. 220–42.

[24] David, *Fraternité et Révolution française*, p. 195. Such a strictly 'ideological' approach tends to show only half the picture; the same can be said of the literary approach, as in the case of André Delaporte's review of the 'idea' of equality in eighteenth-century France, which tends to dwell on utopian visions of equality to the exclusion of the real world: Delaporte, *L'idée d'égalité*, pp. 325–34.

grown-ups, monks and fine ladies, and even the king in person, congregated on the Champ de Mars in Paris, rolled up their sleeves, took up their spades and pick-axes and pushed wheelbarrows to ensure the works were finished on time, in a great and memorable manifestation of the community spirit at work: equality and fraternity vividly brought to life.[25]

Although such classless images are clearly imbued with the message of national reconciliation, they have an economic relevance too, which was again highlighted in August 1793 on the occasion of the national recruitment campaign, the *levée en masse*, in which all classes and ages had their assigned part to play: 'Young men will go to battle; married men will forge the arms ... women will make the tents ... children will ravel old linen into lint; the elders will have themselves borne onto the public squares to excite the courage of the warriors.'[26] The many Jacobin festivals of Year II, dedicated to Friendship, Equality or Labour, appeal to the same virtue of neighbourliness and propound the same image of a happy family united in a common endeavour and, when the labour is done, enjoying a shared meal around a trestle table or dancing to the sound of a fiddle in common rejoicings.

The theme of the 'single family' or 'extended family' is one which will be familiar to most students of French revolutionary texts.[27] It stirred the imagination of the National Convention in early November 1792, at the opening of the long economic debate on the corn trade, when, in the words of the rapporteur Fabre de l'Hérault, it was commonly recognised that without the free exchange of grain and flour, 'a people of brothers would be refusing a surplus which was perishing in their hands to those who are members of the same family'.[28] It was soon to become a cliché, resorted to in times of shortage by the representatives-on-mission as an incentive to the fair apportionment of scarce commodities. Thus, Nicolas Maure, the grocer from Auxerre, reminded his electors of the Yonne department of the need to share their grain 'in the name of brotherliness and good neighbourliness' and took as the basis for all his activities 'the perfect

[25] *Réimpression de l'Ancien Moniteur*, 32 vols. (Paris, 1863–70), 11 and 13 July 1790, vol. V, pp. 95–6, 112; Ozouf, *La fête révolutionnaire*, pp. 44–74.
[26] Decree of 23 August 1793, in Aulard, *Recueil*, vol. VI, p. 72.
[27] P. Higonnet, 'The "Harmonization of the Spheres": Goodness and Dysfunction in the Provincial Clubs', in Baker, *The Terror*, pp. 122–4.
[28] Report of 3 November 1792, *Arch. parl.*, vol. LIII, *Convention*, p. 131.

accord of fraternity'.[29] Pierre Paganel declared to the people of Toulouse in Brumaire that their happiness could only be secured through sharing, it being unthinkable that 'misfortunes should be unequally borne and that surplus should exist side by side with dearth among the children of a common homeland'.[30] Antoine Lanot reminded his listeners in Brive that 'Republicans now make up a large family occupying many places and many houses'.[31] And Jean-Baptiste Bo, who coined the expression 'fraternal popularity', urged the local authorities of the fertile region of Gaillac to divide their grain with the inhabitants of the arid Rouergue, because 'a family of brothers must share both the hardships and the pleasures' and the principle of 'equal shares' should compel them 'spontaneously to deprive themselves of everything that was not momentarily indispensable ... You must submit with your brethren to the most austere economy, we must all suffer momentarily for the priceless reward of our freedom, since we have consecrated the principle of fraternity as the basis of our republican system'.[32]

Similarly, Jean-Baptiste Féraud, on his visit to the sheep-rearing mountainfolk of the upper Pyrenees, endeavoured to make these worthy citizens 'good fathers, good friends, good spouses, good sons, good republicans, compassionate to the misfortunes of their fellow men' and to prepare them to face 'all manner of privation, sacrifice and self-denial in their devotion to their country'.[33] Jean-Marie Goujon, who was appointed to the key post in charge of a wartime ministry of supply during the winter months of Year II, dutifully discharged his mandate in consideration of the fact that 'provisions are the property of the people as a whole, and the people are a family of brothers'.[34] Out in the field, Gilbert Romme instituted food rationing in close liaison with Goujon, mindful of

[29] Letter to the president of the National Convention, Auxerre, 24 September 1793, Aulard, *Recueil*, vol. VII, pp. 48–50.

[30] Toulouse, 5 and 8 Brumaire II, Arch. Nat., AF$_{II}$ 185, Midi, pl. 1531, p. 6; Arch. dép. Dordogne, 1 L 231, Paganel; Lot-et-Garonne, L 152, Paganel.

[31] Arch. dép. Corrèze, L 98, missions, 8 Pluviôse II.

[32] Letters from Figeac, Gaillac and Lavaur, 12, 17 and 20 Germinal II, Arch. dép. Lot, L 12, missions; Tarn, L 132, missions, pp. 7–12; and Tarn-et-Garonne, L 75*, dist. Montauban, f° 45.

[33] Arreau, 3 Germinal II, Arch. Nat., AF$_{II}$ 262, Committee of Public Safety, pl. 2214, p. 9; Aulard, *Recueil*, vol. XII, p. 138.

[34] P. F. Tissot, 'Vie de Goujon', in Fr. Brunel and S. Goujon (eds.), *Les martyrs de prairial: textes et documents inédits* (Geneva, 1992), p. 165.

this maxim which he encapsulated in the term 'fraternal equality'. *Egalité fraternelle* meant sharing without constraint, making spontaneous offerings of chestnuts, dried peas and lentils to those in need, motivated by the 'gentle pleasure which stems from coming to the aid of one's brethren' in a spirit of 'frank and universal brotherhood'.[35] In the rural communities where Romme's proclamations were put to the test, his earnest pleas produced a consistent echo: 'All citizens are brothers and all food supplies must be common to them all and shared accordingly ... Equal consumption among all working folk will enable them to enjoy jointly, and each severally, all the benefits of society.'[36]

The hackneyed theme of the extended family, which served as a leitmotiv to the persuasive republican propaganda of Year II, appealed to the principle of equity rather than strict equality. Equity tolerates an unequal distribution of basic foodstuffs or other commodities, between localities or members of a single family – the old, the young, the working man, the nursing mother – each of whom is called upon to contribute his or her share, by definition unequal, to the common good (from each according to his or her means). Extrapolated to the 'large family' or community, equity counsels neither the hoarding nor the absolute levelling of the primary goods, but a fair and just distribution, with the inequalities such as they are being harmful to none and, in keeping with John Rawls's two principles of justice, beneficial in the long run to all.[37]

The family ethos which emerges from this brand of liberal egalitarianism is not a haphazard by-product of economic necessity and crisis management, but rather the culmination of a long tradition of moral philosophy. Rousseau devotes a full page at the beginning of his article on political economy in Diderot's *Encyclopédie* to a comparison between the cellular family and society, between the *pater familias* in the domestic context and the legislator.[38] And most of Mably's ruminations on temperance and

[35] Resolutions of 19 Ventôse, 23–8 Floréal, 4–8 Prairial II, Arch. Nat, AF$_{II}$ 97, Dordogne, pl. 713, pp. 45–53; Arch. dép. Charente, L 67, missions (Romme) and 1962, missions; Dordogne, I L 233, Romme, pp. 2–9.

[36] Challignac (Charente), Pluviôse II, quoted by F. A. Aulard, 'La commune de Challignac (Charente) en l'an II: documents inédits, du 21 février 1790 à fin thermidor an II', *La Révol. fr.* 36 (1899), p. 549; and *Histoire politique de la Révolution française*, p. 460.

[37] Rawls, 'Justice as Fairness'; Rawls, *Theory of Justice*, p. 60; and Rawls, *Political Liberalism*, pp. 6–7.

[38] J.-J. Rousseau, 'Economie ou œconomie (morale et politique)', in D. Diderot

frugality, inspired by Plutarch, revolve around the family man's need to make ends meet and be content with little ('heureux à peu de frais') and the legislator's duty to husband the scarce resources of the republic in the same manner. Mably calls public magistrates the 'fathers of the country', *pères de la patrie*, their collective task being to manage the estate wisely and fairly as would a *père de famille*.[39] His works were bedside books during the Revolution, read and digested by the republicans of Year II, Robespierre, Saint-Just and Romme among others.[40] Even those passages in Mably devoted to utopian musing, such as Lord Stanhope's desert island in *Des droits et des devoirs du citoyen* or the golden age in *De la législation*,[41] were resorted to in the development of 'fraternal economics'. While Joseph Lakanal, during his long stay in Périgord, claimed to be playing the role of the 'elder son', *l'aîné de la famille*, first among equals, in keeping with the advice given by Rousseau in his draft constitution for Corsica that the magistrate should behave like the consuls of ancient Rome, Marie-Joseph Lequinio clearly took his cue from Mably in declaring on 29 November 1792 that the legislators should assume the role of the 'fathers of the large family' and task the local authorities to become the 'purveyors of the French'.[42] According to Saint-Just as well, the people's representatives to the armies were expected to act as 'fathers and friends of the soldier' and make a great show of *sollicitude paternelle*.[43]

It is significant that Bo explains the meaning of 'fraternal popularity' by referring to the father figure of the honest yeoman 'surrounded by his labourers as he is by his children, who eats with

(ed.), *Encyclopédie: ou Dictionnaire raisonné des sciences, des arts et des métiers*, 28 vols. (Paris, 1751–72), vol. V, p. 337; Rousseau, 'Economie politique' in *Œuvres complètes*, vol. II, p. 290.

[39] G. Bonnot de Mably, *Entretiens de Phocion* (1763); *Doutes proposés aux philosophes économistes* (1768); *De la législation, ou principes des lois* (1776).

[40] Robespierre possessed a copy of *Des droits et des devoirs du citoyen* (1789), Saint-Just a copy of *Principes de morale* (1784) and Romme a copy of *De la législation, ou principes des lois* (1776): G. Bapst, 'Inventaire des bibliothèques de quatre condamnés (Louis XVI, Robespierre, Saint-Just, Couthon)', *La Révol. fr.* 21 (1891), pp. 534–5; F. Ratineau, 'Les livres de Robespierre au 9 thermidor', *Annales hist. Révol. fr.* 287 (January–March 1992), p. 134; J. Ehrard, inventory of the library at Riom (personal communication).

[41] Mably, *Des droits et des devoirs du citoyen*, p. 111.

[42] Lakanal: Labroue, *La mission de Lakanal*, pp. 126–8, 210–11, 530, 563; Lequinio: 29 November 1792, *Arch. parl.*, vol. LIII, p. 659.

[43] Saint-Just's speech of 10 October 1793, in *Discours et rapports*, p. 127.

them as he works with them, treating them as equals and brothers'.[44] The enlarged family seated around a common table sharing a common loaf conjures up a mixed image reminiscent of the Last Supper and the harvest meals at Clarens described in *La Nouvelle Héloïse*, where Saint-Preux, after a hard day's labour, partook of the coarse wine-harvesters' meal 'without exclusion, without preference', or the family table of twenty or more farm-hands in Auxerrois presided over by the Bible-reading yeoman-preacher idealised by Restif de la Bretonne.[45] It takes us back in time to an ideal primitive society of our forefathers, the age of the 'venerable patriarchs' close to the heart of the Reformed pastors such as the Girondin Rabaut Saint-Etienne and the Montagnard Jeanbon Saint-André, who previously had preached a similar message 'in the wilderness'.

I have dwelt at some length on the paradigm of *la grande famille* and its ramifications because the family ethos which emerges helps to fill the fraternal vacuum recorded by Marcel David. It also stands in contrast to the family model suggested by Lynn Hunt, whose vision is fashioned by the sans-culotte battle-cry 'Fraternity or death!', revealing a bellicose, or at least confrontational, conception of brotherhood.[46] Moreover, while the French Revolution in its radical republican phase may have bred no 'founding fathers', or forefathers, or fathers of the republic, like the American Revolution, it may be misleading to suggest, as does Hunt, that the ritual execution of the king resulted in a 'world without fathers', anti-patriarchal in orientation, the 'family romance of fraternity' relegating the patriarch to the past and imagining the political community as a band of brothers bereft of father figures.[47]

Certainly, Maximilien Robespierre was no George Washington, but the National Convention did briefly succeed in projecting itself collectively as 'father of the nation', while the deputies on mission acted as roving patriarchs of sorts and saw themselves as guardians of justice and fair play. If the Law now replaced the King as emblem of authority, as Hunt affirms, *la patrie* was seen as the

---

[44] J.-B. Bo, speech of 13 Pluviôse II, Aurillac, Bibl. Nat., 8° Lb⁴⁰ 2504.

[45] J.-J. Rousseau, *La Nouvelle Héloïse*, ed. R. Pomeau (Paris, 1960), Part V, Letter 7, pp. 588–98; Rétif de la Bretonne, *La vie de mon père*, p. 130.

[46] L. Hunt, *The Family Romance of the French Revolution* (Berkeley, 1992); in French translation, *Le roman familial de la Révolution française* (Paris, 1995), p. 28; see also David, *Fraternité et Révolution française*, pp. 58, 145, 205, 244.

[47] Hunt, *Le roman familial*, pp. 84, 88, 102, 218.

'common mother' whose 'first-born sons', the poor, could not be left to starve (Paganel and Lakanal), or as Jeanbon Saint-André put it: 'the Republic is the mother of all citizens without distinction: she must give a shelter to the unfortunate who have none'.[48] Notwithstanding a tendency to mix their metaphors, the legislators took it upon themselves to assume the fatherly role and fulfil the dream hinted at by Mably and Restif, but without hankering after 'the paternal absolutism of the Good Old Days'.[49] They saw themselves rather as *pères de famille* or *pères de la patrie* without absolutist leanings, as elders of an antique breed whose paternal responsibilities made them first among equals and potential founding fathers,[50] and in whose absence the family ethos would have crumbled, republican 'fraternity' would have appeared a hollow shell and the 'State' might well have taken on the substitute role of some sinister Big Brother.

The family ethos ensured that the Jacobin blueprint was societal in spirit, rather than étatist.[51] It should not be forgotten that the first sentence of the Declaration pasted on the walls of all public buildings proclaimed the aim of society as being 'the common happiness'. Even those who read no further quickly realised that citizens and legislators were embarked together on a joint and pioneering venture, whose outcome was still uncertain but whose success depended largely on mutual co-operation and the team or community spirit. In that sense, Hunt is perfectly justified in pointing to the 'collective representation of revolutionary fraternity'.[52] Perhaps, in the final analysis, the fraternal and paternal discourses can be profitably seen in historical relation to one another, and as referring to different aspects of the same kind of preoccupations with the destruction of the old regime and the re-ordering of the new society. As Colin Jones reminds us, 'the languages of paternity and fraternity were not invented, they came ready-made with a rich variety of differentially distributed cultural

---

[48] Letters of 20 February and 8 June 1793: *Arch. parl.*, vol. LXVI, p. 164; L. Lévy-Schneider, 'Quelques recherches sur Jeanbon Saint-André', *La Révol. fr.* 29 (1895), p. 76.

[49] M. Gutwirth, 'Sacred Father, Profane Sons: Lynn Hunt's French Revolution', *French Historical Studies* 19 (Fall 1995), p. 266.

[50] Hunt, *Le roman familial*, pp. 81, 87–9, 95.

[51] A risk of which Rousseau was well aware, as his misgivings about the passage from the will of all to the general will make clear: Ferry and Renaut, *Philosophie politique 3*, pp. 74, 84, 90.

[52] Hunt, *Le roman familial*, p. 218.

investments'.[53] The synthesis is perfectly achieved in Gilbert
Romme's proclamation to the inhabitants of the south-west in
Prairial II, in which mothers and daughters are also called upon to
fulfil their assigned role alongside the menfolk:

> Old men, whose long and painful experience has placed you on
> the path to virtue; fathers of families, who are both the light and
> the power of the Nation; young men, who are its force; children,
> who are its hope and who shall receive through a good education
> the sacred deposit of the Revolution's achievement, in order to
> pass it on when your turn comes! Women who, placed between
> man and child, are called upon to instil in the latter the lessons
> and examples of the former and to add your own; and you,
> young *citoyennes*, whom nature and virtue have destined to
> become the partners of the Heroes of Liberty! All of you whose
> love for the *patrie* is sacred, heed her call; she requires you to
> serve her each according to your means.[54]

This image of the republican family living in continuity and
harmony from one generation to the next, bridging the old and new
orders, with each member contributing his or her share and looking
after the common heritage, encapsulates the idea of *bonheur*
fashioned by the eighteenth century and socialised by the Revolution.[55] The preamble of the Declaration of 1789 thus made a point
of referring to the 'happiness of all' (a term inspired by Sieyès, La
Fayette and Thoret among others).[56] Robespierre in 1791, when
discussing the principle of universal suffrage, reaffirmed that 'the
aim of society is the happiness of all'.[57] When Saint-Just in Year II
coined the expression 'happiness is a new idea in Europe', he was
painting a picture of a caring community from which no one would
be excluded, in opposition to the pursuit of selfish pleasures and
advantages achieved at the expense of others, which he dubbed 'the
happiness of Persepolis'.[58]

[53] C. Jones, 'A Fine Romance with No Sisters', *French Historical Studies* 19 (Fall 1995), p. 286.
[54] Périgueux, 4 Prairial II, Arch. Nat., AF$_{II}$ 97, Dordogne, pl. 714, p. 17; Arch. dép. Aveyron, 2 L 18, dist. Aubin; Dordogne, 1 L 233, Romme, pp. 5–8; Lot, L 13, missions.
[55] L. Trénard, 'Pour une histoire sociale de l'idée de bonheur au XVIIIe siècle', *Annales hist. Révol. fr.* 35 (1963), pp. 309–30, 428–52; Mauzi, *L'idée du bonheur*, p. 255.
[56] *Les Déclarations*, ed. by Jaume, p. 12.
[57] Robespierre, 'Discours sur le marc d'argent', April 1791, in *Œuvres*, vol. VII, pp. 163–4.
[58] Saint-Just, 'De la nature' in *Théorie politique*, ed. A. Liénard (Paris, 1976),

Although the choice of the adjective *commun* alongside *bonheur* was interpreted in later years as representing a decisive step in the process of radicalisation on the road to collective ownership, it clearly needs to be placed in the context of the enlarged family or community. It was Romme once again who analysed the term, when describing the notion of 'pooling' in his own declaration of rights: 'Men, in joining together in society, pool all their natural rights, in order to wage a common and successful struggle against the various obstacles which stand in the way of their well-being. Social rights are the share each man gets from the common pool [*la mise commune*].'[59] Viewed in this light, the common happiness which is the end goal of society is not the sum total of individual happinesses, nor arbitrary collective happiness organised from above, but material well-being for all achieved through the voluntary sharing of resources between members of the same family. It sets the adventure of egalitarianism within clearly defined limits. Moreover, it acts as a counterweight to narrow sectarianism and intolerance, and is therefore not entirely bereft of a spiritual dimension. As Maure suggested during the summer of 1794, it might well be that providence (i.e. a good harvest), wise legislation and fraternal behaviour combined would suffice to destroy the prejudice of former times, 'for it is up to us to make the people happy here on earth and they will then await without anxiety the uncertain happiness to come'.[60] Such was the daunting task that awaited the fathers of the fledgling republic.

REHABILITATION AND RECONCILIATION

The Rousseauist principle of 'no exclusion, no preference' entailed two important consequences. The first was that a massive denial of freedom and other elementary human rights could not for long be entertained; the second was that the exercise of power should be shared between the new governing class of provincial lawyers,

pp. 52–8; and Reports of 13 and 23 Ventôse Year II in *Discours et rapports*, pp. 150, 164–5.

[59] 'Les hommes, en se réunissant en société, mettent en *commun* tous leurs droits naturels, afin de lutter d'un *commun* effort et avec succès contre les obstacles de tout genre qui s'opposent à leur bien-être. Les droits sociaux sont la part qui revient à chacun dans la mise *commune* [my italics]', Preamble to Romme's draft Declaration, *Arch. parl.*, vol. LXII, p. 267; *Les Déclarations*, ed. by Jaume, p. 244.

[60] Letter to the Committee of Public Safety, Tonnerre, 6 Floréal II, Aulard, *Recueil*, vol. XIII, pp. 58–60.

property-owners and administrators and the working-class sans-culottes. Theoretically at least, the image of a happy family and the replacement of class antagonism by class friendship implied a speedy end to persecution and a rejection of partisan preferences to the benefit of social harmony and political consensus.

In practice, although the months of Terror (from September 1793 to July 1794) witnessed a tightening of the police apparatus and an increase in the state-of-siege mentality, culminating in the terrorist laws of Germinal and Prairial and the wholesale elimination of unfortunate detainees by the Revolutionary Tribunal in Messidor,[61] the pattern of repression in the provinces followed a very different course. The terrorist Jean-Guillaume Taillefer, the first of the hardliners to be taken to task,[62] was recalled to Paris and his action disavowed as early as mid-Brumaire (early November 1793) and a few weeks later the *armées révolutionnaires* were disbanded and the wayward provincial radicals brought to heel (the so-called 'parallel hierarchies', such as those involved in the Schneider affair in Alsace and the Chasles affair in Lille);[63] Robespierre, together with Barère and Billaud-Varenne, gave consent to the concept of a 'committee of justice' or 'committee of clemency' in response to the humanitarian campaign launched by Camille Desmoulins in the *Vieux Cordelier*, its task being to protect patriots from oppression by examining the 'grounds for arrest' of all detainees and releasing all those 'unjustly arrested'.[64]

Arbitrary detention under the infamous Law of Suspects, the Terror in its most invasive and obstructive form, was clearly incompatible with the kind of society envisioned in the Declaration of Rights and could not for long be countenanced by democrats of goodwill. While vagabonds, foreigners, nobles, relatives of émigrés, refractory priests, Federalists and Girondin sympathisers all figured prominently among those considered suspect and therefore detained, the many discharged from custody between Nivôse and

[61] On this subject, see, *inter alia*: Wallon, *Les représentants du peuple*; D. Greer, *The Incidence of the Terror During the French Revolution: A Statistical Interpretation* (Cambridge, Mass., 1935); L. Jacob, *Les suspects pendant la Révolution, 1789–1794* (Paris, 1952).

[62] Carrier, Barras, Fréron and Javogues were to be recalled on 20 Pluviôse II.

[63] Cobb, *Les armées révolutionnaires*, pp. 241, 340, 673, 750–1, 767.

[64] *Le Vieux Cordelier*, No. 3, 25 Frimaire, and No. 4, 30 Frimaire II, in C. Desmoulins, *Œuvres*, ed. A. Soboul (Munich, 1980), pp. 265, 270, 280; Convention, 30 Frimaire, 4 and 6 Nivôse II, *Arch. parl.*, vol. LXXXII, pp. 36–7, 366–79.

Ventôse and again in Floréal, Prairial and Messidor came from widely differing social groups. Although the clergy in general fared badly, the peasantry, the nobility and the administrative bourgeoisie did rather well.[65]

As Jean-Louis Matharan's extensive research has shown, barely three months after the Suspect Law was passed, the liberation programme was well under way in the Parisian *sections*.[66] So too in the provinces. By mid-Nivôse, Nicolas Maure was releasing those detained in Auxerre whom he considered 'weak rather than wicked' and in the wake of a counter-revolutionary uprising in the district of Coulommiers a month later, out of the 700 insurgents arrested, the twenty most 'dangerous' were referred to the tribunal in Paris, but all the others were given their freedom.[67] Elsewhere in France, a similar pattern of restraint emerges: triage of all suspects, release on the nod of those deemed innocent, house arrest for those confirmed suspects considered innocuous and improvement in the conditions of detention for the untrustworthy who remain in custody. Thus, the arrest of several hundred rebel Limousin peasants involved in the Meymac insurrection, but considered 'credulous and led astray by their priests', prompted an early intervention by Jacques Brival and Antoine Lanot, the last batch being released on pressure from Couthon in Floréal and a general amnesty for all farming folk being agreed on the proposition of Vadier in Messidor.[68]

Although the legislation appeared to victimise the former nobility (decrees of 26 March, 5 September and 28 Germinal), branding all nobles found in the border country 'enemies of the Revolution', those further inland were often given the benefit of the doubt. Jean-Baptiste Monestier (du Puy-de-Dôme) rejected out of hand a proposal from the Jacobin club of Guéret which would have made the sentence of deportation set aside for the refractory clergy applicable to all kinsmen of the émigrés, judging it to be 'harmful

[65] Higonnet, ' "Harmonization of the Spheres" ', pp. 128–9.

[66] J.-L. Matharan, 'Suspects et suspicion, 1792–1794', thesis, 3 vols., University of Paris (1985); see also by the same author, 'Suspects', in Soboul, *Dictionnaire historique*, pp. 1004–8.

[67] Maure believed in the use of 'gentle persuasion and instruction' rather than 'force and terror' to achieve the 'necessary reforms': letters of 14 Brumaire, 21 Nivôse and 19 Pluviôse II, in Aulard, *Recueil*, vol. VIII, pp. 237–8, and vol. X, pp. 179–80, 756–7.

[68] *Arch. parl.*, vol. XC, p. 245; F. Arsac, 'Une émeute contre-révolutionnaire à Meymac (Corrèze)', pp. 152–5; M. Eude, 'Le Comité de sûreté générale en 1793–1794', *Annales hist. Révol. fr.* 57 (1985), p. 296.

to the true interests of republican society'.[69] In releasing two gentlemen farmers of noble extraction in the Creuse in Ventôse, Charles Vernerey explained that these brothers of émigrés 'tilled the soil themselves, and were so poor that they were obliged to rent some land from sans-culottes; even before the Revolution, they were married to poor country girls, and one of them is the local veterinary surgeon'. The two wives of émigrés Vernerey set free the same day were opposed to emigration, divorced, poor, mothers of young children, and one of them was about to remarry a sans-culotte: 'Moreover', Vernerey pointed out tellingly, 'ought I to have left among the suspects children worthy of a republican education?'[70]

Among the seventy-one persons detained at Tulle, Limoges and Poitiers, whom Brival released in Germinal, were several divorced wives of émigrés, it being understood 'that a divorcee does not take part in an offence committed by her former husband'. That same month, Jean-Baptiste Bo removed the stigma of suspect from all those petty noblemen of the Tarn, Aveyron and Lot 'who had constantly cultivated their properties' and stressed that refusal to emigrate was in itself a token of innocence rather than guilt. Gilbert Romme secured work and food rations for the 'innocent members of émigré families' of the Charente and the Dordogne, while Pierre Monestier (de la Lozère) reinstated the *ci-devant* nobles of the Agenais deprived of their civic certificates by local officials, and gave orders to release all the elderly, infirm, young children, pregnant women, nursing mothers and divorcees, and likewise émigré kinsfolk employed on the land or at manual trades, whom he readmitted into the Jacobin clubs: 'Their nobility', he stressed, 'is but *an accident of birth*, to which they were never attached [my italics]'; the emigration of their relations 'cannot be imputed to them'.[71]

Despite the reinforcement of the official Terror after Prairial, the

[69] Guéret, 7 April 1793, Arch. dép. Creuse, L 733, Jacobin club of Guéret, f° 15.
[70] Guéret, Aubusson, Felletin and Cusset, 12–26 Ventôse II, Arch. Nat., AF$_{II}$ 95, Creuse, pl. 703, pp. 42–55, and AF$_{II}$, 176, Western Bureau, pl. 1449, p. 15; and Vernerey's account of his mission in AF$_{II}$ 179, Western Bureau, pl. 1467, p. 15; Aulard, *Recueil*, vol. XV, pp. 122–9.
[71] Brival, 20 Germinal II, Bibl. Nat., 8° Lb^{41} 1049, pp. 1–8; Bo, 19 Ventôse and 11 and 30 Germinal II, Arch. dép. Lot, L 12, missions, and L 73, missions; Tarn-et-Garonne, L 75, dist. Montauban, f° 53; Aveyron, 2 L 18, dist. Aubin, and 8 L 16, dist. Sauveterre; Romme, 21 Germinal Year II, Arch. dép. Charente, L 68, Romme, L 1239, dist. Confolens, and L 1962, missions; Monestier, Agen, 29

trend toward relaxation continued unabated and a 'pre-Thermidorian' climate is apparent in many other regions of France, such as the Ain, Jura, Loir-et-Cher, Loiret, Ardennes and Haute-Saône.[72] After all, the younger Robespierre's claim to have been a 'moderate' and to have applied 'the principles of morality and justice' during his mission in Franche-Comté was founded on his elder brother's careful differentiation between indulgence and fairness.[73] 'Without pity for the enemies of the Revolution', mainstream Montagnards such as Brival and Lanot who also professed their belief in morality and justice felt it their duty to defend 'the innocent who have been oppressed, the weak who have been led astray'; they expressly endorsed Camille Desmoulins's affirmation that 'it is preferable for several guilty persons to go unpunished than for a single innocent person to be harmed'.[74] Having set free all the women of Tulle who had been imprisoned without charge, Brival reproached the administrators of the district of Brive for having arrested humble farmers on purely religious grounds: 'Instruct and enlighten the inhabitants of the countryside, but do not embitter them' (here, Brival is quoting the Committee of Public Safety);[75] 'remember that it is always better to prevent the mischief than to punish the guilty'. And in response to a delegation of Jacobins from the Limoges club who were demanding the reincarceration of the suspects he had just liberated, Brival gave a serene answer: 'The arrest and punishment of an innocent person is a calamity, which can only increase the enemies of the Revolution.'[76]

Freedom of opinion and expression implied that it was 'permissible to err'.[77] This was the theme chosen by Pierre Paganel for his peroration in Toulouse cathedral in celebration of the Feast of

---

Germinal and Dax, 1 and 22 Prairial II, Arch. dép. Lot-et-Garonne, L 148, Monestier (de la Lozère) and L 292, missions.

[72] Eude, 'Le Comité de sûreté générale', p. 299.

[73] Mathiez, *Autour de Robespierre*, pp. 25–8, 167–8.

[74] *Le Vieux Cordelier*, No. 3, 25 Frimaire Year II; cf. Chauvin's Report of Germinal Year III, pp. 56, 77, and Wallon, *Les représentants du peuple*, vol. II, pp. 152, 160.

[75] Letter of 26 Frimaire II, Aulard, *Recueil*, vol. IX, p. 441.

[76] 5 and 18 Nivôse, 18 Pluviôse and 5 Ventôse II, Arch. dép. Corrèze, L 105, Suspects, and Haute-Vienne, L 820, Jacobin Club of Limoges; Arch. mun. Tulle, 1 D 2, mun. register, f° 131.

[77] *Le Vieux Cordelier*, Nos. 3, 5 and 6, in Desmoulins, *Œuvres*, vol. X, pp. 262, 320–4, 327–37.

Reason on 20 Frimaire and widely disseminated throughout the Midi: 'Even religious errors', he said, 'in the eyes of the Legislator ... are a right of ownership.' To hold an opinion, he further explained to the citizens of Castres, whether one is a landowner or a farm-hand, cannot in the absence of any other charge be considered an offence justifying confinement. Implicitly, Paganel was championing the values of a true democracy where everyone would be free to affirm his difference.[78]

The reference to freedom of opinion was of course of direct relevance to those detained for political reasons, who included the many local officials who had sympathies with the Girondin cause and who, after the fall of Brissot and his friends, had sided with the Federalist uprising in the provinces. The Federalist movement naturally carried with it the majority of bourgeois notables who wielded influence within the clubs, local government and the economic life of their regions, but the systematic political purges and detentions instigated by the Montagnards in the wake of the rebellion had little lasting effect. After the arrest of the 'fugitive' Girondin deputies such as Pétion, Guadet, Valady or Sanadon and their most vociferous supporters in the departmental hierarchies,[79] the programme of dismissals, already highly selective in any case, petered out well in advance of the implementation of the revolutionary government (law of 14 Frimaire).

François Ingrand, on his visit to Châteauroux in September, confirmed the administrators of the Indre in their posts while adding to their number; Roux-Fazillac, during his stay in Angoulême, expressed his confidence in the Charentais officials; Lanot and Brival paid tribute to those of Corrèze who had not discontinued giving valuable service to their country.[80] Where changes did

---

[78] P. Paganel, *Discours prononcé au temple de la Raison de Toulouse, 20 frimaire an II*, Bibl. Nat., 8° Lb⁴¹ 3577; proclamation, Toulouse, 16 Nivôse II, Arch. dép. Lot-et-Garonne, L 151, Paganel and Garrau, p. 11; proclamation, Saint-Affrique, 26 Pluviôse II, Arch. Nat., AF$_{II}$ 172, Western Bureau, pl. 1410, p. 41; Arch. dép. Aveyron, 2 L 18, dist. Saint-Aubin; Paganel, *Essai historique*, vol. II, pp. 136, 200; cf. J.-P. Bertaud, 'An Open File: The Press Under the Terror', in Baker, *The Terror*, p. 307.

[79] Wallon, *La Révolution du 31 mai*, vol. II, chapters 7–22, pp. 34–424; A. Forrest, *Society and Politics in Revolutionary Bordeaux* (Oxford, 1975); M. Lyons, *Revolution in Toulouse: An Essay on Provincial Terrorism* (Bern, 1978); and P. R. Hanson, *The Federalist Revolt of 1793: A Comparative Study of Caen and Limoges* (Berkeley, 1981).

[80] Arch. Nat., AF$_{II}$ 168, Western Bureau, pl. 1380, pp. 33–4; pl. 1383, pp. 4–7; pl. 1386, p. 4; and AF$_{II}$ 169, Western Bureau, pl. 1386, pp. 18–21, and pl. 1387, p. 6

occur, a return to the *status quo ante* was not long in coming. Thus, reinstatement awaited those who were judged to be 'weak or misled' (Tallien in Lot-et-Garonne); those who, 'though misled, had repented', were 'relatively good citizens' and 'appeared sincere' (Paganel, in the Tarn and Aveyron); public servants who were 'feeble rather than disloyal' (Bo, in the Cantal), who were 'devoid of revolutionary character', yet displayed integrity and a faultless patriotism, 'albeit lacking in warmth' (Vernerey, in the Creuse). Roux-Fazillac was of the opinion that the committees of surveillance of the Dordogne whom he had himself regenerated remained 'moderantist even after purging'; and Brival, in Limousin, faced with the choice of keeping the 'notables' or appointing 'citizens without any talents', opted for the notables. Finally, Lakanal was perfectly content to reappoint officials in the district of Bergerac who were 'patriots of 1789', i.e. who had been at the helm in unbroken succession since that time.[81]

Robespierre himself urged the deputies to 'preserve for the country men who, rescued from their wayward conduct, could still serve it in good faith and with zeal'.[82] Linked to this consolidation of the revolutionary establishment was the utilitarian consideration that the prosperity of a city or region depended on bourgeois economic initiative. The 'former federalists who had repented' and who were allowed to practise their professions under the supervision of the authorities in Limoges and Poitiers included not just lawyers, but merchants, businessmen and engineers. In answer to Robespierre's query, Brival expressed his liberal conviction that the imprisonment of entrepreneurs, manufacturers, shopkeepers and artisans, allied to the absence of their employees drafted into the army, could only mean the stagnation of industry and the destruc-

(Ingrand); Arch. Nat., AF$_{II}$ 93, Charente, pl. 685, pp. 18–31 and Arch. dép. Charente, L 500*, Roux-Fazillac; Arch. Nat., AF$_{II}$ 95, Corrèze, pl. 694, pp. 1–55; 171, Western Bureau, pl. 1400, p. 14 and pl. 1404, p. 4; Arch. dép. Corrèze, L 103, Brival and Lanot.

[81] These opinions were expressed between the beginning of September 1793 and Floréal Year II: Arch. Nat., AF$_{II}$ 37, Committee of Public Safety, and 171, 175, 175A, 175B, 176, Western Bureau, and 192, Midi Bureau; Arch. dép. Lot-et-Garonne, L 150, Paganel and Garrau, and 283, Paganel and Monestier (de la Lozère); Arch. dép. Tarn, L 131, missions; Arch. dép. Creuse, L 105, missions; Arch. mun. Tulle, I D 2, mun. register, f° 114; Aulard, *Recueil*, vol. IX, p. 223; Labroue, *La mission de Lakanal*, p. 107.

[82] Letter to Roux-Fazillac, 10 Pluviôse II, Arch. Nat., AF$_{II}$ 37, Committee of Public Safety, pl. 297, p. 56; Aulard, *Recueil*, vol. X, p. 510.

tion of commerce.[83] Moreover, although it is customary to consider the Ventôse decrees as a reinforcement of the Terror, the Committee of General Security was primarily charged with sorting the detainees and releasing all patriots unjustly detained, an objective ostensibly in keeping with Camille Desmoulins's humanitarian campaign.[84]

While during Year II more than 3,000 new *sociétés populaires* appeared and the sans-culottes were admitted into the urban political clubs in large numbers,[85] this enlargement of democratic space did not correspond to an enduring transfer of power to their class outside the capital and resulted in precious little power-sharing. Despite some radical changes in personnel, such as the renewal of the Cher tribunals by Laplanche, who replaced the 'old wig-heads' with 'enlightened men', vine-tenders, cobblers, roofers and tailors,[86] there are few signs of the takeover by 'country clowns ... not able to read or write' predicted by Edmund Burke in 1790,[87] let alone the 'tyranny of the plebs' denounced in Year III. Paganel, writing during the Empire, subscribed to this myth, claiming that the Jacobin era spurned science and promoted the illiterate, took the ploughman from his field and the worker from his workshop to administer justice and make the laws of the land; yet Paganel himself had made some 'popular' appointments in the Albigeois, at Puycelci for instance, where he replaced two notaries as municipal

---

[83] Correspondence of 5–13 Ventôse II, Arch. Nat., AF$_{II}$ 37, Committee of Public Safety, pl. 298, p. 38 and AF$_{II}$ 176, Western Bureau, pl. 1445, p. 29; *Arch. parl.*, vol. LXXXII, p. 36; Aulard, *Recueil*, vol. XI, pp. 375, 518.

[84] S. Garnier, 'Les conduites politiques en l'an II: compte rendu et récit de vie révolutionnaires', *Annales hist. Révol. fr.* 295 (January–March 1994), p. 19.

[85] Merchants and *gens à talents* made up 30 per cent of the membership of the clubs at Albi and Castres in Year II, with the shopkeepers and tradesmen some 70 per cent; at Bergerac, Tulle and Montauban, the percentage of small artisans and industrial workers exceeded 35 per cent: P. Duperon, 'Etudes sur la société populaire de Castres d'après les procès-verbaux de ses séances (1er avril 1792–14 vendémiaire an II)', *Revue du Tarn* 13 (1896), p. 343, and 14 (1897), pp. 40, 146, 183 and 316; H. Labroue, *La société populaire de Bergerac pendant la Révolution* (Paris, 1915); *Documents inédits sur la vie économique de la Révolution française: le Club des Jacobins de Tulle, procès-verbaux (1790 à 1795)*, ed. by V. Forot (Tulle and Paris, 1912); J. Boutier and Ph. Boutry, 'La diffusion des sociétés populaires en France (1789–an III): une enquête nationale', *Annales hist. Révol. fr.* 266 (September–October 1986), pp. 366–98; Woloch, 'Contraction and Expansion of Democratic Space', p. 314.

[86] Bourges, 27 September and 6 October 1793, Aulard, *Recueil*, vol. VII, pp. 120, 261.

[87] Burke, 'Reflections', p. 397.

officers with a baker and a tailor.[88] However, in terms of their access to political power, the 'triumph of the poor' proclaimed by the delegates of Taillefer turned out to be an exceptional and ephemeral phenomenon, with the *gens à talents* continuing to monopolise the management of public affairs.

Nonetheless, the policy pursued in the field by democrats prepared to forgive and forget and rehabilitate men of their own ilk, associated with a deliberate if symbolic gesture toward the 'people', seems to announce a pluralism of sorts, encompassing patriots of all sides conscious of belonging, in the words of Jean-Paul Bertaud, to 'a composite political nebula' and representing a 'multiform opinion'.[89] This incipient pluralism was reinforced by the carefully promoted image of a conciliatory Mountain, a redeemable Gironde[90] and an amnestied nobility. Those among the nobles, especially, who by resisting the temptation to emigrate had resigned themselves to throw in their lot, for better or for worse, with the Republic, were now divested of their former privileges, treated as equals and assimilated into the throng of ordinary working citizens. Neither the 'accident of their birth', nor the crimes of their ancestors, nor the emigration of their kin could prevent them from enjoying their rights and assuming their obligations, nor from taking their rightful place alongside others, domestic servants included, who were now placed on an equal footing with their former masters.[91] Why should not their children, as Vernerey suggested, mingle with others in the republican classroom? The vision of a society without exclusion, far removed from the divided nation of the old regime and the bitter conflicts of the Revolution, emerges from the political confusion of Year II: the single family of tomorrow.

[88] Albi, 13–24 Pluviôse II, Arch. dép. Tarn, L 131, missions; and Paganel, *Essai historique*, vol. II, p. 76.

[89] Bertaud, 'Press Under the Terror', p. 307; J.-P. Bertaud, 'La presse de l'an II: aperçu des recherches en cours', *Annales hist. Révol. fr.* 300 (April–June 1995), p. 171.

[90] The Committee of Public Safety would have preferred to spare if not the Girondin leaders, at least those in the second rank, those 'more deceived than guilty' in the words of Saint-Just, men such as Bertrand L'Hodiesnière or Rabaut Saint-Etienne who shared the Jacobin concept of an austere and caring Republic: see J. Chaumié, 'Saint-Just et le procès des Girondins', in A. Soboul (ed.), *Actes du Colloque Saint-Just, Sorbonne, 25 juin 1967* (Paris, 1968), p. 33; and by the same author, 'Les Girondins', in A. Soboul (ed.), *Actes du Colloque Girondins et Montagnards, Sorbonne, 14 décembre 1975* (Paris, 1980), pp. 19–60.

[91] Article 18 of the 1793 Declaration of Rights.

3. *Food rationing, collectivism and the market economy*

> I see everywhere public stores containing the riches of the republic; and the magistrates, truly fathers of the country, have barely any other function than to maintain the *mores* and distribute to each family the things they require.
>
> Mably, *De la législation ou principes des lois*, 1776[1]

THE RIGHT TO EXISTENCE

The fair distribution of the 'fruits of the earth' represented the acid test of Jacobin egalitarianism, relegating all the other social and economic reforms to second place. The primary goal of society, according to Marat, was 'bread for all'. The 'right to subsistence' which La Rochefoucauld-Liancourt had wanted to see included in the Declaration of 1789, the 'right to existence' demanded by Robespierre, the 'right to live' defended by Thuriot, the 'preservation of life' considered the first of all human rights by Romme, 'equality of consumption' proclaimed by Harmand[2] – all amounted to a principle that pre-empted all others: that of each person's entitlement to food. The Jacobin rhetoric of subsistence was indistinguishable in this respect from that of the sans-culotte militants: 'The life of men', Jacques Roux proclaimed, 'is the most sacred of properties.'[3] Was it permissible in these circumstances for a consumer's right of appropriation to extend with impunity to staple foodstuffs beyond individual entitlement, or should it be subordi-

---

[1] Mably, *Sur la théorie du pouvoir politique*, p. 217.
[2] Rist, 'Les rapports du Comité de mendicité', p. 267; draft declarations in *Les Déclarations*, ed. by Jaume, pp. 244, 251, 258; Coquard, *Jean-Paul Marat*, p. 355.
[3] J. Roux, *Le publiciste de la République française*, No. 259 (8 August 1793), cited by Sewell, 'Sans-Culotte Rhetoric of Subsistence', pp. 253–4.

nated to the common welfare? 'Did you not know', Rousseau had asked, 'that a multitude of your brethren are perishing or suffering from their need of what you have in excess, and that you required the explicit and unanimous consent of mankind to appropriate from the common subsistence all that exceeded your own?'[4] To what extent should the state concern itself with supply and demand or intervene in the marketplace to regulate the sale and storage of corn? Was it justifiable to call on the military to protect freedom of trade and put down by force any disturbance to the peace caused by shortage, rising prices and hunger?

These were burning issues which had troubled not only Rousseau, but also Mably, Turgot and Necker, among others, in the decades prior to the Revolution, notably during and in the immediate aftermath of the so-called 'flour war' of 1775.[5] Turgot, for his part, epitomises a very French brand of liberalism combining *laissez-faire* and protectionism.[6] If grain producers, especially those he called the 'entrepreneurial farmers' of northern France, could be left to themselves to supply the market without constraint or regulation of any sort, a natural equilibrium would be struck and prices would remain stable.[7] Necker's publicly expressed concern with the ill effects of precipitate liberalisation and consequent price speculation on consumers and smallholders alike was interpreted by Turgot as 'a demagogic appeal to the populace'.[8] Be that as it may, the experience of physiocracy in action during the 'flour war' shows that the law of supply and demand sits uneasily with the concept of 'fair shares for all'.

[4] J.-J. Rousseau, 'Discours sur l'origine et les fondements de l'inégalité' (1755), in *Œuvres complètes*, vol. II, p. 233.

[5] S. L. Kaplan, *Bread, Politics and Political Economy in the Reign of Louis XV*, 2 vols. (The Hague, 1976); Gauthier and Ikni, *La guerre du blé*.

[6] 'At all times, the desire of commerce in all nations has been contained in these two words: *liberty* and *protection*, especially liberty. As M. Le Gendre said to M. Colbert: *laissez-nous faire*': Turgot, 'Eloge de Vincent de Gournay' (1759), in *Œuvres de Turgot, et documents le concernant*, ed. by G. Schelle, 3 vols. (Paris, 1913–19), vol. I, p. 620.

[7] Turgot's liberalising edict was issued on 13 September 1774; see his '6e Lettre sur le commerce des grains à Terray' (1770), in Turgot, *Ecrits économiques*, ed. by B. Cazes (Paris, 1970), p. 327; Fl. Gauthier, 'De Mably à Robespierre: un programme économique égalitaire, 1775–1793', *Annales hist. Révol. fr.* 57 (1985), p. 266.

[8] J. Necker, *Sur la législation et le commerce des grains*, 2 vols. (Paris, 1775); Galante Garrone, *Gilbert Romme*, pp. 70–4; R. D. Harris, *Necker, Reform Statesman of the Ancien Régime* (Berkeley, 1979), pp. 61–2.

Fraternity – the readiness to share the primary economic goods with others in the greater interest of the community at large – necessarily injects communal restraints and ethical correctives into a market economy governed by *laissez-faire*, turning it into a 'moral economy'. It remains to be seen, however, whether the emerging Jacobin model of a moral economy is necessarily 'anti-liberal', as Florence Gauthier suggests.[9] Turgot's reforms, after all, were ethically motivated and conceived of as utilitarian rather than anti-social; and E. P. Thompson concedes that Adam Smith's model of a self-adjusting market economy cannot be branded as 'immoral'.[10] Indeed, if the *Wealth of Nations* were divested of moral imperatives, there would be no 'Adam Smith problem', which stems directly from the author's professed belief in the virtue of altruism.[11]

'Transcending any system of ethics', writes Olwen Hufton, 'is the obligation to stay alive.'[12] The symbolic presence of women in the forefront of the revolutionary struggle for existence claiming their right to the ownership of food, such as those who marched on Versailles in October 1789, is clearly of relevance in the context of the extended family and the obligation to feed all hungry mouths. The Constituents retaliated against aggressive behaviour sparked by female discontent with successive versions of the Riot Act forbidding unlawful assembly and ordering the militia to disperse food rioters by force.[13] The image of angry housewives demon-strating in defence of their vital interests is a far cry from the *banquet public* of Year II, where food was shared out equally to all comers and women joined in a jig with the menfolk, irrespective of class or condition. That moment of redemption was long in coming and when it did, it lasted but a short while: women were once again

---

[9] Gauthier, 'De Mably à Robespierre', pp. 282–6.

[10] E. P. Thompson, 'The Moral Economy of the English Crowd in the Eighteenth Century', *Past and Present* 50 (February 1971), pp. 89–90.

[11] Smith's belief in the virtue of altruism (*Theory of Moral Sentiments*, 1759) is matched (in the *Wealth of Nations*, 1776) by his belief in the virtue of self-control in the selfish acquisition of wealth; his view of the division of labour is a moral, not just an economic, view: G. Jorland, 'Le problème Adam Smith', *Annales ESC* 39 (1984), pp. 831–48; Werhane, *Adam Smith and His Legacy*.

[12] Hufton, *The Poor*, p. 367.

[13] Laws of 21 October 1789 and 23 February 1790, followed by the Le Chapelier laws of 14 June and 20 July 1791, inaugurating a 'period of liberal economic terror' in the words of Gauthier, *Triomphe et mort du droit naturel*, p. 57.

in the front line leading the bread rioters during the hard winter and spring of 1794–5.[14]

When the National Convention first assembled in Paris on 21 September 1792, the women of Lyons, for their part, were in no mood for jesting. As Roland, the minister of the interior, reported to the house the next day, these *citoyennes* had invaded the city shops to fix the prices of vital commodities, bread, meat, butter and eggs, at what they considered a 'fair price', that is half the published value, without so much as a protest from the local officials. Marie-Joseph Chénier proposed that clear instructions be conveyed to the mayor of Lyons on the maintenance of free trade, and the house decided to send to the city a delegation of its own members accompanied by an armed militia to re-establish law and order.[15]

September 1792 was a critical month, during which a vision of wanton fratricide – the September massacres – coincided with a vision of sans-culotte anarchy – arbitrary price controls imposed by shrieking housewives in flagrant violation of the rules governing a free market economy. The economic debate which ensued and lasted several months, involving as it did all political persuasions and spilling over from parliament into the provinces, is one of the most revealing and fascinating series of exchanges to be found in the political records of the period. For the discussion soon transcended the basic concern of food availability and encompassed supply and demand in general, the desirability of price regulations, the role of the state and state intervention in the means of production, distribution and exchange, the advisability of limiting private ownership and free enterprise, the erosion of individual liberties, and the extent to which public inquiry, inquisition and the power of search could be tolerated. The very concept of the republican regime was at stake, the issue of a liberal pattern of social and economic arrangement. And the debate demonstrated the enduring influence of Turgot, Dupont de Nemours and the physiocratic school, Adam Smith (whose views had by now been fully assimilated in France),[16] Rousseau and especially Mably.[17]

---

[14] Hunt, *Le roman familial*, p. 173.

[15] *Arch. parl.*, vol. LII, *Convention*, pp. 98–9.

[16] French translations of the *Wealth of Nations* appeared in 1778–9 (?abbé A. Morellet), 1779–81 (J. L. Blavet) and 1788–90 (J. A. Roucher).

[17] Mably's works of particular economic relevance in this context include *Des droits et des devoirs du citoyen*, written in 1758 and published in 1789, 'Du commerce des grains', written in 1775 at the time of the 'flour war' and published in 1790 in the

As Jeanbon Saint-André was to express it in putting the motion on the corn trade to the vote on 3 December 1792, it was basically a question of deciding whether freedom was to be 'limited' or 'unlimited'.[18] This was an issue which had just been the subject of extensive correspondence between the citizens of Montauban and their new deputy. As a Protestant pastor and son of a local millowner, Saint-André was well acquainted with the wool trade and the living conditions of the fullers in his home town. He considered a 10 per cent increase in the mill-workers' wages justified on account of the high cost of bread, but his entrepreneurial background caused him to take account of the profitability of the bakery business. He was staunchly opposed to price controls such as a *maximum* on food, because the people of Lyons 'in their blindness' had allowed consumer goods to be taxed at uncompetitive prices, with the result that traders were withholding commodities from sale. The Jacobin club of Montauban was highly critical of this market approach which was bound to drive the price of bread up to 7 sols per pound: that was 'a calumny', Saint-André replied, adding that he was wedded to the principle of equality and his heart bled for the manual workers who lived in constant anxiety because of the high price of food: 'The poor man must live and we must spare no effort to ensure he is able to supply his needs.'[19]

'Il faut que le pauvre vive': the poor man must live. That is the moral non-partisan view of economics as propounded by a man whose loyalties are as yet divided between the political groupings: among Saint-André's close associates in the south-west was the Girondin shipowner Pierre Seys (president of the Gironde department in 1793). Condorcet, who was considered at this time as loosely adhering to the party of Brissot, also advocated a rise in workers' wages in keeping with increases in corn prices.[20] This presupposes that concessions of one kind or another have to be made, and demonstrates a readiness to entertain a shift from

so-called *Œuvres posthumes*, and *De la législation ou principes des lois*, published in 1776.

[18] *Arch. parl.*, vol. LIV, p. 61.

[19] Correspondence between Jeanbon Saint-André and the municipality of Montauban, 23 September 1792, 23 November 1792 and 20 February 1793, in 'Quelques recherches sur Jeanbon Saint-André', L. Lévy-Schneider, *La Révol. fr.* 29 (1895), pp. 64, 72, 76; see M. H. Darrow, 'Economic Terror in the City: The General Maximum in Montauban', *French Historical Studies* 17 (1991), p. 498.

[20] Articles in the *Chronique de Paris*, 5, 18 and 28 November 1792: cited by Badinter and Badinter, *Condorcet*, p. 574.

unrestricted liberty toward greater equality. Fabre, the spokesman of the joint committee on agriculture and commerce, put it another way in opening the debate in the Convention on 3 November: 'Property is a sacred right, but ...' That single word 'but' encapsulates the economic challenge of the years 1792–4. However, Fabre was careful to weigh his words in order to allay mounting fears: 'Every citizen owes to the general interest the sacrifice of a small part of his property so that he may enjoy the remainder in peace.'[21]

Those who endorsed this view included radicals like Marie-Joseph Lequinio, who was in favour of dividing up the large farms and increasing the number of smallholdings, and Georges Couthon, a moderate politician who had built himself a reputation as an 'advocate of the poor',[22] but also several whose affiliation lay right of centre. One such was Louis-Etienne Beffroy, a deputy from the Aisne who was to side with the Plain, but who refused to ignore the interests of the 'indigent portion' of the people: whether the shortage was real or caused by speculation was largely irrelevant, he believed; what mattered was that it served as a pretext for the farmer to withhold his grain or to increase his prices by virtue of the precious 'property right'. But, Beffroy asked, 'is not *existence* itself the first, the most incontestable, the most legitimate, the most essential of properties?'[23] Beffroy was appointed rapporteur for the subcommittee in favour of 'limited freedom', in opposition to the 'economists' (or disciples of the physiocratic school) who were in favour of unrestrained freedom of the corn trade.

It was Robespierre, however, true to his reputation of voicing the concerns of the common people, who brought all his eloquence to bear on the issue of principle. The first 'social law' which overrode all others, he claimed, was 'that which guaranteed the means of existence to all members of society'; ownership was but a means to achieving this end, to ensuring life, and thus ownership could never be in opposition to man's subsistence. Robespierre thus spelled out the basic tenet of Jacobin egalitarianism: that everything which was essential to preserve life was 'a property common to society as a whole', and 'only the surplus' could be considered 'an individual

[21] *Arch. parl.*, vol. LIII, p. 131.
[22] Lequinio's speech of 29 November 1792, *ibid.*, p. 658; Couthon was also a defender of the farming community, as his mission to the Loir-et-Cher in November 1792 clearly shows: R. Schnerb, 'Notes sur les débuts politiques de Couthon et des Monestier'.
[23] Beffroy's speech of 16 November 1792, *Arch. parl.*, vol. LIII, p. 440.

property'. Common sense dictated that every man should be able to produce or purchase consumables vital to his and his children's subsistence. Whereas for all other commodities the principle of unfettered freedom could apply, it was indefensible in the case of foodstuffs, where people's lives were at stake, to try and impose the market economy 'at bayonet-point'.[24]

Although the Girondin brand of liberalism was far from insensitive to humanitarian arguments, the debate hinged on the delicate issue that Robespierre had chosen to highlight, namely the advisability of limiting the right of ownership, and herein lay the difference of opinion.[25] And when the long debate ended on 8 December 1792, the Girondin lobby finally won the day. Public grain distribution and price controls were dismissed as an intolerable infringement of individual liberty. Powerful pleas from Vergniaud, Barbaroux, Boyer-Fonfrède and Creuzé-Latouche resulted in a majority vote in favour of 'complete freedom of commerce' safeguarded by 'martial law', i.e. the death penalty or forced labour for those who obstructed it.[26] The oversimplified picture of a return to physiocratic economics à la Turgot does not really do justice to the leaders of the Gironde, as Marcel Dorigny has emphasised:[27] they shunned the prospect of a static economy based on fair distribution, and favoured instead a dynamic economy based on the production and exchange of more and more goods generating ever-greater growth and prosperity to the benefit of all; theirs was a utilitarian approach which sought inspiration from the British example. They were, moreover, preaching to the converted, since none in the Convention seriously questioned the advantages of free enterprise.

Those who had misgivings or who were as yet uncommitted, like the young Louis-Antoine de Saint-Just, were liberals at heart who

---

[24] Speech of 2 December 1792, in *Œuvres de Maximilien Robespierre*, vol. IX, pp. 109–20.

[25] M. Dorigny, 'Les Girondins et le droit de propriété', *Bulletin d'histoire économique et sociale de la Révolution française* (Paris, 1983), p. 19; and by the same author, 'Quel libéralisme pour la Gironde?', in 'Soutenance de thèse sur travaux', *Annales hist. Révol. fr.* 290 (October–December 1992), pp. 601–4.

[26] Decree of 8 December 1792, *Arch. parl.*, vol. LIV, p. 688. See also Vergniaud's intervention of 3 November, Boyer-Fonfrède's of 16 November, Barbaroux's and Creuzé-Latouche's of 8 December, *ibid.*, vol. LIII, pp. 130, 443, and vol. LIV, pp. 670, 676.

[27] Dorigny, 'Les Girondins et le droit de propriété' and 'Quel libéralisme?'; see also S. Meysonnier, *La balance et l'horloge* (Paris, 1988).

feared the abuse of liberty (for instance, the freedom to hoard grain at the expense of the hungry poor). Saint-Just criticised those who, like Féraud, were content to rely on the theories of Montesquieu and Adam Smith, or like Roland simply repeated the well-worn advice of the *économistes*. He found it difficult to reconcile the view that self-interest was the proper criterion of economic action with the fact that 'hard men who live only for themselves' continued to elude the lessons of 'virtue' and that freedom ran the risk of being stifled by anarchy. For individual liberty to come into its own, there was lacking a necessary prerequisite, namely 'social harmony'.[28] The question, then, that remained to be resolved at the end of this theoretical debate was whether virtue could be instilled by precept and example, and social harmony achieved peacefully and amicably, or whether the outrage to natural justice posed by unequal apportionment and the stubborn resilience of economic individualism necessitated direct intervention on the part of the legislators.

That question, which in practical terms revolved around fair prices for consumer goods, was thus at the top of the revolutionary agenda well before the Paris sugar riots of February 1793. It was partly answered between 31 May and 2 June 1793, with the fall of the Gironde.[29] By the time the harvest was in store that same summer, the members of the Convention realised that, as *pères de la patrie*, they had immense responsibilities which could not be evaded in this vital area of public concern: 'The matter of food supplies', they wrote to Du Bouchet and Maure, 'is of such great importance that it cannot warrant too much attention.' And the deputies agreed to a man: 'Peace at home and the triumph of liberty', wrote Paganel, 'depend on this salutary movement of provisions', while Bo admitted to his colleague in private that sufficiency, if not abundance, was 'the only weapon' they had to win over those, not just in the large cities, but also in the far-flung provinces, who still doubted that the Revolution had been worthwhile.[30] If fair shares

---

[28] Saint-Just, 'Sur les subsistances', 29 November 1792, in *Discours et rapports*, pp. 75, 80.

[29] Sewell, 'Sans-Culotte Rhetoric of Subsistence', pp. 265–6.

[30] Committee of Public Safety, September 1793, Aulard, *Recueil*, vol. VI, p. 556; Paganel, Toulouse, 29 Nivôse II, Arch. dép. Tarn-et-Garonne, L 75, dist. Montauban, f° 36; Arch. nat., AF$_{II}$ 116, Lot, pl. 879, p. 39; Bo, letter to Paganel, Figeac, 11 Ventôse II, Arch. nat., AF$_{II}$ 176, Western Bureau, pl. 1444, p. 43; Aulard, *Recueil*, vol. XI, p. 489.

could be ensured for all, they fondly imagined, everything else would run like clockwork, notwithstanding certain obvious obstacles, such as the profit motive, human selfishness, greed, deceitfulness and pig-headedness.

THE FAILURE OF PRICE CONTROLS AND ECONOMIC COERCION

Behind the inspiring image of the noble savage and the hard-working country yokel,[31] there lurked a fierce beast, recalcitrant and impervious to the plight of his fellow men: the yeoman-farmer, stockowner, miller and village worthy, often elected local mayor or councillor, staunchly defending the inward-looking concerns of his rural community against all comers. On the one side, the virtuous, honest and respectable countryman painstakingly preparing the cornucopia for the townsfolk, and once the coin was flipped, there stood the country *muscadin*, the rich landowner or 'agricultural Croesus' whose 'cupidity' knew no bounds, the 'livestock banker' renting out his fat oxen at exorbitant prices, bleeding his sharecroppers 'like rust corrodes iron'.[32] Yet the country poor, exploited though they were, belonged to a closely knit community whose economic interests were indivisible; faced with the prospect of requisition and further privation, they quickly rallied to the banner of village solidarity[33] in refusing to release their meagre surpluses.

In the French provinces, the 1793 crop carry-over or 'hungry gap' (*soudure*) proved a trial especially for the urban poor. When the first price regulations were enacted in May, bread in Figeac was selling at 9 sols 3 deniers a pound; in Bordeaux, 8 sols for the first quality, 5 sols for the third; in Agen, 8 sols for black bread, the only type authorised; at Périgueux, in early June, white bread was selling

---

[31] See, for example, Bo's praise of 'ce bon père de famille qui cultive la terre, qui élève ses enfants au travail et à la vertu ... Vivons comme les habitants des campagnes!': Speech at Aurillac, 13 Pluviôse Year II, Bibl. Nat., 8° Lb⁴⁰ 2504; this image belongs to a long literary tradition perpetuated by *inter alios* La Bruyère and the chevalier de Jaucourt: J.-P. Gross, 'L'idée de pauvreté dans la pensée sociale des Jacobins', *Annales hist. Révol. fr.* 54 (1982), p. 207.

[32] Bo, Lanot, Lequinio, Laignelot, Tallien, Ysabeau and Vernerey, who habitually overlook the inherent solidarity of the village community: P. Massé, 'Baux à cheptel dans la Vienne sous la Révolution', in A. Soboul (ed.), *Contributions à l'histoire paysanne de la Révolution française* (Paris, 1977), pp. 210–13.

[33] See J.-P. Jessenne, *Pouvoir au village et Révolution: Artois, 1760–1848* (Lille, 1987), p. 108; Jessenne, 'Land', pp. 230–1.

at 5 sols 2 deniers, brown bread (*pain bis*) at 4 sols, black bread at 2 sols 10 deniers. But at Limoges and Guéret, shortly before the corn harvest, a pound loaf of rye was selling for as much as 18 sols, 'though as black as the chimney'.[34]

In these circumstances, the *maximum* decreed on 4 May 1793 was off to a poor start. Any attempt to tax the price of bread at 3 sols a pound nationwide and maintain free circulation of grain ran the risk of paralysing the market. While a distinction had always been made between free trade for *grain* and price regulations for *bread* in the cities, where municipal supply policies had been in place for centuries, the maximum legal price, as Judith Miller has demonstrated, was traditionally understood to mean a 'fair market price'.[35] The price of 3 sols demanded by the women of Lyons in September 1792 was certainly no longer a fair market price in September 1793 when Baudot decided to impose it in Toulouse. To attempt to impose a price in the city without controlling the sources of supply or the prices in the surrounding countryside was seriously to court the risk of famine.[36]

Faced with this regulatory measure, the farmers of the grain-rich district of Grenade-Beaumont simply refused to sell their grain and withdrew it from the market. In the Agenais, the local authorities claimed they were 'forced to abolish the *maximum*' as early as July.[37] In general, the federalist or federalist-sympathising departments were strongly opposed to pricing regulations, claiming that the law of 4 May was prejudicial to the right of ownership and damaging to agriculture and trade.[38] In the prosperous Loiret and Seine-et-Marne, wheat was converted into flour and sold at prices

---

[34] Arch. Nat., AF$_{II}$ 146^A, Vienne; 167 and 169, Western Bureau; Bibl. Nat., 8° Le[39] 36; Arch. mun. Périgueux, D 4, mun. council; A. Mathiez, 'La Révolution et les subsistances: l'application du premier maximum', *Annales révol.* 11 (1919), pp. 294–321 and 500–1; L. de Cardenal, 'Les subsistances dans le département de la Dordogne (1789–an IV)', *La Révol. fr.* 82 (1929), p. 243.

[35] J. A. Miller, 'Politics and Urban Provisioning Crises: Bakers, Police and Parlements in France, 1750–1793', *Journal of Modern History* 64 (1992), pp. 227–62; cf. Thompson, 'Moral Economy', p. 79.

[36] Toulouse, 27 September 1793, Arch. Nat., AF$_{II}$ 184, Midi Bureau, pl. 1525, p. 13.

[37] J. Donat, 'Le maximum et son application dans un district de la Haute-Garonne', *Revue hist. Révol. fr.* 14 (1919–22), pp. 20, 178, 241; M. Pastre, *Le district de Grenade-Beaumont de 1790 à 1795* (Toulouse, 1948).

[38] R. Baticle, 'Le plébiscite sur la Constitution de 1793: la réunion des assemblées primaires; le vote des armées; le recensement et le résultat; les amendements économiques', *La Révol. fr.* 58 (1910), p. 402; H. Calvet, 'Subsistances et fédéralisme', *Annales hist. Révol. fr.* 8 (1931), p. 229.

well above the maximum, while the people of Montargis prepared themselves for 'a kind of combat between the inhabitants of town and country'. In the Haute-Vienne, the law provoked endless squabbling among the administrators, while in the Creuse, a grain-poor department at the best of times, the 'murderous law' was suspended as inoperative, and at Bourganeuf and Boussac, it was not even *printed*.[39]

After the harvest, in September, bread was selling at 11 or 12 sols a pound in these parts of the country. On receiving the text of the decree of 11 September standardising the *maximum* on grain and flour, Roux-Fazillac in the Charente confessed his anxiety since all the local officials were landowners with corn to sell, and Vernerey, on observing that a revolutionary committee in the district of Guéret was chaired by a miller who owned two flour-mills, came to the conclusion that the maximum price was 'inexecutable'.[40] And with the enactment of the 'general maximum' on most common consumer commodities, allied with the enforced currency of the *assignat*, there quickly grew up a parallel economy based on barter, bacon being traded for cheese, honey for oil, eggs for soap, an underground trade in kind subject to tacit commercial agreements between whole communities, depriving normal market outlets of their source of supply.[41]

Resorting to force of arms to break the vicious circle proved as counterproductive as it was democratically harmful. The municipality of Montauban's success in enforcing price controls on bread and meat and preventing the total collapse of the paper currency without excessive coercion[42] generated little emulation elsewhere in France. The brand of 'economic Terror' practised by Fouché in the Nièvre and surrounding areas with the help of a 'people's army' drafted among levellers from the Cordeliers in Paris drove scarce commodities further underground and incensed the landowners, while imposing atheism 'at bayonet-point' added spiritual insult to

[39] Arch. Nat., AF$_{II}$ 95, Creuse, pl. 703, p. 13; 168, Western Bureau, pl. 1380, p. 34; Aulard, *Recueil*, vol. VI, p. 303; V. Fray Fournier, *Le département de la Haute-Vienne, sa formation territoriale, son administration, sa situation politique pendant la Révolution*, 2 vols. (Limoges, 1909), vol. I, p. 303.

[40] Angoulême, 27 September 1793 and Guéret, 26 Ventôse II, Arch. Nat. AF$_{II}$ 169, Western Bureau, pl. 1386, p. 38; and 176, Western Bureau, pl. 1449, p. 15; Aulard, *Recueil*, vol. VII, p. 91 and vol. XII, p. 6.

[41] Cobb, *Les armées révolutionnaires*, p. 435.

[42] Darrow, 'Economic Terror in the City'.

material injury, provoking hostile and often violent reactions from the pious country folk. Thus, Maure and Du Bouchet had difficulty in quelling the spillover effect of exactions demanded by Parisian army troopers, who triggered serious riots at Coulanges-sur-Yonne and likewise in the fertile Brie near Rozay and Provins, an area of strategic importance since it served as bread-basket to the capital.[43] Conversely, in Rouergue, one of the poorest regions of France already subject to religious unrest, the punitive expedition undertaken by Taillefer's *armée révolutionnaire* of 5,000 levies from the Lot and Cantal reaped untold havoc, draining the land of scarce grain supplies through their voracious incursions and increasing the risk of famine.[44]

The short-lived military operation mounted by Paganel in the Haute-Garonne was a serious attempt by a moderate 'Girondin' to raise food for the capital of the Midi. Soldiers were billeted in the houses of twenty-one suspect farmers in the district of Grenade and some 4,300 quintals of wheat were conveyed to Toulouse before the Committee of Public Safety brought the operation to a halt. Paganel conceived of the idea as a preventive exercise, in the hope that the threat of force, rather than force itself, would produce the desired effect: it was up to the rural mayors to explain to their constituents whose grain-stores were full that 'among the children of the same fatherland, surplus cannot exist next to dearth'. Though the armed detachments were authorised to enter 'the dark retreats where cupidity and avarice plot their plebicide profit', the Sword would be preceded by the Law and the markets supplied since 'common interest and gentle fraternity would finally bind together the owners of the land with the industrious citizens of the cities'.[45] Proof that Paganel's coercive supply policy was plausible is provided by the companies of men he drafted as an urban police force in his native Villeneuve-sur-Lot and at Agen to supervise the

[43] Auxerre, 14 Brumaire, and Dammartin, 17 Brumaire II, Aulard, *Recueil*, vol. VIII, pp. 237–8, 273; Cobb, *Les armées révolutionnaires*, pp. 37, 105, 141, 168–9, 239–40, 242, 268–9.
[44] Cobb, *Les armées révolutionnaires*, pp. 50, 237–55, 279, 302, 324–47, 438, 453, 460, 562, 979.
[45] Toulouse, 5 and 8 Brumaire II, Arch. Nat., AF_{II} 185, Midi Bureau, pl. 1531, p. 6; Arch. dép. Dordogne, 1L 231, mission of Paganel, pp. 1–3; Lot-et-Garonne, L 152, mission of Paganel; P. Gérard, 'L'armée révolutionnaire de la Haute-Garonne (septembre 1793–nivôse an II)', *Annales hist. Révol. fr.* 31 (1959), pp. 7–18, 29–37; Mme. Darroux, 'La société populaire de Grenade-sur-Garonne de 1790 à 1794', unpublished dissertation, University of Toulouse (1959).

local markets and the river traffic, and to ensure that provisions travelled freely and price regulations were complied with: they acted with exemplary forbearance and obtained some limited success.[46]

Robespierre, however, was quick to realise that enforcement of this kind was fraught with risks. In the letters he drafted to Paganel and Maure on behalf of the committee, he made his view clear that 'a revolutionary army ... might become a force of terror lending itself to abuse to the detriment of liberty itself'; 'left to its own devices, it could become very dangerous and turn against liberty' especially since it was apt to run astray and 'preach philosophy by force of arms'. He therefore urged his colleagues in the field to disband the armies and not let 'this instrument of power wander out of your hands'.[47] Paganel hastily complied and put an end to an anti-liberal deviation which had in any case proved inconclusive, while Maure, who had also resorted to coercive means to mobilise supplies in the district of Tonnerre,[48] needed little convincing that 'gentle persuasion' brought better results than 'force and terror'.

Having effectively abandoned their faith in price controls as a viable economic policy and having renounced the use of force to regulate supply and demand, the mainstream Jacobins found themselves looking for palliatives to attenuate the incidence of shortages on the poor. Favourite among these were subsidies geared to making up the difference between the cost of production and the market price of bread. Funded by progressive taxes levied on the wealthy, these subsidies presented the twofold advantage of making bread affordable to the urban poor whenever prices exceeded the *maximum* and charging the mark-up to those who could afford to pay, or as Vernerey expressed it, placing 'the burden of public distress squarely on those who had contributed to producing it' by their disdain for price regulations and their desire for profit.[49] The main thrust of economic action, however, lay in the area of resource management.

[46] F. de Mazet, *La Révolution à Villeneuve-sur-Lot* (Villeneuve, 1894), p. 139; Cobb, *Les armées révolutionnaires*, pp. 255, 279, 453, 570, 760.
[47] Committee of Public Safety to Maure and Paganel, Paris, 4 Frimaire II, Aulard, *Recueil*, vol. VIII, pp. 238–9, 675–7.
[48] Auxerre, 25 Brumaire II, *ibid.*, pp. 451–3.
[49] Guéret, 24 Pluviôse II, Arch. dép. Creuse, L 734*, Jacobin Club of Guéret; Arch. Nat., AF$_{II}$ 95, Creuse, pl. 703, pp. 32–3. Cf. similar measures taken by Laplanche at Bourges, Bo at Aurillac and Figeac, and Monestier de la Lozère at Agen.

STORES OF PLENTY AND EQUAL DISTRIBUTION

In 1755, Rousseau had suggested that public grain-stores be established to prevent scarcity during the lean years.[50] At the time of the 'flour war' in 1775, Mably took the idea further by proposing to set up regional grain-stores known as 'stores of plenty' (*greniers d'abondance*) in all the main cities of the kingdom, charged with 'corresponding' with each other, that is effecting reciprocal shipments of grain and avoiding any surpluses being wasted.[51] Replenished after every crop at the market price, these public grain-stores would supply local needs in times of shortage, curb price rises and protect the consumer. Conceived of as a sort of buffer stock, which would only be released when prices reached a previously determined threshold, the mechanism would be triggered by an 'intervention price' rather than a 'maximum price'; in other words, it was interventionist in modern parlance rather than illiberal, its avowed aim being not to 'enforce ascetic austerity' but to balance supply and demand and sustain the market.[52]

The economic debate of November 1792 had convinced Montagnards and Girondins that French agricultural production overall was largely in excess of consumption and that the shortages which occurred were 'artificial'. It is interesting to note that the theme of *disette factice* was not just repeated in sans-culotte texts like an incantation, as William Sewell emphasises,[53] but likewise propounded by political leaders on the left and the right, notably Robespierre and Vergniaud. The latter, it is true, prescribed the physiocratic remedy of non-interference, namely 'free circulation' which he considered 'the only sure way of supplying the poor department with the surplus of the rich department'.[54] Others, however, found Mably's buffer stock scheme attractive. Fabre and

---

[50] Rousseau, 'Discours sur l'inégalité', part II, § 1, and 'Economie politique', *Œuvres complètes*, vol. II, pp. 228, 288.

[51] G. Bonnot de Mably, 'Du commerce des grains', in *Œuvres complètes*, 14 vols. (London, 1789–91), vol. XIV; reproduced in *Sur la théorie du pouvoir politique*, p. 265.

[52] Talmon, *Origins of Totalitarian Democracy*, pp. 61–2; Gauthier, 'De Mably à Robespierre'; J. P. Gross, 'L'économie fraternelle: les greniers d'abondance de l'an II', in Fl. Gauthier (ed.), *Colloque Mably: la politique comme science morale, Vizille, 6–8 juin 1991*, 2 vols. (Bari, 1995–), vol. II (forthcoming).

[53] Sewell, 'Sans-Culotte Rhetoric of Subsistence', p. 256.

[54] Vergniaud, 3 November 1792, *Arch. parl.*, vol. LIII, p. 130; cf. Robespierre, 2 December 1792, *ibid.*, vol. LIV, p. 45.

Beffroy had suggested that private granaries be earmarked for public use, Saint-Just that the stores belonging to émigrés be taken over and converted into municipal assets, and more recently Jeanbon Saint-André, in a letter to Barère, had proposed a 'general recruitment of all grain' in every administrative district, with a view to establishing 'public grain-stores made up of private surpluses, the owners being paid a fair price for the value of the commodity'.[55] The decree of 9 August 1793 organising the 'stores of plenty' was presented to the Convention by Barère and faithfully reproduced Saint-André's proposal: one grain-store per district; 100 million livres set aside for the purchase of grain surpluses; émigré houses used for storage; bread ovens set up in the city *sections*; bakeries requisitioned.[56] Although the decree could not apply to the 1793 crop and the 'stores of plenty' were officially left pending till the following spring,[57] the principle of 'correspondence', or equal distribution, was to be entrusted to a national Commission des subsistances for speedy implementation, and the representatives in the field were to be empowered to take emergency measures.

The three-man Commission established on 1 Brumaire was faced with the awesome task of organising a wartime ministry of supply. Its leading member, Jean-Marie Goujon, who was to side with Romme during the food riots of Prairial Year III, had come to the attention of the Convention in November 1792 when, as the young author of a petition on behalf of the electors of the Seine-et-Oise, he had defended the principle of 'fair proportion between the cost of grain and the wage for a day's labour'.[58] As Catherine Kawa and Françoise Brunel have shown, Goujon, together with co-members Brunet and Raisson, working twelve to sixteen hours a day, now set about drawing up the statistics of a would-be command economy, including pricing tables for a wide range of commodities and departmental allocation quotas for the two staple crops, wheat and rye.[59] These were far from ready, however, before the spring of

---

[55] Moissac, 26 March 1793, Arch. Nat., AF$_{II}$ 167, Western Bureau, pl. 1369, p. 42; Aulard, *Recueil*, vol. II, pp. 532–5; L. Lévy-Schneider, *Le conventionnel Jeanbon Saint-André, membre du Comité de salut public, organisateur de la marine de la Terreur, 1749–1813*, 2 vols. (Paris, 1901), vol. I, pp. 260–75.

[56] *Arch. parl.*, vol. LXX, p. 585.

[57] Decree of 12 Germinal Year II, *Réimpression de l'Ancien Moniteur*, vol. XX, p. 114.

[58] Fr. Brunel, 'Présentation de Goujon', in Fr. Brunel and S. Goujon (eds.), *Les martyrs de prairial: textes et documents inédits* (Geneva, 1992), pp. 26–33.

[59] *La Commission des subsistances de l'an II: procès-verbaux et actes*, ed. by P. Caron

1794, by which time glaring inequalities in stockpiles had made provisioning precarious in many disadvantaged areas, and the prescribed quotas were seldom put into effect, but they provide a good illustration of the interventionist nature of the policy of 'perequation' (see table 3).

Historians of the *maximum* have largely chosen to ignore the parallel pursuit of a co-ordinated egalitarian food policy which, in Paganel's words, promised no less than 'the equal distribution between all Frenchmen of all the resources of the Republic'.[60] In the light of such a policy, confrontation between regions with surpluses and those with shortfalls was inevitable. On his arrival at Provins, in the fertile Seine-et-Marne, Du Bouchet was dismayed to find the grain-store assigned to Paris standing empty, while Maure expressed his disgust that the district of Sens, 'the most agricultural of the Yonne department' should show such 'unbrotherly conduct' toward the district of Auxerre which was sorely lacking.[61] So too, Paganel and Bo were forced to wage an uphill struggle to overcome the refusal of the rich districts of Gaillac and Lavaur in the Tarn to transfer more than token consignments of rye, in the name of 'suffering humanity', to their brethren in the Aveyron 'expiring from the horrors of starvation'. Indeed, 'nature, humanity and justice demand a more legitimate levelling and the surplus of one department must make up the deficit of another'.[62]

Richard Cobb has shown that the struggle was not so much one between town and country as one which pitted city against city. The mayors of Villeneuve-sur-Yonne and Joigny stopped laden barges heading upstream for Auxerre and Avallon on the assumption that their own needs were greater. The citizens of Cahors doubted the needs of Toulouse, which they thought must be overflowing with grain. The officials of Moissac on the Tarn and Tonneins on the Garonne halted shipments on their way to

(Paris, 1925); review by C. Bloch in *La Révol. fr.* 79 (1926), pp. 71–3; C. Kawa, 'Le fonctionnement d'une administration en l'an II: la Commission des subsistances', thesis, Institut d'histoire de la Révolution française, Paris (1984); Brunel and Goujon, *Les martyrs de prairial*, p. 26.

[60] Toulouse, 2 Pluviôse II, Arch. dép. Aveyron, 2 L 18, dist. Aubin.

[61] Du Bouchet, Melun, 15 October 1793, and Maure, 10 Frimaire II, Aulard, *Recueil*, vol. VII, p. 424 and vol. IX, pp. 71–2.

[62] Rodez, 1 Ventôse; Aubin, 1 Germinal; Gaillac and Lavaur, 3–18 Germinal, 8–11 Floréal II: Arch. dép. Tarn, L 132, missions, 3, 4, 8 and 10; L 855, dist. Gaillac; Aveyron, 8 L 18, dist. Aubin; and 8 L 16, dist. Sauveterre; Arch. Nat., AF$_{II}$ 177, Western Bureau, pl. 1454, p. 18 and pl. 1458, p. 11.

Bordeaux, and the city of Albi saw no reason to bow to the requirements of the great Atlantic port, notwithstanding news of its 'alarming status' and the arrival of *commissaires* charged with 'breaking the circle of prejudice which prevents the movement of supplies'.[63]

Taillefer took the trouble of analysing this 'circle of prejudice' within a single department, the Lot. Montauban was one of those provincial cities, like Cahors, whose administrative district was too small and too poorly endowed to supply its needs by itself. So Montauban habitually encroached on its neighbours, such as Moissac, 'as easily as an army general raises contributions from a conquered land'. While Montauban 'looted' Moissac, the latter 'invaded' the district of Lauzerte. The other local seats were careful not to lower their guard, the affluent district of Figeac ('le faubourg Saint-Antoine du Lot') giving short shrift to the Montauban *commissaires* and preparing to 'repel them by force'.[64] It is worthy of note that these were neighbouring towns, situated within a single province, prepared to take matters to the point of economic warfare, and in these circumstances Cahors, by the winter of 1793, found herself in a state of siege and 'in the throes of starvation', a famine barely remedied by the energetic measures of Bo and Paganel (table 1).

Equal distribution required detailed knowledge of resources, and these in turn required reliable statistical returns, a near impossibility in the climate of suspicion which reigned. Inquiries met with a stubborn refusal to co-operate. The farmer instinctively refrained from declaring at least part of his stock of grain; individual deceit was institutionalised by the *communes*, which supplied the *districts* with the arguments they required to justify their inability to help outsiders. Cobb's analysis of the economics of dearth makes it abundantly clear that one of the bitter lessons of Year II was the

---

[63] Arch. Nat., F⁷ 4563, Committee of General Security; Arch. dép. Tarn, L 130, missions; Aulard, *Recueil*, vol. XIII, pp. 473–4; J. Adher, *Département de la Haute-Garonne: le Comité de subsistances de Toulouse (12 août 1793–1er mars 1795)* (Toulouse, 1912), pp. i–xlviii; P. Becamps, 'La question des grains et de la boulangerie à Bordeaux de 1793 à 1796', *Actes 83e Congrès national des sociétés savantes, Aix-Marseille, 1958* (Paris, 1959), p. 260; Cobb, *Les armées révolutionnaires*, p. 433.

[64] Rodez, 5 Brumaire II, Arch. Nat., AF_{II} 89, Aveyron, pl. 659, p. 35; Aulard, *Recueil*, vol. VIII, p. 45; Darrow, 'Economic Terror in the City', pp. 498–525.

Table 1. *Reluctant famine relief, Lot, Nivôse–Pluviôse II (Bo and Paganel)*

Supplier district	Beneficiary district	Initial amount (quintals)	Reduced amount (quintals)	Deliveries (quintals)
Lauzerte	Cahors	2,500	1,250	1,038.45
Montauban	Cahors	3,000	1,500	321.86
Gourdon	Cahors	1,500	750	200
Total		7,000	3,500	1,560.31

Sources: Arch. Nat., AF$_{II}$ 116, missions, Lot, pl. 879, p. 39; Arch. dép. Lot, L 12, missions; Tarn-et-Garonne, L 75*, missions, Register, ff. 36–7, 45–6, 55.

tacit understanding among officials never to allow grain to leave the territory of their district.[65]

The Montagnards spared no effort in devising ways of circumventing this wall of deception. Some, such as Lanot, played on the Limousins' love for the staple fare of chestnut and their growing familiarity with potato in order to entice them into depositing their surplus grain in the public stores. In the Charente and Dordogne, Roux-Fazillac established central supply committees charged with checking and releasing local holdings, and ensuring their 'equal and proportional distribution' into public grain-stores throughout the two departments. Similarly, Maure in the Yonne appointed a central commission with liaison officers in each of the seven districts of the department as the 'only sure means of sharing grain, stored at regular sites, among all the constituents'. Romme, who had sponsored private grain-storage initiatives in his home village of Gimeaux in 1791 to enable the small folk to cushion the effects of price fluctuations and even make a small profit at the end of the day,[66] realised that the key to fair distribution resided with

[65] Cobb, *Les armées révolutionnaires*, p. 435; R. C. Cobb, 'Plaintes des paysans du Cantal, nivôse an III', *Annales hist. Révol. fr.* 33 (1961), pp. 99–102; and on the famines of Years III and IV, R. C. Cobb, 'Dearth, Famine and the Common People', in *The Police and the People: French Popular Protest, 1789–1820* (Oxford, 1970), section III; cf. the economics of dearth in England in 1795 and 1800–1: Thompson, 'Moral Economy', pp. 98, 127–8.

[66] Lanot, Tulle, 7 Brumaire II; Roux-Fazillac, 27 September 1793 and 13 Brumaire II; Maure, 10 and 19 Frimaire II: Arch. Nat., AF$_{II}$ 95, Corrèze, pl. 694, p. 54; 169, Western Bureau, pl. 1386, p. 38; 170, Western Bureau, pl. 1394, p. 44; Arch. dép. Dordogne, 1 L 228, Roux-Fazillac, and 3 L 24, dist. Bergerac, ff. 67, 158; Aulard, *Recueil*, vol. IX, pp. 71–2, 297; Romme, 31 March 1791, in Galante Garrone, *Gilbert Romme*, p. 266.

Table 2. *Redistribution of grain, Charente, Germinal II (Romme)*

Supplier district	Shipments (quintals)	Beneficiary district	Deliveries (quintals)	Total (quintals)
Barbézieux	8,000			
Cognac	8,000	Angoulême	21,000	
Ruffec	5,000			
				32,000
Confolens	6,000			
Ruffec	4,000	La Rochefoucauld	11,000	
Cognac	1,000			

Sources: Arch. dép. Charente, L 1239, dist. Confolens; L 1962, missions, Year II; Haute-Vienne, L 110, Romme.

the communes and the districts, not the departments. Dismayed by the Charentais peasants' failure to respond honestly to repeated inquiries and by their habit of keeping whole grain for themselves while selling the 'siftings' to their city brethren, Romme decided to launch a large-scale inquiry which he dubbed *recensement géneral révolutionnaire* and entrusted to thirty officials per district chosen by the Jacobin clubs. His innovation was to have these officials conduct their mission in the communes of the *neighbouring* district: those from Ruffec in the district of Angoulême, those from Cognac in the district of La Rochefoucauld, those from Barbézieux in that of Confolens, etc. Following their investigations, which he considered conclusive, Romme proceeded to 'level' the grain between the districts, to the advantage of those in greatest need, Angoulême and La Rochefoucauld (table 2).

Romme proceeded likewise in the Dordogne, where he found the recommendations of Goujon's commission unrealistic (table 3). After an exhaustive survey conducted by no fewer than 592 officials covering every single commune, but always operating away from home in a neighbouring district to ensure impartiality, he launched a levelling exercise which entailed a transfer of grain between the nine districts, Périgueux being entirely exempt on account of its large shortfall, while Belvès, Sarlat and Ribérac in return were asked to bear the brunt of the sacrifice.[67]

[67] Angoulême, 19 Ventôse and Périgueux, 8 Prairial II, Arch. dép. Charente, L 1239, dist. Confolens and 1962, missions; Haute-Vienne, L 110, missions; and Dordogne, 1 L 233, Romme, p. 9; L. de Cardenal, 'Les subsistances', p. 36.

Table 3. *Redistribution of grain, Dordogne, proposed by the*
Subsistence Commission in Germinal and revised by Romme on
1 Prairial II

Supplier district	Requisition (quintals)	Shipments (quintals)	Beneficiary district	Deliveries (quintals)
Belvès	5,000	5,000	Bergerac	—
Périgueux		2,000	Bergerac	1,600
Périgueux		5,000	Montignac	950
Périgueux	34,500	12,500	Sarlat	—
Périgueux		15,000	Excideuil	650
Ribérac		4,000	Nontron	1,500
Ribérac	8,000	4,000	Mussidan	—

Sources: La Commission des subsistances de l'an II: procès-verbaux et actes, ed.
P. Caron (Paris, 1925), pp. 376, 487, 618; L. de Cardenal, 'Les subsistances dans le
département de la Dordogne (1789–an IV)', *La Révol. fr.* 83 (1930), pp. 23–32.

Bo was to follow Romme's example on his arrival in the Tarn in
the spring. The twelve officials per district he selected from the
local clubs were expected to act with 'loyalty, delicacy and
fraternity' but always outside their home district, those from
Castres in the district of Albi, those from Albi in the district of
Gaillac, and so on. The results (table 4) authorised the department
to conclude it could not afford to ship grain beyond its borders,
but could just meet its own requirements by redistributing the
Lavaur surplus and if the need arose, part of the grain stored at
Gaillac. In the Lot-et-Garonne, Pierre Monestier ordered all
supplies still available before the 1794 harvest to be 'equally
divided' between the nine districts of the department, which meant
that the more affluent districts of Marmande, Monflanquin and
Lauzun were obliged to make sacrifices.[68]

In acting thus, the deputies were knowingly courting the risk of
riots, triggered by a conservative reflex in the farming community
wherever cereal stocks were not yet depleted, and such events did
indeed occur at Meymac in the district of Ussel (Corrèze) and at

[68] Gaillac, 17 Germinal, Agen, 3 Germinal and 12 Floréal, Paris, 15 Prairial II:
Arch. dép. Tarn, L 132, missions, p. 7; Arch. Nat., AF$_{II}$ 117, Lot-et-Garonne, pl.
888, p. 19, and 192, Midi Bureau, pl. 1586, p. 32; Aulard, *Recueil*, vol. XII, p. 134
and vol. XIV, p. 164.

Table 4. *Dubious statistics of redistribution, Tarn (wheat and millet), Germinal II*

District	Population	Grain in storage (quintals)	3 months' consumption (quintals)	Shortfall (quintals)	Surplus (quintals)
Castres	73,605	21,803.90	84,239.82	62,435.92	—
Albi	64,130	11,984.85	73,393.21	61,408.36	—
Gaillac	57,520	62,317.78	65,828.44	3,510.66	—
Lavaur	39,040	65,657.11	44,679.10	—	20,978.01
Lacaune	28,974	4,367.54	33,159.12	28,791.58	—
Total	263,269	166,131.18	301,299.69	156,146.52	20,978.01
Total shortfall			135,168.51		

Source: Arch. dép. Aveyron, 1 L 989, food supplies, Year II.

Salvagnac in the district of Gaillac (Tarn), with the farmers, led by their mayors, marching to the public grain-stores to retrieve their grain.[69] Nevertheless, the policy of *nivellement* or levelling was relatively successful in those areas where supplies were quite plentiful and where requisition orders from the army had already been catered for. But in the poorer areas, where the 'hungry gap' started early and could last several months, it was soon realised that containment was the only tenable course of action. Pierre Garrau, who was charged with feeding the Army of the Pyrenees, accused his colleague Romme of imposing an 'embargo' on all outward shipments of corn from the Charente and Dordogne departments.[70] Equal distribution during the *soudure*, as stocks dwindled, entailed jealous husbanding of resources, inward-looking autarky and a closed economy. The euphemism 'stores of plenty' inevitably gave way to a more traditional notion: that of food rationing.

[69] Ussel, 15 Nivôse II, Arch. dép. Corrèze, L 98, missions; C. Berriat-Saint-Prix, *La justice révolutionnaire: août 1792 à prairial an III, d'après des documents originaux, la plupart inédits* (Paris, 1870), pp. 351–4; Wallon, *Les représentants du peuple*, vol. I, pp. 316–17; Arsac, 'Une émeute contre-révolutionnaire', pp. 152–5.
[70] Letter to Carnot, Sainte-Foy, 17 Prairial II, Arch. Guerre, Armée Pyrénées occidentales: Aulard, *Recueil*, vol. XIV, p. 164.

THE FAMILY GRAIN-STORE AND THE
BREAD OF EQUALITY

The poor country folk, accustomed to chronic penury and obsessed by the fear of going short, were loath to see precious corn leave their village.[71] As a former country priest, Paganel was keenly aware of this reticence and it prompted him to institute the *communal* grain-store. Close to their homes and the local market-place, these warehouses, which he likened to 'family stores', would serve as village depot to which all the peasants would bring their bags of surplus corn, having kept enough to feed themselves and their families for one month. Once in store, the grain could be held and distributed in a manner which was 'self-evident'; a register would be kept of the names of all the contributors and the quantities and types of grain handed in: wheat, *méteil* or mixture, rye, barley, millet, oats and buckwheat. Established throughout the departments of the Aveyron and the Tarn, the 'family stores' were each to be managed by a 'communal subsistence board' whose task was to ensure transparency (*y voir clair*), assess the real stocks held and monitor their distribution.[72]

A similar policy was pursued by Pierre Monestier in the Lot-et-Garonne, whose communal depots were funded by the proceeds of forced loans levied on the rich; in the Gers, where Dartigoeyte invited the communes to set up public granaries to house all provisions in grain and flour purchased from the producers at *maximum* prices; and in the Dordogne, where Romme organised the pooling of each commune's grain in a single store and the baking of a common bread in the communal oven, or the distribution of flour rations to families to bake their own bread at home, all in the name of 'fraternal equality'. He who refused to deliver his grain was branded not a suspect as in the early days of Romme's mission, but henceforth 'an egoist and a bad brother'.[73]

---

[71] Cobb, *Les armées révolutionnaires*, pp. 427–40.

[72] On his return to Paris, Paganel continued to receive records of corn transfers made by the municipal grain-stores of the Tarn and Aveyron: Toulouse, 2 Pluviôse; Castres, 6 and 7 Pluviôse; Albi, 10 Pluviôse; and Rodez, 1, 2 and 10 Ventôse II: Arch. dép. Aveyron, 1 L 183, Paganel; 1 L 354, Paganel; 2 L 8* and 18, dist. Aubin; Tarn, L 136, missions, p. 1; and Tarn-et-Garonne, L 2*, dist. Castelsarrasin.

[73] Cf. the 'foundry grain-stores' set up by Romme for the workers in industry, chapter 6 in this volume. Monestier, Marmande, 1 Ventôse; Dartigoeyte, Auch, 23 and 29 Floréal; Romme, Périgueux, 28 and 30 Floréal, 4 Prairial and 2

Communism, understood as the collectivised takeover not of the means of production, but of the means of distribution and exchange of vital commodities, was thus a fact of life in the villages and small towns of south-western France, at least during the carry-over period from one crop to the next. It in no way ran counter to the tradition of a 'regulated social economy' prevalent in many rural communities.[74] Its impact was more widely felt than any timid attempts made to implement the *loi agraire*. It was also put into practice, if less systematically, by Jeanbon Saint-André, in the maritime ports of Brest, Cherbourg and Toulon, with a view to eking out scarce resources and equalising consumption in the urban context of a large municipality.[75] Municipal collectivism, albeit in a restricted format, can thus be considered an integral part of Jacobin democracy.

Rousseau had explained to his contemporaries that while the land belonged to no one, its fruits belonged to all, and Mably had developed this idea in a long meditation on common ownership on a desert island, 'where all equal, all rich, all poor, all free, all brothers, our first law would be to possess nothing in person', the fruit of collective labour would be deposited in public warehouses and constitute both 'the treasure of the state and the patrimony of each citizen', while regular distributions by elected stewards would ensure each family received their fair share according to need.[76] The main feature of this brand of communism appears to be equality of consumption, or the sharing out of commodities in fixed quantities, i.e. food rationing. What is significant is that the Jacobins of Year II, in forsaking the stores of plenty recommended by Mably in 1775, did so to the benefit of Mably's 'utopian' dream

Fructidor II: Arch. Nat. AF$_{II}$ 106, Gers, pl. 789; 117, Lot-et-Garonne, pl. 885, p. 14; 172, Western Bureau, pl. 1413, p. 40 and pl. 1414, pp. 2 and 6; 179, Western Bureau, pl. 1475, p. 4; Arch. dép. Charente, L 67, missions; Dordogne, 1 L 233, Romme, pp. 2–3; 3 L 25, dist. Bergerac, ff. 178, 183; Lot-et-Garonne, L 148, Monestier (de la Lozère); Wallon, *Les représentants du peuple*, vol. II, pp. 378–9.

[74] See G. R. Ikni, 'Crise agraire et révolution paysanne: le mouvement populaire dans les campagnes de l'Oise, de la décennie physiocratique à l'an II', 6 vols., thesis, Sorbonne, Paris (1993).

[75] Lévy-Schneider, *Jeanbon Saint-André*, vol. II, *passim*; cf. Aulard's comments on the collectivist leanings of the commune of Challignac (Charente) in *La Révol. fr.* 36 (1899), pp. 549–53, and Aulard, *Histoire politique de la Révolution française*, pp. 459–60.

[76] J.-J. Rousseau, *Discours sur l'origine et les fondements de l'inégalité parmi les hommes*, ed. by J.-L. Lecercle (Paris, 1965), p. 108; Mably, *Des droits et des devoirs du citoyen*, p. 111.

Table 5. *Rationing scheme, south-west France, Ventôse–Floréal II: dwindling flour rations*

Time-scale 1794	Adult (yearly in lb.)	Manual trades (monthly in lb.)	Manual trades (daily in oz.)	Unemployed (daily in oz.)	Women (daily in oz.)	Pregnant and nursing mothers (daily in oz.)	Children (daily in oz.)
1 March	500	50	24	16	16	16	16
20 March	—	50	24	12	12	16	12
20 April	—	30	20	8	8	16	8
20 May	—	25	16	8	8	16	6
1 June	—	25	16	8	8	16	4

Sources: Arch. Nat., AF$_{II}$ 95, Corrèze, pl. 694–5; 117, Lot-et-Garonne, pl. 885, p. 14; 172, Western Bureau, pl. 1413, p. 13; 192, Midi Bureau, pl. 1586, p. 32; Arch. dép. Aveyron, 1 L 183, missions, 2 L 18, dist. Aubin; Dordogne, 3 L 25, dist. Bergerac, f° 151; Haute-Vienne, L 110, missions; Lot-et-Garonne, L 148, missions; Tarn, L 132, missions, pp. 3–8.

of 1758, which they found relevant in practice and applicable to the poorer regions of provincial France during the hungry gap of 1794.

Rationing in time of war or shortage is the product of necessity and is subject not to the rational rules of arithmetic, but to a process of empirical change, as shown by the curve of degressive consumption (table 5). Starting with a theoretical average annual consumption of 5 quintals, or 500 pounds, of flour per adult, it was estimated that the manual worker required a basic minimum of 50 pounds per month or one and a half pounds (24 oz.) per day, while others would have to make do with one pound or 16 ounces. But in order to ensure a smooth carry-over to the harvest, a reduction was felt necessary as from the end of Ventôse (20 March) and others were to follow. From 1 Floréal (20 April), daily allowances were reduced by half for some, to 8 oz., while children were restricted to 6 oz. in May and finally 4 oz. in June.

Rations varied not only according to the class of consumer (worker, unemployed, nursing mother, child), but also in the light of additional foodstuffs available: chestnuts, dried peas and lentils or meat. The local authorities issued individual ration cards bearing the allowances received and *billets* or coupons entitling the holder to meat rations from his butcher in each commune.[77]

[77] Romme, Périgueux, 4 and 21 Prairial II, Arch. Nat., AF$_{II}$ 97, Dordogne, pl. 714,

The survival ration of 8 oz. for grown-ups and 4 oz. for children under twelve would appear to correspond to the 'vital minimum', the threshold at which all men are equal in the face of starvation, the point at which no one can become poorer or less equal than his fellow for any length of time without incurring the risk of death. It is here that the Jacobin view of elementary justice can be said to be strictly or purely egalitarian, i.e. where the process of downward 'levelling' becomes absolute: equal shares, rather than fair shares, for all. The further, however, we move away from the irreducible threshold of basic necessities, the further we progress up the scale from absolute to relative deprivation and from acute to decent poverty, the more fairness comes into its own, taking over from equality, and the more graduated the process of distribution becomes.[78]

Although the idea of a 'bread of equality' was first floated by Fouché in western France in March 1793 and then proposed to the citizens of Nevers, Moulins and Lyons in September and October, the first detailed guidance on the subject was the decree of 25 Brumaire prepared by Goujon. It prescribed a single type of bread with a high bran content, composed of three-quarters wheat germ and one-quarter rye or barley.[79] This prescription was adapted in the Midi to local cropping patterns, with a mix of two-thirds rye and one-third wheat. Already in 1789, the city of Périgueux had prohibited white loaves and increased the regulation price for a single loaf. Roux-Fazillac in early Brumaire prevented the bakers of Périgueux, Tulle and Brive from making puff-pastries, cakes, waffles or fancy buns from white flour, but only as from late Floréal, during the *soudure*, did he extend this prohibition to bread, which henceforth could only be made from wholemeal (*en tout son*), that is meal from which not more than 15 pounds of bran content per quintal had been removed.[80] Romme, for his part, reduced the

pp. 5–10; AF$_{II}$ 172, Western Bureau, pl. 1414, p. 6; Arch. dép. Dordogne, 1L 233, Romme, pp. 2, 3, 9; and 3 L 25, dist. Bergerac, ff. 178, 225.

[78] Cf. chapter 5 on progressive taxation.

[79] Report by Barère and decree of 25 Brumaire II, *Arch. parl.*, vol. LXXIX, pp. 286–7; A. Mathiez, *La vie chère et le mouvement social sous la Terreur*, 2nd edn, 2 vols. (Paris, 1973), vol. II, p. 68.

[80] Roux-Fazillac, Périgueux, 5 Brumaire, and Tulle, 24 Germinal and 2–13 Prairial II: Arch. Nat., AF$_{II}$ 95, Corrèze, pl. 695, p. 57; Arch. dép. Corrèze, L 96, Roux-Fazillac; Arch. mun. Périgueux, D 4, mun. register, f° 105; Cardenal, 'Les subsistances dans la Dordogne', p. 327; Arsac, 'Une émeute contre-révolutionnaire', pp. 152–3.

removable amount to 7 pounds. This now became the statutory bread consumed in the cities of Limousin and Périgord, and was distributed free of charge to the indigent who had obtained their ration cards from the commune, until such time as the new crop was harvested and safely in store.

In rural areas, a single type of country loaf of the coarser type was the rule in any case. In the farming households of the Auxerrois, according to Restif de la Bretonne, writing in 1778, 'everybody ate the same bread; the odious distinction between white bread and brown bread did not occur'.[81] Nevertheless, Romme was insistent that, in the villages of the south-west, 'the selected grain of the rich shall be mixed with the poor grain of the needy and taken together to the mill, from which each shall remove weight for weight in flour what he has brought in grain, so that all shall eat the bread of equality'. On several occasions, he recommended that all the grain be mixed and milled together, the whole grain together with the siftings, so that the notion of real sharing be fully put into practice and understood by all.[82] If equality was the child of necessity, it should in his view be governed by the principle of the 'pooling of common resources' (as in his own draft declaration of rights), by the principle of 'share and share alike', which extended to all without exception, including for example the army officers and NCOs in transit in the area, who were all obliged to resign themselves to the same ration as the other ranks.[83]

It may be useful at this stage to move from the quantitative to the qualitative aspects of rationing. What, if anything, differentiates Romme's bread of equality from Fouché's? At face value, the two schemes are identical, both dictated by the state of war and the 'command economy', both aiming to supply to all consumers a common loaf at a stable price, and fulfil the dream of a three-sols loaf throughout the Republic. Under closer scrutiny, however, singular differences appear. Chronologically, Fouché launched his scheme in mid-September 1793, that is after the harvest, at a time when a 'bumper crop' (Goujon) might well have justified the free

[81] Rétif de la Bretonne, *La vie de mon père*, p. 130.
[82] Romme, Angoulême, 19 Ventôse; Périgueux, 23 Floréal and 4 Prairial II: Arch. dép. Charente, L 1239, dist. Confolens, and L 1962, missions; Dordogne, 3 L 25, dist. Bergerac, f° 151; Haute-Vienne, L 110, missions.
[83] Resolution of 23 Floréal II, Arch. Nat., AF$_{II}$ 97, Dordogne, pl. 713, pp. 45–51 and 54–5; Arch. dép. Dordogne, 3 L 25, dist. Bergerac, f° 151.

circulation of grain and the making of three sorts of bread (*pain blanc, pain bis, pain noir*). Secondly, September 1793 was the month the Terror was formally introduced, essentially as an economic weapon, with the Convention acquiescing to a series of anti-liberal coercive measures, including the prosecution of forestallers and hoarders of grain as suspects and public enemies, the levying of people's armies to scour the countryside and seize provisions, and the use of the guillotine as an instrument of persuasion.

In this context, as Elisabeth Liris has demonstrated,[84] Fouché's bread of equality quickly became a symbol not of national solidarity, but of class war, a war against the consumers of white bread, the urban bourgeoisie, with the main battlefield soon transferred to the counter-revolutionary city of Lyons: 'Wealth and poverty being equally destined to disappear with the reign of equality', Fouché's proclamation had read, 'there shall no longer be made a bread of fine flour for the rich and a bread from bran for the poor.'[85] Since those who tried to circumvent the edict would have their properties sequestrated, the levelling process would not be limited to the 'fruits of the land', but would extend to the land itself. Fouché and his Enragé friends such as Chaumette, the ardent advocate of economic terror,[86] saw themselves as embarking upon a major social revolution which would give short shrift to the sacrosanct right of private ownership.

In Romme's case, however, nine months later, the redistribution was 'commanded by shortage', confined to foodstuffs and limited to the hungry gap. The frugality and self-denial he asked of his fellow citizens was to be the fruit of exhortation rather than threat, 'rationing' being understood as 'sharing'. His is an appeal to reason and sensibility, the cardinal virtues of the Enlightenment: 'to follow the counsel of reason should suffice to friends of equality', writes Romme the mathematician, carefully counting the rations to ensure there are enough to go round; but he adds that voluntary sharing brings its own rewards, 'coming to the aid of one's brothers is the source of sweet pleasure' and 'individual happiness is only assured in the happiness of all'.[87] His hope was that by treating the people

---

[84] Liris, 'On rougit ici d'être riche', pp. 297–9.
[85] Proclamation by Fouché and Collot-d'Herbois, 24 Brumaire II, in Madelin, *Fouché*, p. 132.
[86] Sewell, 'Sans-Culotte Rhetoric of Subsistence', p. 258.
[87] Resolutions of 28 Floréal and 4 Prairial II: Arch. dép. Charente, L 67, missions; Arch. Nat., AF$_{II}$ 97, Dordogne, pl. 714, pp. 5–10.

as 'a family of brothers', they would, with a little persuasion, behave like one and not question the restrictions of food rationing. Terrorism clearly ran counter to such an ethic. Again, while Fouché's bread of equality served as a curtain-raiser to bloodthirsty repression in Lyons, Romme's in contrast, which was introduced after the disbanding of the *armées révolutionnaires* and after the trial of Hébert and Chaumette, was accompanied by specifically pacificatory and *anti*-terrorist measures: welfare relief to the kin of émigrés, aid to the suspects detained in gaol whose properties were now threatened by the Ventôse decrees and to whom safeguards were offered so that those 'declared innocent might reclaim their revenues'.[88]

The fair shares policy pursued by Romme during his long mission in the provinces in Year II sheds an instructive light on his role and that of his colleague Goujon a year later when, during the terrible dearth of 1795, he took the floor in the Convention to demand, on behalf of the people of Paris who loudly cheered him on from the public gallery, a general prohibition on the making of cakes, buns and all types of pastry, a door-to-door search for flour, and a 'single sort of bread' equally distributed to all consumers.[89] His parliamentary colleagues, in the changed political climate of Prairial Year III, failed or refused to understand the principle of 'fraternal equality' underlying his intervention. Knowingly or not, they confused his bread of equality with that of Fouché (he too being implicated, albeit indirectly, in the popular uprisings of that year). If, as Bronislaw Baczko suggests, the Thermidorian reaction to terrorism was characterised by the attempt to reconcile legal equality with de facto *in*equality, then any reference to equal shares was bound to be interpreted as a wilful revival of the Jacobin Terror.[90]

Romme's egalitarianism was neither that of a terrorist nor that of a 'true' leveller, as was Fouché's or subsequently Babeuf's. But here a word of caution is in order. Babouvism, according to Georges Lefebvre, was essentially 'a communism of consumption that aimed to put into effect the socialised distribution of vital

[88] Resolutions of 21 Germinal and 20 Floréal II: see chapter 4, pp. 114 and 119.

[89] 'Défense de Gilbert Romme', in Brunel and Goujon, *Les martyrs de prairial*, p. 393; and Tissot, 'Vie de Goujon', *ibid.*, p. 165.

[90] B. Baczko, 'Thermidoriens', in Furet and M. Ozouf, *Dictionnaire critique*, pp. 435–6.

commodities, especially bread, which was expected from the revolutionary government's policy of requisition and price regulations and which remained so incomplete and so imperfect'; and further, 'Babouvist communism ... resides in the placing of the crop in the communal warehouse'.[91] Mably had not argued otherwise in his description of the golden age, which unexpectedly turns out to be relevant to a pre-capitalist private-ownership market economy in which exchange entitlements break down[92] and price controls and the use of force prove ineffective. There is an interesting continuity here, in the recognition that the voluntary pooling and sharing of staple commodities is the only safe and effective way of eliminating the risk of manipulated scarcity and establishing an economy of provision free from inequalities.

[91] G. Lefebvre, review of A. Galante Garrone, *Buonarroti e Babeuf* (Turin, 1948), *Annales hist. Révol. fr.* 22 (1950), pp. 81–2.
[92] Sen, *Poverty and Famines*, pp. 45–51.

4. *Land tenure, shelter and the right of ownership*

It is certain that the right of ownership is the most sacred of all the rights of the citizen and more important in certain respects than liberty itself.

Rousseau, 'Economie politique', in *Encyclopédie*, vol. V, 1755

Beware of listening to that impostor: you are lost if you forget that the fruit belong to all and the land belongs to no one!

Rousseau, *Discours sur l'origine et les fondements de l'inégalité*, 1755[1]

The fair apportionment of essential commodities entailed no common ownership of the means of production, no wholesale redistribution of the land, no 'agrarian law' and few if any curtailments of individual property rights. Nevertheless, declarations of principle decreed at regular intervals by the Convention make it clear that while no erosion of the sacrosanct right of ownership would be tolerated, the 'red scare' was very real and the risk of such erosion taking place was clearly perceived. At its very first sitting, on 21 September 1792, Danton had moved to much acclaim that all 'territorial, individual and industrial properties would be eternally maintained'; on 18 March 1793 the death sentence was imposed on whomsoever proposed a *lex agraria* or 'any other law subversive of territorial, commercial and industrial properties', while on 7 May the people's representatives-on-mission were charged with 'affirming liberty and ensuring the guarantee of properties' and on 21 September, as the Terror was inaugurated, the spectre of arbitrary land redistribution was once again squarely laid to rest.[2]

[1] Rousseau, *Œuvres complètes*, vol. II, pp. 228, 286.
[2] Danton, *Œuvres*, ed. by A. Vermorel (Paris, 1866), p. 120; C. Desmoulins, *Les*

Although Montesquieu had situated the issue of land partition in distant antiquity and envisaged 'equalisation' only in the context of income redistribution,[3] and Rousseau's thoughts on common ownership were confined to a theoretical age before the invention of private property,[4] historical or utopian musings of this kind could, in a revolutionary context, prove dangerously subversive. Hence the pains taken by Montagnards and Girondins alike to show that freedom and property were one. According to Saint-Just, 'man was born to possess'; he firmly believed, in the wake of John Locke, that property alone conferred independence and the capability of self-fulfilment: 'a plough, a field, a cottage protected from taxation, a family sheltered from the cupidity of a brigand, *voilà le bonheur.*'[5] Although Robespierre, as we have seen, voiced his opposition to 'unlimited' freedom, that is possessive individualism at the expense of others, he too roundly condemned the 'extravagant' notion of common ownership. As a consequence, in conceding that property was inviolable and equality of ownership 'fundamentally impossible in civil society',[6] he was in effect subscribing to the maintenance of inequality, a position which did not deter him from being a staunch egalitarian.

The *représentants* who in the spring and summer of 1793 set about the delicate task of defusing the agitation in the provinces thus found themselves preaching the inviolability of private property and reassuring their listeners that they stood for law and order. Monestier du Puy-de-Dôme and Jeanbon Saint-André promised to be ruthless with those who transgressed this rule and who became the 'disorganisers of social order', while Lakanal a year later

---

révolutions de France et de Brabant, part II, 30 September 1792, in *Œuvres*, vol. IX, pp. 5–8; M. Robespierre, 'Lettres à ses commettans', in *Œuvres de Maximilien Robespierre*, vol. V, p. 24; R. B. Rose, 'The "Red Scare" of the 1790s: The French Revolution and the "Agrarian Law"', *Past and Present* 103 (1984), pp. 113–30; Hirsch, 'Terror and Property', p. 215.

[3] Montesquieu, 'Comment les lois établissent l'égalite, dans la démocratie', book V, chapter 5, *De l'esprit des lois*, vol. I, pp. 51–4.

[4] 'Commençons par écarter tous les faits, car ils ne touchent point à la question': Rousseau, 'Discours sur l'inégalité', in *Œuvres complètes*, vol. II, p. 212.

[5] Saint-Just, 'De la nature', in *Frammenti sulle istituzioni repubblicane*, ed. by A. Soboul (Turin, 1952), pp. 149–51; and report of 23 Ventôse II, in *Discours et rapports*, p. 165.

[6] Robespierre, 'Discours sur le marc d'argent', 20 April 1791; *Le Défenseur de la Constitution*, No. 4, 7 June 1792; and speech of 24 April 1793, *Œuvres*, vol. IV, pp. 116–19; vol. V, p. 165; and vol. IX, pp. 459–71; see C. Brough Mackenzie, *Property: Mainstream and Critical Positions* (Oxford, 1978), pp. 15–27.

reminded the citizens of Bergerac that respect for property was the basic principle governing 'civilised society', that 'anarchy always resulted in servitude' and that those who plundered the possessions of others should be locked up 'with the enemies of the people'.[7] Interestingly, Roux-Fazillac, an energetic Montagnard intent on radical land reform, was quite scrupulous in respecting the property rights enshrined in the constitution, for when his planned enlargement of the Tulle arms factory required the expropriation of a number of residents on the left bank of the Corrèze, he made sure full and adequate compensation was paid to them in advance, in accordance with article 19 of the 1793 Declaration of Rights.[8]

Roux-Fazillac even promised a bonus to the expropriated smallholders who belonged to the 'precious class of sans-culottes', those who 'work with their hands', in order to assist them in quickly acquiring a new holding. Indeed, access to property ownership was the cornerstone of government policy and Romme held the view that a man's labour should suffice to secure such access: 'Every man who works is really a proprietor ... We speak of capital as property. And why do we not speak of the worker's wage? His arms are his capital ... everything a man reaps from his labour makes up his property.'[9] Likewise, Robespierre's view of 'honourable' poverty was based on the limited ownership of material possessions, including the 'fruits of one's labour', and culminated in the concept of 'legitimate property', guaranteed by law, designed to meet the needs of the working man, the right of appropriation being therefore 'limited by the obligation to respect the rights of others'. Saint-Just was in favour of 'giving some land to everybody'; what the Robespierrists sought but never managed to achieve was a limited right of ownership that entailed both a minimum and a maximum entitlement,[10] in keeping with Rousseau's stated belief that a ceiling to acquisition could and should be

---

[7] Monestier, Guéret, 20 April 1793, Arch dép. Creuse, L 105, Jacobin Club of Guéret; Saint-André, Périgueux, 17 April 1793, Arch. dép. Dordogne, 1L 225, mission of Saint-André; Lakanal, Floréal II, Arch. mun. Bergerac, Box U, mun. papers, 1.42, p. 36; and Labroue, *La mission de Lakanal*, p. 257.

[8] Tulle, 13 Thermidor II, Arch. dép. Corrèze, L 260*, arms factory, f° 1.

[9] Romme's definition of property on 17 April 1793 led to a change to the wording of article 16 of the Declaration, Condorcet's term 'capitaux' being replaced by 'fruit de son travail': Galante Garrone, *Gilbert Romme*, p. 300; *Les Déclarations*, ed. by Jaume, pp. 242, 301.

[10] Saint-Just, 'Quatrième fragment' and 'Institutions rurales', *Frammenti sulle istituzione*, pp. 59, 94–5; cf. Robespierre, 24 April 1793, *Œuvres*, vol. IX,

determined by law, provided legally acquired property was always respected: 'No law can deprive anyone of any part of his estate; the law can only prevent him from acquiring more.'[11]

The curbs to possessive individualism felt necessary did not automatically imply a shift toward agrarian radicalism of a fundamental kind nor an abandonment of liberal economic principles. Of course, it cannot be denied that the Mountain did pursue a vigorous policy of redistributive land reform, as Peter M. Jones, Jean-Pierre Jessenne and others have shown.[12] Some deputies, such as Le Bon, Coupé, Dartigoeyte, Isoré and possibly Roux-Fazillac, were prepared, such was their desire to satisfy the legitimate aspirations of the country poor, to go beyond Marat's 'democratic maximum': thus, Joseph Le Bon's persecution of large producers in the Pas-de-Calais 'constitutes a notable case of fusion of agrarian policy with the Terror'.[13] But the majority felt it necessary to reconcile their egalitarian leanings with the belief they professed in human rights: Augustin Robespierre, for example, showed particular leniency toward worthy farmers in the Haute-Saône who had been removed from office and imprisoned.

In these circumstances, the democratic options open to would-be reformers were limited in number and scope. They included the reform of inheritance law, the division of the commons, the sale of émigré properties in small parcels, the liquidation of the royal parks and farms and the demolition of *châteaux-forts* for the provision of building materials. The Convention also seriously considered the feasibility of dividing large holdings into smaller tenancies and increasing the number of small holdings in keeping with traditional modes of land tenure, especially *métayage*. In the process they envisaged the sequestration and exploitation of property belonging to the detained suspects found guilty of connivance with the counter-revolution. An assessment of the lengths to which they were prepared to take this reform programme may enable us

---

pp. 459–71; M. Dommanget, 'Saint-Just et la question agraire', *Annales hist. Révol. fr.* 38 (1966), pp. 33–60.

[11] Rousseau, 'Projet de constitution pour la Corse', *Œuvres complètes*, vol. III, pp. 510, 512.

[12] P. M. Jones, *The Peasantry in the French Revolution* (Cambridge, 1988), pp. 148, 164; P. M. Jones, '"Agrarian Law"'; Jessenne, 'Land', pp. 235, 239; see also Ikni, 'Jacques-Michel Coupé, curé jacobin'.

[13] Jessenne, 'Land', p. 239.

to make a balanced judgement about the democratic nature (or otherwise) of Jacobin egalitarianism.

INHERITANCE LAW REFORM AND THE INADMISSIBILITY OF EQUAL SHARES

The least painful and most effective way of redistributing property and wealth for future generations was by reforming the law governing inheritance. Montesquieu's advice in this respect appeared quite unambiguous: 'A very good law in a trading republic', he prescribed, 'is that which gives all children an equal portion of their fathers' legacies. It thereby transpires that, whatever fortune the father made, his children, always less rich than he, are induced to shun luxury and work as hard as he.'[14] Gary Kates has described how members of the Cercle Social made this a strong point of Girondin policy, with Lanthenas recommending abolition of the right of entail for the first-born and equal division of all legacies, and he and Clavière opting for stringent progressive inheritance and legacy duties, while Pétion considered it elementary justice that children should be deemed 'equal in the eyes of the law by sharing equally the estate of their fathers'.[15] Few if any of the Girondins felt there lay a conflict here with the liberal principles which they cherished. After all, John Stuart Mill was later to concede that progressive legacy duties were 'quite unobjectionable'.[16]

Legislation in the Constituent and Legislative Assemblies had already paved the way to the revolutionary view of inheritance.[17] Most of those elected to the Convention in 1792 considered it desirable to aim for real equality in the transmission of property to the next generation: Saint-Just, for instance, who considered it a

[14] Montesquieu, *De l'esprit des lois*, book V, chapter 6, vol. I, p. 55.
[15] J. Pétion, 'Discours sur les testaments en général, et sur l'institution d'héritier dans les pays de droit écrit en particulier', in *Œuvres*, 3 vols. (Paris, 1791–2), vol. III, pp. 357–79; cf. Lanthenas, *Inconvénients du droit d'aînesse* (1789): M. Dorigny, 'Recherches sur les idées économiques des Girondins', in A. Soboul (ed.), *Actes du Colloque Girondins et Montagnards, Sorbonne, 14 décembre 1975* (Paris, 1980), pp. 79–102; G. Kates, *The 'Cercle Social', the Girondins and the French Revolution* (Princeton, 1985), p. 213.
[16] In contrast, Mill roundly condemned progressive income tax as 'a mild form of robbery': J. S. Mill, *Principles of Political Economy, with Some of Their Applications to Social Philosophy*, 2nd edn, 2 vols. (London, 1849), vol. II, p. 355.
[17] For example, the decrees of 15 March 1790 and 8 April 1791.

foil against usurpation and serfdom, and Saint-André who made it the cornerstone of republican society. It was 'unfair', the latter claimed, to 'treat unequally the children of a single father whom nature has made equal'; if all estates were divided on inheritance between the direct offspring, then 'inequality of wealth would necessarily diminish, and possessions, spread out between a larger number of hands, would produce a more general affluence: the rich would be less proud and the poor would be consoled'. Allied to progressive taxation, social welfare and free schooling, which would 'mingle the classes', equality of inheritance would 'establish an order of things such that no citizen would endure the horrors of absolute deprivation'.[18]

Jean-Louis Halpérin has shown that the Jacobins stopped short of supporting the most unsettling proposals, such as calls to limit the wealth children could inherit, with the state confiscating the rest for the poor. Even spokesmen for the militant sans-culottes wanted wealth to remain within the family.[19] Nonetheless, the inheritance legislation introduced by Cambacérès – which overturned centuries of tradition and 'pulverised' Roman law,[20] abolishing wills and codicils, divesting men of property of the faculty of disposing freely of their assets, severely curtailing legacies, equalising all direct descendants, including illegitimate children, then those in collateral line, breaking up estates piecemeal into ever smaller portions – ran up against the most massive disavowal the new regime experienced at grass-roots level.

Although radicals did not seek to make any legal provision retroactive before 14 July 1789, the fact that the principle of retroactivity to that date was endorsed on 12 Brumaire, in flagrant contradiction to article 14 of the newly amended Declaration of Rights, incensed all the beneficiaries of recently divided estates. The precursors and effects of 'equalisation of inheritance' have been reviewed in some depth by Margaret Darrow in the context of

---

[18] Jeanbon Saint-André, *Réflexions sur l'éducation nationale*, Paris, 20 December 1792, Bibl. Nat., 8° Le[38] 2259, pp. 10–14; cf. Saint-Just, 'De la nature', *Frammenti sulle istituzione*, pp. 152–3.

[19] J.-L. Halpérin, *L'impossible code civil* (Paris, 1992), reviewed by L. R. Berlanstein in *Journal of Modern History* 66 (September 1994), pp. 616–17, and by J. Bart, *Revue d'hist. mod. et cont.* 41-3 (July–September 1994), pp. 537–9.

[20] The principal decrees were those of 25 October and 14 November 1792, 4 January and 7 March 1793, 5 and 12 Brumaire and 17 Nivôse Year II: see Sagnac, *La législation civile*, pp. 223, 225, 229–43.

southern France.[21] Many of the primary assemblies called upon to vote in the referendum of June–July 1793 on the new constitution voiced their discontent. They declared the new laws to be in violation of the right of ownership enshrined in the Declaration; others insisted that fathers could not be divested of the freedom to dispose of their possessions as they thought fit; many that the right of the first-born, or the principle of one privileged child per family, was essential to preserving the economic viability of the estate, that the new laws meant the ruin of entire families, the dawning of a new age of pauperism, of disrespect for parents, whose children would no longer be 'held to obedience in expectation of a settlement'. And in those areas where the soil was too sterile to support several families, how could the inheritance be divided up in equal parts between eight, nine or ten children?[22]

Whereas in practice, as Saint-André ruefully noted, passive resistance and procrastination succeeded in foiling its implementation, in some cases the legislation gave rise to open revolt. What passed for religious unrest during the period of active dechristianisation frequently turned out to be an anti-egalitarian protest triggered by inheritance reform, in which frustrated testators and disgruntled inheritors voiced their grievances; thus, in a hill-farming region such as the district of Gourdon in the Lot, angry Quercynois smallholders took Taillefer to task for spearheading the Convention's policy of 'dividing up the land' after 'abolishing the right of the first-born and enacting equality of succession'.[23] That the last-born *cadets* of Gascony should be shown favour was a source of indignation to proud fathers and elder children alike. That a young Normandy girl from the district of Saint-Lô should marry and enjoy her dowry, yet still deprive her brothers of the land they had tilled and fertilised with their labour, was the subject of bitter recrimination. The storm of protest unleashed everywhere, the numerous real or simulated sales and other schemes contrived to circumvent the retrospective effect of the

---

[21] M. H. Darrow, *Revolution in the House: Family, Class and Inheritance in Southern France, 1775–1825* (Princeton, 1989).

[22] Baticle, 'Le plébiscite', *La Révol. fr.* 58 (1910), pp. 398–9.

[23] Saint-André, letter to the Convention of 25 June 1793, *Gazette Nationale ou le Moniteur universel*, 24 vols. (Paris, 1789–Year VIII), vol. XVI, p. 642; Taillefer, Cahors, 29 September 1793, Arch. Nat., AF$_{II}$ 169, Western Bureau, pl. 1387, p. 10; Aulard, *Recueil*, vol. VII, p. 122.

law,[24] the many family disputes which were carried to the bar of the Convention, provide ample proof of the deep-seated opposition to these reforms.

But still the assembly refused to budge. A repeal of the inheritance laws would have amounted to a renegation of the principles of the Revolution itself. It was strongly felt in Jacobin circles that to entitle a poor younger child, boy or girl, to an equal share of their father's estate was not only fair, but it was to bestow on them the gift of emancipation, their passport to freedom and independence through the blessing of ownership: property for all understood as 'liberty made visible', in the words of Philippe Sagnac.[25] The Jacobins indeed were confirmed liberals in their determination to defend individual rights and ensure that no one was left out in the cold: their concept of the family as 'building block' of the Republic was all-encompassing.[26]

All the offspring were now lumped indiscriminately together into a single category, including those born out of wedlock, the *enfants de la nature*,[27] a startling and truly egalitarian innovation which was not to survive the Civil Code of 1804. In the opinion of Jean Bart, the fact that the members of the Convention were careful to avoid 'inquisitorial' practices in the establishment of parenthood and gave the putative father the right to recognise or not his natural-born child is symptomatic of the 'liberal individualism' that permeated revolutionary civil legislation at a time when egalitarian demands were at their strongest: in the conflict between the equality of the children and the liberty of the father, liberty won hands down.[28] Lynn Hunt, for her part, comes to a similar conclusion for the opposite reason: in her view, the liberal notion of the individual during the Revolution is also to be found in a model of the family in which the autonomy of the child was recognised, both sexes treated equally and natural children assimilated with legitimate children.[29] At all events, the notion of absence of discrimination

[24] These are recorded in Arch. Nat., AD XVIII, Laws and Decrees, and C. 326, Convention: Sagnac, *La législation civile*, p. 238.
[25] *Ibid.*, p. 243.
[26] L. Hunt, 'Male Virtue and Republican Motherhood', in Baker, *The Terror*, pp. 199, 201, 204.
[27] On illegitimate children under the *ancien régime*, see Hufton, *The Poor*, pp. 320–9.
[28] J. Bart, 'Les anticipations de l'an II dans le droit de la famille: l'intégration des "enfants de la nature"', *Annales hist. Révol. fr.* 300 (April–June 1995), pp. 192–3.
[29] Hunt, *Le roman familial*, pp. 104, 223.

which today prevails in the jurisprudence of the European Court of Human Rights has a distant precursor in the Jacobin project of Year II.[30]

The image of a property-owning democracy, a happy community of individual smallholders farming equal plots and content with little in the tradition of Fénelon's *Télémaque*, was a fond illusion, albeit an original and tenacious one, which Saint-André and Cambacérès were to continue to cherish long after the advent of the Empire and the adoption of the Napoleonic code, and which Honoré de Balzac was subsequently to caricature at the end of his novel *Les paysans*. Here, in a historical time-loop, the peasants of lower Burgundy are portrayed as enjoying their new-found 'poverty' in the Jacobin style, finally reaping the benefits of the gospel according to Jean-Jacques: 'The country was no longer recognisable. The mysterious woods, the avenues of the park, all had been cleared; the landscape looked like a tailor's pattern-card. The peasant had taken possession of the land as victor and conqueror. It was divided up into more than a thousand lots.'[31]

GOD'S LITTLE ACRE: THE DIVISION OF THE COMMONS

Balzac's jaundiced view of the peasantry's rise to small ownership included their appropriation of common land. Whereas the ambitious egalitarian changes made to the law on inheritance in Year II promised long-term benefits which would only be felt, in theory at least, by the generations to come, the partition of communal properties, in contrast, seemed to herald immediate or short-term relief for the rural poor. This significant aspect of agrarian reform, warmly recommended by Enlightenment agronomists[32] and already instigated by the expiring Legislative Assembly amid popular acclaim in August 1792, was brought to the statute book by the Montagnard Convention on 10 June 1793, during the period of intensive social legislation that followed the fall of the Gironde. It encountered conflicting reactions from the rural community.

---

[30] Bart, 'Les anticipations de l'an II', p. 196.

[31] H. de Balzac, *Les paysans*, ed. by P. Barbéris (Paris, 1970), p. 373.

[32] See the numerous reforms proposed between 1761 and 1777: H. Sée, 'Le partage des biens communaux en France à la fin de l'Ancien Régime', *Revue d'histoire du droit français et étranger* (1923), cited by A. Bourde, *Agronomie et agronomes en France au XVIIIe siècle* (Paris, 1967), p. 1079.

While everywhere in France the peasants were attached to their customary common pasture rights which they considered essential to their survival,[33] and while they were unanimous in claiming back common lands annexed by their *seigneurs* in virtue of the *droit de triage*, village communities were split between the agrarian individualism of the wealthy stockowners, who were in favour of maintaining collective grazing for their flocks, a greater readiness on the part of the smallholders to entertain some form of division, and a clear preference for egalitarian *partage* from the landless who had nothing to lose.

The detailed if somewhat patchy research undertaken by, *inter alios*, Florence Gauthier and the late Guy Ikni in Picardy, J.-M. Sallman in Artois, Roland Marx in Alsace, Gabrielle Richert in the Haute-Garonne and Peter M. Jones at Versailles and in the Orne[34] reveals a very uneven pattern of division: failure to divide in the Somme, where community cropping and grazing practices were paramount, outright success in lower Alsace where handouts were numerous, or at Versailles where extensive tracts of the royal estates were shared out in one-*arpent* plots, and partial success in the Oise, Artois and Midi Toulousain, where some loss of common pasture proved tolerable. These results seem to demonstrate that the success or failure of division was largely determined by geography, tenure and agrarian practice, such as the open-field cropping system in the north or sharecropping in the south-west, which was on the increase since the abolition of feudal rents.[35]

The arguments against partitioning made sense. In Limousin and the Massif in general, regions well endowed with commons, the unsuitability of wasteland, badlands or sterile moorland for dis-

[33] A. Ado, 'Le mouvement paysan et le problème de l'égalité', in A. Soboul (ed.), *Contributions à l'histoire paysanne de la Révolution française* (Paris, 1977), p. 137.
[34] G. Lefebvre, *Les paysans du Nord pendant la Révolution française* (Paris, 1924), p. 523; G. Richert, 'Biens communaux et droits d'usage en Haute-Garonne pendant la réaction thermidorienne', *Annales hist. Révol. fr.* 23 (1951), pp. 274–84; J. M. Sallman, 'Etude sur l'Ancien Régime agraire: la question des biens communaux en Artois de la fin du XVIIe au début du XIXe siècle', thesis, University of Paris (1974), p. 218; R. Marx, *La Révolution et les classes sociales en Basse-Alsace* (Paris, 1974), pp. 425–31; Fl. Gauthier, *La voie paysanne dans la Révolution française: l'exemple picard* (Paris, 1977), pp. 194–203; G. R. Ikni, 'Sur les biens communaux', *Annales hist. Révol. fr.* 54 (1982), pp. 71–94; P. M. Jones, *Peasantry*, pp. 148–54; P. M. Jones, '"Agrarian Law"'.
[35] Roux-Fazillac, letter of 13 Brumaire Year II, Aulard, *Recueil*, vol. VIII, pp. 210–11; P. M. Jones, *Peasantry*, p. 164.

memberment into arable plots was the obvious cause for rejection. Sheep-farming in the district of Uzerche required unimpeded access to vast tracts of heath. Smallholders who owned a team of oxen to till their farms needed to put their animals out to graze, while the poor who had no oxen and plough could not benefit from division on account of their inability to clear the land.[36] Village worthies in the Cantal and Aveyron, often supported by the smallholders, found it 'unnatural' for simple farm-hands to acquire land and 'only right' that a few households should rule the roost; it was in any case inevitable that after ten years, when sales became lawful, the fragmented parcels would be reunited under one ownership; if division there had to be, then one-third of the commons could be divided equally by hearth, and two-thirds between the existing landowners in proportion to their properties.[37]

Arguments in favour of partition were to be heard in those areas where common land was unsuitable for grazing and could usefully be reclaimed for cropping, as in the districts of Tulle and Cahors. Here, according to the future Montagnard Jean-Baptiste Cavaignac, writing in December 1791, the mode of *partage* favoured by the majority was equal division between all the heads of families, the aim being firstly to return to the 'pre-feudal equality of possession' eroded by exchanges, and secondly to prevent 'the man who has much to increase his wealth at the expense of the one who has nothing' and to enable the latter to 'acquire something'. As for encroachments on common land, while large landowners who consolidated their estates in this way should be taken to court, it would be wrong to dispossess those who 'having no property at all or only a modest amount' had wrongfully seized a plot and farmed it for several years, and whose share on partition should preferably be assigned from the territory they had appropriated.[38]

The decree of 10 June 1793, moved by Fabre, stipulated that shares should be assigned by ballot and per head rather than per

[36] Reasons advanced by the administrators of the Corrèze, Haute-Vienne and Aveyron departments between November 1790 and July 1792: *Le partage des biens communaux*, ed. by G. Bourgin (Paris, 1908), pp. 37, 47–8, 51–3, 69, 311 and 442.
[37] Creuse, Cantal, Corrèze and Aveyron: Baticle, 'Le plébiscite', pp. 398–9; C. Alhéritière, *Les communaux en France, spécialement en Creuse* (Paris, 1912), p. 100; M. Chamboux, *Répartition de la propriété foncière et de l'exploitation dans la Creuse* (Paris, 1956), pp. 1–60.
[38] Cahors, 28 December 1791, in *Le partage des biens communaux*, ed. by Bourgin, pp. 132–5.

hearth, thus giving equal status not just to the landowners but to the farm-hands, labourers, plough-boys and milkmaids, that is all those whose silent aspirations to a plot of land had until now been overlooked. That women were given equal rights to vote on this important economic issue is a sign that the distant prospect of 'universal' suffrage was not, even at this early stage, a flight of fancy. However, the per capita approach led to all manner of difficulties in practice since most households preferred to hold their share in a single territorial unit. While many village assemblies would have preferred a division between families rather than individuals, some complied with the letter of the law. Thus, Verdun-sur-Garonne split its commons into tiny portions between all the 681 adult inhabitants. The small commune of Marignac near Beaumont-de-Lomagne tried to inject greater fairness into the deal by marking out the commons into 267 lots which were 'equal *and comparable* with respect to the quality and soil of the terrain [my italics]'. In keeping with Fabre's sceptical view that the rural poor were not of necessity driven by the property-owning instinct and preferred a sum of money 'and the momentary pleasure it brings to an allotment that he would have to cultivate', the nearby commune of Comberouges decided to rent out its small commons on a single annual lease and share out the cash among the villagers, while the commune of Pazayac in the Dordogne put its land up for auction and distributed the proceeds of the sale to all the inhabitants, male and female, equally.[39]

Division of the common land thus proved very uneven and in the long term disappointing. Mathematical division did not necessarily mean viable apportionment. Just how individually cost-effective was the land parcelling carried out in the 100 villages of the Oise recorded by Ikni, or the one-third of the 309 rural communities in Artois sampled by Sallman? To whose ultimate advantage was the elimination of 9,564 hectares of commons out of a total of 35,240 estimated by Richert for the Haute-Garonne? In so many cases, the poor were tempted to dispose of their holdings at the earliest opportunity, often before the statutory ten-year

---

[39] Decree of 10 June 1793, *ibid.*, pp. 728–39; Arch. dép. Tarn-et-Garonne, L 37, dist. Grenade-Beaumont, 17 Pluviôse II and 20 Prairial III; R. Laffon, 'La commune de Pazayac (Dordogne) pendant la Révolution', *La Révol. fr.* 66 (1914), p. 342; Ikni, 'Sur les biens communaux', pp. 93–4; P. M. Jones, ' "Agrarian Law" ', p. 119.

period had elapsed. The 1,546 plotholders in the former Grand Parc at Versailles were among these. Jones has shown that land consolidation had begun well before the Napoleonic decree of 9 Ventôse Year XII (29 February 1804), which legitimised the acquisitions made under *partage*. A stone cutter from the Vosges who petitioned the Convention in Year III to allow him to clear some wasteland pointed out that the quarter-*arpent* allotment he had received on partition (i.e. about 1,000 square metres) was quite inadequate to support his family of five young children.[40] The women of the district of Sarlat who during the hungry gap of Floréal Year III 'invaded the cemeteries' for their own needs, making 'insidious speeches demanding the partition of the land', were acting, according to the Thermidorian Boussion, at the instigation of the 'agents of anarchy and terror, brigandage and robbery'.[41] Shades of the *loi agraire* yet again.

There are some success stories, however, which seem to indicate that the partition law of 10 June 1793 did not completely miss the mark. P. M. Jones has recorded the cases of humble labourers of the Orne who cleared and enclosed strips of common land which previously produced nothing but rushes and weeds and converted them to crops such as barley or planted them with fruit trees: ten years on, they boasted a house, garden and small pear-orchard enclosed by a neatly clipped hedgerow, husbandry of the kind Arthur Young would have approved of.[42] One of the Versailles *partageurs* described his *arpent* plot as 'more honourable than profitable', a revealing phrase which shows that ownership was understood not as acquisitive individualism, but as 'useful tenure', to borrow Georges Lefebvre's term, as access to a fair share of arable land rather than title to property, within the framework of a village community and cropping system which continued to include, as in the past, collective practices and customary rights. If the aim was not to promote the profit motive but to 'make poverty

[40] P. M. Jones, *Peasantry*, p. 154 and '"Agrarian Law"', pp. 128–30.
[41] The preparatory decree of 6 June 1793 converted graveyards around churches into a 'communal à partager': *Le partage des biens communaux*, ed. by Bourgin, p. 728; Boussion, 30 Floréal III, Arch. Nat., AF$_{II}$ 180, Western Bureau, pl. 1483, p. 39; Aulard, *Recueil*, vol. XXIII, p. 350.
[42] P. M. Jones, '"Agrarian Law"', p. 130; cf. A. Young's description of the hill farmers of Béarn, in *Travels in France and Italy*, ed. by T. Okey (London, 1976), p. 52.

honourable',[43] the small allotment was doubtless conducive to this end.

SELLING THE ÉMIGRÉ PROPERTIES AND DISMANTLING THE CASTLES

Although the *représentants* did not involve themselves during their peregrinations with the division of communal properties, a matter they left to the village communities, they were very active in supervising the sales of émigré estates. Placed at the disposal of the nation by the Brissotin-dominated Legislative Assembly to cover the costs of waging war, the sequestrated lands of the émigré nobility were finally released for sale on 3 June 1793. The Montagnards went about this business with entrepreneurial enthusiasm, delighting in the unexpected profits made at auction and displaying thereby both their satisfaction at the transfer of landed wealth from aristocracy to bourgeoisie, and their implicit faith in the virtues of the market economy.

Bidding was so active in the Saintonge that a typical sale of émigré farm-land yielded 200,000 livres, as compared to an estimate of 80,000; at Rochefort, the first two sales almost doubled the estimates, with figures reaching 123,000 livres against an estimate of 69,000, and 34,000 against 18,000. Five small vineyards in Auxerrois measuring 2 *arpents* 58 *perches* and estimated 2,528 livres, were sold for 17,285 livres, 'a very high price indeed', commented Maure. And while profits in Poitou exceeded valuations by about a third overall, the income from land sales over five months in the small district of Bellac in the Haute-Vienne totalled nearly 1,340,000 livres. Roux-Fazillac noted that bidders were 'anxious' to buy, while Paganel considered that the 'alacrity' shown at auction was a sign that the purchasers were finally prepared to throw in their lot with the Revolution.[44] There appears to have

---

[43] B. Minzes, *Die Nationalgüterverausserung während der französischen Revolution mit besonderer Berücksichtigung des Department Seine und Oise* (Jena, 1892), p. 82, n 278, cited by P. M. Jones, '"Agrarian Law"', p. 130; M. Bloch, *Caractères originaux de l'histoire rurale française*, 2 vols. (Paris, 1952), vol. I, p. 134; G. Lefebvre, 'Répartition de la propriété et de l'exploitation foncières à la fin de l'Ancien Régime', in *Etudes sur la Révolution française* (Paris, 1954), pp. 201–22; Robespierre, speeches of April 1791 and 24 April 1793, *Œuvres*, vol. VII, p. 165, and vol. IX, p. 459.

[44] Bernard, Guimberteau, Lequinio, Maure, Ingrand, Brival, Roux-Fazillac and Paganel, 25 June, 16 September, 9 and 12 October 1793, 4 and 17 Brumaire, 23

been little awareness at this stage that the émigré properties had in effect already lost a great deal of their value through encroachment, poor management and discriminatory fiscal valuation, that collusion between purchasers and local authorities was now giving rise to innumerable cases of fraud and that the ten-year period accorded for payment in unstable *assignats* meant that the *biens nationaux* were actually being sold off for derisory amounts.[45]

Active bidding at auction was a sign at least that the landed bourgeoisie were intent on both rounding off their possessions and finding a secure and potentially profitable outlet for their devalued paper money. Although Maure was delighted to report that a nobleman's property at Chastellux-sur-Cure on the edge of the Morvan, an 'arid and sterile land', had been acquired *in toto* by 'his former vassals',[46] the small peasantry in general were outflanked by the propertied classes. Research conducted in the region of Montauban by Daniel Ligou shows that the nationalised lands purchased by 137 merchants, 26 public officials and 10 constitutional priests amounted to nearly 60 per cent of sales, while the acquisitions made by 163 farmers and artisans made up only 20 per cent.[47] The proportion in the Bordelais was even less favourable, while in the Toulousain, 60 per cent of the buyers were city dwellers who secured over 80 per cent of the 3,200 lots up for sale, representing an area of 10,240 hectares, or 86 per cent of the total acreage.[48]

Possessive individualism on this scale clearly thwarted the avowed aim of Montagnard legislation, which was to favour mini-proprietors and first-time buyers. The sale of national land in 'very small lots', that is enough to sustain 'a family of cultivators', was a notion of long-standing radical pedigree favoured by, among others, La Rochefoucauld-Liancourt and François de Neufchâ-

Nivôse II, in Aulard, *Recueil*, vol. V, p. 80; vol. VI, p. 527; vol. VIII, pp. 280, 331; vol. IX, p. 193; vol. X, p. 206; first *Supplément*, p. 194; second *Supplément*, p. 174.

[45] Aftalion, *French Revolution*, p. 158.

[46] Auxerre, 11 Frimaire II, Aulard, *Recueil*, vol. IX, p. 88.

[47] D. Ligou, 'La structure agraire de la banlieue montalbanaise' and 'Biens nationaux dans le district de Montauban', *Bulletin de la Société des sciences naturelles de Tarn-et-Garonne* (1952), reviewed by G. Lefebvre in *Annales hist. Révol. fr.* 25 (1953), p. 375.

[48] M. Marion, J. Benzacer and H. Caudriller, *Département de la Gironde: la vente des biens nationaux*, 2 vols. (Paris, 1912), vol. II, reviewed by A. Mathiez, *Annales révol.* 6 (1913), p. 730; H. Martin, *Documents relatifs à la vente des biens nationaux dans la Haute-Garonne: le district de Toulouse* (Toulouse, 1916), pp. i–lxxxvii.

teau.[49] The decree of 3 June 1793 required the local authorities in communes which contained émigré properties but lacked commons to mark out and exclude from auction a quantity of land 'sufficient to allow the grant of one *arpent* on a perpetual lease' to every household not owning land to this amount, the surplus being subdivided for auction in separate small lots corresponding to whole fields, meadows or vineyards, which could not then be consolidated.[50] However, the one-*arpent* land grant and exemption from bidding for poor householders were cancelled on 13 September and replaced by the issue of interest-free credit vouchers of 500 livres, reimbursable over twenty years, to assist them in placing their bids at auction. This new provision, as Mathiez emphasised,[51] was socially retrograde and disadvantaged the farm labourers or craft workers who neither paid taxes nor owned property, since the requirement to purchase now superseded the offer of a tenancy: the poor preferred to rent rather than buy, for they were not accustomed to buying and could rarely afford to do so. The voucher system did not exempt them from auction and the sum of 500 livres was not enough to enable them to acquire a sizeable holding.

Despite this unequivocally liberal shift in policy, prompted by commercial considerations, and which underscores the Montagnards' adherence to market values, the Convention continued to bear the interests of the rural poor in mind. Merlin de Douai claimed it was essential to divide the nationalised lands into portions of sufficient size to support a family, and on 2 Frimaire the deputies voted to break up all the émigré estates into small lots and extended this measure to include ecclesiastical properties.[52] Recognising that the 500-livres vouchers were especially aimed at the poor peasants who were enlisted in the army, Brival recommended that the Limoges authorities set aside the relief payments due to soldiers' families under the new welfare legislation to augment the funds available for purchasing a plot of land: 'You

---

[49] *Le partage des biens communaux*, ed. by Bourgin, p. 397; H. Sée, 'Les conceptions économiques et sociales du Comité de mendicité de la Constituante', *Annales hist. Révol. fr.* 3 (1926), p. 332.

[50] *Arch. parl.*, vol. LXVI, p. 10; A. Mathiez, 'La Révolution française et les prolétaires: la loi du 13 septembre 1793, ses antécédents et son application', *Annales hist. Révol. fr.* 8 (1931), p. 485; P. M. Jones, ' "Agrarian Law" '.

[51] Mathiez, 'La loi du 13 septembre 1793', p. 486.

[52] *Arch. parl.*, vol. LXXIX, p. 647; Sagnac, *La législation civile*, pp. 179–82.

cannot take too much care to ensure these sums are turned into capital used to make them proprietors.'[53]

Cavaignac and Dartigoeyte pointed out to the newly appointed government officials in the Gers that the object of parcelling out the national estates was to ensure that those who had received at least one *arpent* from the partition of the commons should be able to 'complete their share' by purchasing an additional parcel of émigré land. The Committee of Public Safety, which in Ventôse launched an inquiry into the progress of land distribution, issued a circular in Floréal recalling the availability of credit notes aimed at 'making all Frenchmen participate in the advantages of republican government' so that 'no one should be a stranger in the land where he was born and each should be able to have a property'.[54] Renewed efforts were made to ascertain how many citizens had received and made use of the 500-livres vouchers. Maure reported from Avallon that the district of Joigny had been painstaking in its efforts to divide up émigré properties into 'lots and small portions' but that the auctioneers had not been prepared to accept bids from soldiers' parents with proxies from their sons to buy land in accordance with the provisions of the law of 13 September 'to the value of the service gratuity to which they shall be entitled'.[55]

On the strength of negative returns such as this, Collot-d'Herbois took up Brival's Limoges initiative in Prairial and proposed on behalf of the committee that welfare benefits to servicemen's families be paid in kind rather than cash: henceforth, pensions and allowances would be 'liquidated so that they could be exchanged for *biens nationaux* and so as to enable the defenders of the *patrie* to purchase portions of these properties through agents acting in their name. Then, everything that their families are entitled to receive from the Nation can easily be *converted* into a fertile plot of land [my italics].'[56] This important piece of legislation was subsumed into the 'territorial assistance' programme discussed below, but it clearly shows that those in power were aware of the limitations of the voucher scheme and the need to supplement it in such a way as

---

[53] Limoges, 18 Pluviôse II, Arch. dép. Haute-Vienne, L 820, Jacobin Club of Limoges.

[54] 22 Ventôse and 14 Floréal II: Mathiez, 'La loi du 13 septembre 1793', p. 483; G. Lefebvre, *Questions agraires au temps de la Terreur*, 2nd edn (Paris, 1954), pp. 57–60; P. M. Jones, ' "Agrarian Law" ', p. 115.

[55] 29 Floréal II, Aulard, *Recueil*, vol. XIII, p. 600.

[56] Decree of 13 Prairial II, *Arch. parl.*, vol. XCI, p. 208.

to secure viable holdings for the small peasantry. The same is true of the efforts undertaken in Fructidor and the following Vendémiaire to ascertain the numbers of households who had taken advantage of the facilities to acquire national properties. While such efforts no doubt reflected a 'relentless pursuit of the goals of social Jacobinism', they did not herald a shift toward a bolder form of agrarian radicalism: on the contrary, it was openly recognised that non-proprietors could only 'become owners by the same route as the rich', that is 'without upsetting or overturning the process of property transfers'.[57]

Respect for legal conveyancing practices was a basic tenet of Jacobin land reform. It meant that legal obstacles could not be swept aside or circumvented, nor were they. The local administrators dutifully drew up listings of beneficiaries of the voucher scheme, which read as a roll call of the rural poor, and P. M. Jones has given an indication of the proportion of these credit notes used in exchange, or in part exchange, for national property in various parts of France.[58] An interesting facet of this survey is that non-rural artisans and manual workers bulk large as potential buyers in a number of the medium-sized manufacturing towns, such as Elbeuf in Normandy (previously studied by Marc Bouloiseau), Sens, Alençon and Nérac. Likewise, in the arms-manufacturing town of Tulle, Roux-Fazillac reported that the factory workers were keen to claim their entitlement to a 500-livres voucher. Conversely, in the country areas of Aquitaine, where the most widespread form of land tenure was sharecropping, smallholders tended to stay away from the sales, although this may well have been in part due to the small size of the lots reserved for non-proprietors, which, according to the district of Casteljaloux, required enlargement.[59] The long-suffering class of *métayers* had few if any benefits to expect from the new social legislation, although

---

[57] District of Versailles, 26 Germinal II, P. M. Jones, ' "Agrarian Law" ', pp. 115–16.

[58] Gironde, Drôme, Nord, Lot-et-Garonne, Seine-et-Oise, Yonne, Orne, Creuse and Calvados: P. M. Jones, ' "Agrarian Law" ', tables 2–3 and map 2.

[59] Arch. mun. Tulle, 1 D 2, mun. register, ff. 126 and 153–4 (16 Pluviôse and 1 Thermidor II); M. Bouloiseau, *Le séquestre et la vente des biens des émigrés dans le district de Rouen, 1792–an X* (Paris, 1937), pp. 247–53; Mathiez, 'La loi du 13 Septembre 1793', p. 486; M. Secondat, 'L'affermage des terres en Périgord au XVIIIe siècle (bassin de la Vézère et ses affluents)', *Actes 82e Congrès national sociétés savantes, Bordeaux, 1957* (Paris, 1958); P. M. Jones, ' "Agrarian Law" ', table 3.

Roux-Fazillac, together with Dartigoeyte, was able to obtain a decree (1 Brumaire II) restricting the unfair demands that owners could lay upon their sharecrop tenants, such as rent liability in case of harvest loss. Moreover, as we shall see, sharecropping as the preferred mode of tenure was to prove a valuable asset when it came to implementing the Ventôse decrees, making land accessible to a greater number.

Provision of shelter for the homeless and building materials for home improvement was to have been a welcome spin-off from the disposal of émigré properties. In fact, much depended on the terms of the demolition programme voted by the Convention, which was quite limited in scope and a far cry from the widespread revolutionary 'vandalism' disparaged by the nineteenth century.[60] The main targets for demolition were the fortified castles and keeps which, on the model of the Bastille, were considered symbols of tyranny and feudalism, and whose materials were singularly ill suited to the refurbishment of the modest country cottage. Nonetheless, it proved a challenge that aroused the revolutionary ardour of Du Bouchet in Brie, Brival and Lanot in Limousin, Roux-Fazillac in Périgord, Chateauneuf-Randon in Auvergne, and Tallien, Paganel and Monestier de la Lozère in Gascony. Outraged by the many 'Gothic fortifications' they encountered on their travels ('You cannot take a step here without finding one', wrote Roux-Fazillac from Périgord), they invited all the villagers to seize a hammer and devote their rest-day, Sunday and later *décadi*, to taking part in this highly instructive 'republican diversion': the materials thus gathered would be distributed among the citizens 'in proportion to their needs and the labour supplied by each'.[61]

Brival was one of the first to resolve that the poor without shelter, or whose homes required urgent repair, should be entitled to their share of all the necessary building materials free of charge. It was in the interest of the community, he instructed the authorities at Brive, to enable the poor to build a home for themselves, for

---

[60] Decrees of 21 December 1792, 18 and 21 March and 6 August 1793, 18 and 28 Vendémiaire, 4 Brumaire and 13 Pluviôse II. The decree of 4 Brumaire urged the *commissaires* to avoid gratuitous damage resulting from 'ignorance' or 'cupidity'. In contrast, the churches and monasteries suffered more extensive degradation from the iconoclasts of the dechristianisation movement.

[61] Arch. dép. Dordogne, 3 L 24, dist. Bergerac, f° 167; Lot-et-Garonne L 292, missions, and 293, castle demolition; Lot, L 12, missions.

then they would think seriously about buying a plot with their savings and the credit facilities put at their disposal. The Jacobin news-sheet *Journal de la Haute-Vienne*, published by the club of Limoges, reproduced Brival's resolution in full, thus giving it widespread publicity throughout Limousin.[62] Free distribution of materials to the poor was on a par with the one-*arpent* rental scheme for commons or émigré allotments: it established a safety-net-cum-springboard that went beyond the requirements of economic survival and promised a chance of self-promotion.

In most cases, however, the materials from the castles were put up for auction in bulk lots, like the émigré properties themselves, at the expense of the poor. Lanot expressed his dismay at the 'egoism' of the rich who cornered all the benefits of the Revolution to their own advantage without sparing a thought for the provision of welfare. On the high plateau of Millevaches, he came face to face with the new 'bourgeois aristocracy' and its dealings at the sale of materials from the château de Treignac sponsored by the authorities. Here, a group of local worthies, including two members of the municipal council, had organised an auction ring and bought up all the valuable objects, including the stacks of slate roofing-tiles, in order to retail them subsequently at a profit. Lanot declared the transactions null and void and gave orders for the materials to be sold again in small lots so that 'the sans-culottes may profit from the remains of the haunts of their former tyrants'.[63] However incongruous the proud slate of the seigneur's ancestral home might appear on the roof of the craftsman's humble cottage, the fact that it had in the process been removed from the grabbing hands of the bourgeois profiteer provides a perfect illustration of the spirit of Jacobin redistribution: a clear social commitment, a rejection of the 'unacceptable face of capitalism', but compliance with the rules of the game and attention to fair play.

Demolition was partial and selective. The first to be attacked

[62] Tulle, Uzerche and Limoges, 6, 8, 13, and 19 Nivôse II, Arch. Nat., AF$_{II}$ 171, Western Bureau, pl. 1404, pp. 4, 25 and AF$_{II}$ 95, Corrèze, pl. 694, p. 26; Arch. dép. Corrèze, L 97, missions; Haute-Vienne, L 195, castle demolition, and L 818, *Journal de la Haute-Vienne*, No. XVIII, p. 149, and L 820, Jacobin Club of Limoges; C. Leymarie, 'Le Journal de la Haute-Vienne (1793)', *Le Bibliophile limousin* (July–October 1901).
[63] Ussel, 12 Nivôse and Treignac, 9 and 11 Ventôse II, Arch. Nat., AF$_{II}$ 171, Western Bureau, pl. 1405, p. 29; Arch. dép. Corrèze, L 779, Jacobin club of Treignac, ff. 27–30.

were the great medieval fortresses, such as the massive keep of Mareuil on the borders of Angoumois and Périgord, or the stronghold of Bonaguil on the southern edge of Quercy, a masterpiece of fifteenth-century military architecture, whose towers were decapitated rather than torn down. Chateauneuf-Randon, who, despite his name and aristocratic ancestry, was a keen demolisher, began the dismantlement of the walls of Saint-Flour, the 'suspect' fortified city of the Cantal, which stood as 'odious barriers raised between brothers'; he also severely took to task the fortress of Sévérac-le-Château and the inaccessible citadel of Najac in the forests of Rouergue. While most of these acts were demonstrative and more labour-intensive than they were socially profitable, Romme used the materials of the château de Monelard to furbish the new cannon foundry he established at Abzac on the confines of the Gironde, and Lakanal used those from the château de La Force, which he 'razed to the ground', to lay the foundations for the new stone bridge over the Dordogne at Bergerac.[64]

The re-use of stones and tiles to mend country cottages or equip public works gave a plausible humanitarian and utilitarian veneer to ostensible acts of vandalism. To propose, as did Roux-Fazillac in his proclamation of 27 Frimaire, the absolute levelling of structures that 'stray from the limits imposed by nature' and thereby place 'all Frenchmen on a same level'[65] was to demand the impossible. In this sense, the *guerre aux châteaux*, which more often than not confined itself to 'decapitating' or 'discrowning' feudal fortresses, reflects symbolically the real limitations of revolutionary egalitarianism.

The management of natural resources offered by émigré properties often proved more cost-effective than their alienation. Lakanal requisitioned not just the joists and floorboards from the *châteaux*, but also all the walnut trees growing on the national estates of the Dordogne to supply wood for rifle-butts in the new small arms factory at Bergerac. Roux-Fazillac did likewise at Tulle. Romme found plentiful firewood for the furnaces under his supervision in

---

[64] Châteauneuf-Randon, 26 Frimaire II, Aulard, *Recueil*, vol. IX, p. 443; Labroue, *La mission de Lakanal*, pp. 604–25; A. Jouanel, 'La démolition du château de La Force', *Bulletin de la Société historique et archéologique du Périgord* 86 (1959), p. 183.

[65] Arch. Nat., AF$_{II}$ 97, Dordogne, pl. 717, pp. 44–7, and AF$_{II}$ 171, Western Bureau, pl. 1403, p. 17; Arch. dép. Dordogne, 3 L 24, dist. Bergerac, f° 167; Labroue, *La mission de Lakanal*, pp. 602–4.

the forests where the seigneurs of old had once hunted with impunity and which now supplied the Republic with both the 'civic tree of liberty' and the fuel for the arsenals needed to prosecute the war.[66] They also requisitioned the contents of émigré grain-stores to provide supplementary rations for the foundry-workers, émigré townhouses to provide lodgings (*casernes d'ouvriers*) for the additional labour force required in the armaments industry and émigré furniture to equip the offices of the workshop managers.[67] Indeed, as time passed, the emphasis was laid less on the profitability of private sales and more on the collective exploitation of resources and short-term tenancy arrangements.

Surrender of title gave rise to a legal objection which could not simply be brushed aside. While revolutionary logic stipulated that the nobility who had fled the land and joined the enemy had openly forsaken their heritage, which could now rightfully be redistributed to the poor and needy or sold to the highest bidder, the same could not be said of their relatives who had remained behind and whose presence signified a refusal to quit, and hence a theoretical attachment to the values of the new Republic. Roux-Fazillac was too hasty in assimilating the émigrés and their kin and wanting to be rid of both: he could not but recognise that the 'rights claimed' by the wives and mothers of the Charentais émigrés were proving a serious obstacle to the liquidation of their kinsmen's estates.[68] Both traditional jurisprudence and the legitimate property rights recently reaffirmed in the Declaration of the Rights of Man ran counter to this revolutionary form of distributive justice. An account was given at the end of chapter 2 of the exemplary moderation shown to the *ci-devant* nobles by Bo, the two Monestiers and Romme. Romme even awarded welfare benefits to the 'innocent' relatives of Charente and Dordogne émigrés as an 'indemnity' to compensate them for the loss of their confiscated properties.[69] Romme's

[66] Lakanal, Pluviôse II, Arch. dép. Dordogne, 3 L 25, dist. Bergerac, f° 41; Roux-Fazillac, 3 Brumaire, 12 Pluviôse, 14 Ventôse and 12 Floréal II, Arch. dép. Corrèze, L 258 A, Tulle arms factory, ff. 261–2, 367–74, and 258 B, f° 581; Romme, Périgueux, 4 Prairial II, Arch. dép. Dordogne 1 L 233, Romme, pp. 5–8.
[67] Roux-Fazillac, 16 Pluviôse and 1 Thermidor II, Arch. mun. Tulle, 1 D 2, mun. register, ff. 126 and 153–4; Romme, 4 Prairial II, Arch. Nat., AF$_{II}$ 95, Corrèze, pl. 695, p. 58; Lakanal, 8 Messidor II, Arch. dép. Dordogne, 3 L 25, dist. Bergerac, f° 230; Galante Garrone, *Gilbert Romme*, p. 344.
[68] Angoulême, 16 September 1793, Aulard, *Recueil*, vol. VI, p. 527.
[69] Angoulême, 21 Germinal II, Arch. Nat., AF$_{II}$ 97, Dordogne, pl. 713, p. 5; Arch. dép. Charente, L 68^1, Romme, and L 1239, dist. Confolens.

'fraternal' gesture reflects a concern for human rights, a recognition that legal redress was justified and an awareness that the democratic option entailed far-reaching moral obligations.

THE VENTÔSE DECREES AND THE REJECTION OF EXPROPRIATION

It was widely felt in the spring of 1793 that no stone should be left unturned in the 'mobilisation of unknown resources' and that the state of emergency empowered the government to make 'direct and personal requisitions'.[70] The popular press, notably the *Père Duchesne*, interpreted this as including the confiscation of conspirators' properties in order to provide an endowment or life annuity for the valiant sans-culottes, and Albert Soboul has shown that this became a current theme in the Parisian sections during the summer.[71] Baudot, adept at exploiting popular feeling, suggested to the Jacobins on the eve of his mission to the Midi that the sans-culottes were entitled to 'assume ownership of everything they might lay hold of, by force', and on arrival in Montauban, true to his word, he arrested the millowners as Girondin sympathisers and urged the fullers to take possession of their workshops. Dartigoeyte asked for the immediate sequestration of property belonging to officials who had taken part in the Federalist uprising, while Roux-Fazillac wanted to seize the estates of the suspects who went into hiding. He even suggested to the Committee of Public Safety in Brumaire that the 'confiscation of all the suspects' properties' would provide 'further collateral for our *assignats*' and oblige the suspects to 'contribute their share to the prosperity of the Republic'.[72]

The principle of confiscation was therefore in the air at the time the infamous Suspect Law was voted, long before the month of

---

[70] Robert Lindet, author of the circular of 7 May 1793, Aulard, *Recueil*, vol. IV, p. 42. This section is based on research undertaken in the 1980s and published as 'Note sur la portée des décrets de ventôse dans le centre et le sud-ouest', *Annales hist. Révol. fr.* 275 (January–March 1989), pp. 16–25.

[71] *Le Père Duchesne*, No. 289; cited by A. Soboul, *Les sans-culottes parisiens en l'an II* (Paris, 1958), pp. 461–9, 710–13.

[72] Baudot, Jacobins, 21 July 1793; L. Lévy-Schneider, 'Le socialisme et le Révolution française', pp. 131–2; Ligou, 'L'épuration', p. 60; Dartigoeyte, Auch, 7 September 1793, Aulard, *Recueil*, 2nd *Supplément*, p. 89; Roux-Fazillac, 16 September 1793 and 13 Brumaire II, *ibid.*, vol. VI, p. 527 and vol. VIII, p. 211.

Ventôse II, and it was continually said to be applicable to suspects who took flight or escaped detention and were therefore assimilated to the émigrés and counter-revolutionaries, and likewise to the conscripts who evaded military service or deserted from the forces, *muscadins* branded as cowards whose property should be forfeited.[73] The Committee of Public Safety appeared to concur with radical Jacobin opinion when they wrote to Roux-Fazillac on 26 Pluviôse that the time had come to attend to the property of suspects whose

> fortunes should at least be of service to the cause of liberty: the coward who withdraws from the social contract cannot claim its benefits, nor does society owe anything to him who does nothing for it. Alone to exercise true ownership, it has distributed fortunes on the express understanding that they contribute to the greatest advantage of all its members. The man who fails to respect that sacred clause shall be dispossessed; society shall reassert its rights: it can never entertain their prescription.[74]

Fine words indeed, imbued with utilitarian innuendoes, and culminating in a frightening perspective. But to what extent was the committee referring to expropriation, or a gradual redistribution of monetary wealth? Were there not alternatives to outright spoliation?

In the provinces, as in Paris, the mood was for strong action. Bo threateningly told the Auvergnats that no enemy of liberty should escape punishment: 'he must pay his want of good citizenship with his head or his properties'.[75] And Saint-Just echoed this ominous warning in his report of 8 Ventôse, in which he proposed the sequestration of the estates of the detainees found guilty of counter-revolutionary sympathies: the course of the Revolution, he said, 'leads us to recognise this principle, that he who has shown himself to be the enemy of his country may not own property in it'. This could mean only one thing: confiscation, to the benefit of the poor. It was high time indeed for the 'suffering indigent to recover the

---

[73] Resolutions by Tallien, Ysabeau, Baudot, Paganel, Chaudron-Rousseau, Leyris, Dartigoeyte, Pinet, Monestier du Puy-de-Dôme and Roux-Fazillac, 20 September, 19 October 1793 and 10 Frimaire II, Arch. dép. Dordogne, 1 L 227, missions, 1 L 228, Roux-Fazillac, and 3 L 24, dist. Bergerac, ff. 83, 149, 162; Arch. dép. Lot, L 10, missions.

[74] Arch. Nat., AF$_{II}$ 37, Committee of Public Safety, pl. 297, p. 154; Aulard, *Recueil*, vol. XI, p. 147.

[75] Bo's speech delivered at Aurillac, 13 Pluviôse, Montauban, 17 Ventôse and Castres, 8 Floréal II, Bibl. Nat., 8° Lb^{40} 2504 .

property usurped by crime and rightfully theirs'.[76] It is understandable that Albert Mathiez, writing in 1928 at the time of 'dekulakisation' in the Soviet Union, should have interpreted the Ventôse scheme as promising 'a vast expropriation of one class to the benefit of another' and equated the means employed with the dictatorship of the proletariat.[77] Jean-Pierre Hirsch has recently set the record straight in this regard.[78]

Nevertheless, there are signs that some revolutionaries took the project very much to heart. Under the dynamic supervision of Roux-Fazillac, the districts of Thiers in the Puy-de-Dôme and Brive and Tulle in the Corrèze set to work drawing up lists of the suspects in their jurisdiction and the grounds for their detention. Robert Schnerb has highlighted the feverish haste with which the officials of Thiers filled in the tables supplied by the Committee of General Security.[79] This missionary zeal was altogether exceptional, however, and attributable to the forceful presence of Roux-Fazillac, the main instigator of the scheme, who was evidently prepared in this instance to go beyond broadly accepted democratic limits. Elsewhere, apart from pious declarations of intent, the majority of local authorities showed evident reluctance when it came to implementation. Much depended, of course, on the guidance received from the government in Paris and this turned out to be evasive or ambiguous. Thus, the table with vertical columns sent out for completion asked for details of the suspects' *income* before and after 1789. And the circular prepared by Saint-Just requested information about the real estate and movable property of the detainees with a view to ascertaining their global assets, and emphasised it was 'important to specify their revenues' in order to 'establish the pledge of the Republic'.[80] It looked very much as if,

---

[76] Saint-Just, *Discours et rapports*, p. 145; and committee circular of 20 Ventôse II, Aulard, *Recueil*, vol. XII, p. 70; C. Gaspard, 'Saint-Just et la force des choses', in A. Soboul (ed.), *Colloque Mathiez-Lefebvre* (Paris, 1978), pp. 371–80.

[77] A. Mathiez, 'La Terreur, instrument de la politique sociale des Robespierristes', in *Girondins et Montagnards*, 2nd edn (Paris, 1988), pp. 109–38.

[78] Hirsch, 'Terror and Property', p. 211.

[79] R. Schnerb, 'L'application des décrets de ventôse dans le district de Thiers (Puy-de-Dôme)', *Annales hist. Révol. fr.* 6 (1929), pp. 24–33; Schnerb, 'Le Club des Jacobins de Thiers et l'application des décrets de ventôse', *ibid.*, pp. 287–8; 'Les lois de ventôse et leur application dans le département du Puy-de-Dôme', *ibid.* 11 (1934), pp. 405–11.

[80] 16 Ventôse and 22 Germinal II, in Schnerb, 'Les lois de ventôse', pp. 408–9 and 411.

in official circles at least, a fiscal alternative was being prepared to the Ventôse legislation.

Two powerful arguments militated against confiscation. Firstly, the persons detained without charge under the law of 17 September were still presumed innocent under articles 13 and 14 of the 1793 Declaration of Rights; and secondly, as we have seen, the kith and kin of the émigrés together with the 'misled' supporters of the ousted Gironde were now the beneficiaries of an intense campaign of rehabilitation. Among mainstream Montagnards it was strongly felt that alternative means, fiscal or otherwise, had to be found to the threat of expropriation.

Vernerey, in the Creuse, suggested that former church property, wherever possible, should be put to immediate use for the benefit of the landless. He applauded the initiative of the district of Evaux which was renting out village presbyteries and their dependences on one-year leases to the 'suffering poor' so that they might cultivate the vegetable gardens and *demi-arpents* presently lying fallow. Lanot endorsed the district of Saint-Léonard's proposal to rent the properties of the suspects of Eymoutiers to tenants among the sans-culottes who had participated in the quelling of the Meymac uprising.[81] One-year rentals and similar leasing deals limited to short-term occupancy had already been discussed by the Convention the previous year in the context of the royal parks. Now the idea re-emerged as a panacea to the thorny problem of disposing of estates covered by the Ventôse decrees.

By the month of Floréal, Bo and Romme, acting severally but in concert, had elaborated the provisions which were to regulate the disposal of suspects' properties sequestrated in the departments of the Tarn, Aveyron, Lot, Cantal, Dordogne and Charente, in respect of both farmland and industry. Thus, farming tenancies would continue as before and so too would sharecrop leases, except that livestock could not be sold without the authorisation of the local authorities. The local authorities would pay the wages of farm labourers and gamekeepers employed on the estates. In the case of land producing grain, hay or pulse crops, rents would be paid in kind, whatever the form of tenancy. The districts would be charged with reopening and managing workshops and factories and re-

---

[81] Guéret, 19 Germinal II, Arch. dép. Creuse, L 232, primary schools; Meymac, 3 Nivôse II, Arch. dép. Haute-Vienne, L 109, Lanot; Arsac, 'Une émeute contre-révolutionnaire', pp. 154–6.

leasing and supplying raw materials. Leasing arrangements would give preference to one-year renewable rentals, as opposed to the traditional three-, six- or nine-year lease. The management of properties belonging to suspects was to be kept separate from the management of émigré properties. This distinction was fundamental, since a suspect who had not yet been heard and who might well be cleared could expect to obtain the restitution of all his rights and possessions. In the meantime, the government would be acting as trustee to his estate.[82]

Further provisions covered the personal needs of the suspects during their detention: each detainee would receive a daily subsistence allowance of 30 or 40 sols, to be paid out of the cumulative total of sequestrated assets in each district, while their relatives not in custody would receive allowances proportional to the revenue of the sequestrated estate of the head of the family; they would have free access to their lodgings and essential furniture; job opportunities would not be denied them; and the elderly and infirm would be entitled to poor relief like ordinary citizens, for reasons of 'justice and humanity'.

The very flexible transitional arrangements set in motion by Bo and Romme in central and south-western France ensured cost-effective management of the seized assets, while avoiding injury to the rights and interests of the suspects themselves, pending their release if found innocent or summary conviction if found guilty, and in the latter case, whatever the length of their prison sentences. Since the landed properties of the small nobility and urban bourgeoisie were already mostly subject to tenancy agreements, sharecropping was the ideal formula, in keeping with the traditional farming system. Their sharecrop tenants could continue farming as in the past, with the express proviso that leases were renewable every year. Alternatively, the holding could be entrusted to a landless labourer or artisan from the nearby town, or a soldier whose gallantry deserved recognition, in accordance with the terms of the Ventôse decrees, which did not stipulate that the beneficiaries of plot handouts should necessarily become landowners.

---

[82] Bo, Castres, 7 Floréal II and Romme, Périgueux, 20 Floréal II: Arch. dép. Aveyron, 1 L 181, Bo; 2 L 18, dist. Aubin; 8 L 16, dist. Sauveterre; Arch. dép. Charente, L 68¹, Romme, and L 1239, dist. Confolens; Arch. Nat., AF$_{II}$ 97, Dordogne, pl. 713, pp. 33–41; see also letter of Bo, 8 Floréal II, in Aulard, *Recueil*, vol. XIII, p. 108.

Furthermore, since half of the produce would be paid in rent to the state as trustee, *métayage* provided an easy means of accumulating stocks of grain in the public stores and thus allowing the distribution of poor relief in kind to the citizens without land or unable to farm. The advantages were numerous: it laid to rest the threat of a *loi agraire* by dispensing with the need to expropriate and redistribute the land; it made rural leases available to those who could put them to good use; it allowed the pooling of half the crops as food aid for the poor; and although it deprived the owner temporarily of the use and enjoyment of his property, it did not deprive him of his right of ownership. Thus Bo found it perfectly logical to declare that the enemies of liberty should expect to see their estates sequestrated, and in the next breath to invoke the republican constitution whose 'great and eternal bases are liberty, equality and *property* [my italics]'![83]

Saint-Just's plan to establish a 'public domain' made up of the proceeds of taxation and the produce of the national lands, including the émigré properties, is not without relevance in this context. The public estates included in this scheme were to be leased to 'those who have no land'. Like many of his colleagues, Saint-Just, who had grown up in the Soissonnais, a region of large farms, was in favour of splitting up not the ownership of properties, but the tenancies. His stated object was to destroy mendicity by distributing small holdings to the able poor and foodstuffs to those who could not farm. For this reason, it was essential to dispose of public revenue 'in kind'.[84] The measures taken by his colleagues Bo and Romme in a very different part of France, where land tenure was already characterised by small holdings and half shares, evidently reflect the same concerns.

Georges Lefebvre was of the opinion that, apart from a small group of isolated radicals, the Mountain in its majority refused to be swayed by the Ventôse laws which they considered a 'political manoeuvre' or even worse, yet another 'terrorist measure'.[85] The ineffectual action taken in the Puy-de-Dôme and Corrèze, and the 'total lack of implementation' recorded by Jean-Pierre Jessenne in

[83] Bo's speech of 13 Pluviôse, 17 Ventôse and 8 Floréal II, Bibl. Nat., 8° Lb⁴⁰ 2504.

[84] Saint-Just, *Frammenti sulle istituzione*, pp. 59, 108; cf. the opinions of his Aisne colleague Beffroy and Lequinio, 16 and 29 November 1792, *Arch. parl.*, vol. LIII, pp. 442, 658; Dommanget, 'Saint-Just et la question agraire'.

[85] Lefebvre, *Questions agraires*, p. 57, and review of P. Derocles (a pseudonym of A. Soboul), *Saint-Just* (Paris, 1938), in *Annales hist. Révol. fr.* 16 (1939), p. 353.

the Haute-Marne or the Pas-de-Calais, no doubt reflect these suspicions.[86] But in a sense, this is a secondary consideration. What is surely significant is that a number of deputies in the provinces, who had serious doubts as to the admissibility of terrorist legislation vis-à-vis the suspects and their property, but who were faced with the very real difficulty of implementing government policy, were seeking conditions of alienation in keeping with the spirit of the decrees yet compatible with democratic principles.

The agrarian *status quo* was thus preserved in the depths of the French countryside, and the ultimate repeal of Jacobin land reform legislation in the following years[87] reinforced the inbuilt resistance to structural change. Nonetheless, although the Ventôse decrees were suspended soon after Thermidor, the provisions enforced by Bo and Romme were not immediately repealed. They were found convenient by the Thermidorians Perrin and Goupilleau in the Aveyron and Pellissier in the Dordogne, where estates belonging to the 'aristocracy' and 'enemies of the people' continued to be rented to the 'poor in need' on one-year renewable sharecrop leases:[88] a discreet mechanism geared to maintaining the uneasy balance between the sacred debt of society and the freedom of the landlord, before the reaction let it tilt in favour of the latter. During this short period of time, the poor peasants of Rouergue and Périgord could entertain the hope of modestly cultivating a 'little acre' as their ancestors had in the past.

---

[86] Jessenne, 'Land', p. 240.

[87] The decree of 13 September 1793 on émigré property was revoked on 12 Prairial III, after the Parisian uprising of that month; the partition of the commons decreed on 10 June 1793 was suspended on 21 Prairial IV and the decree of 1 Brumaire II on sharecropping finally succumbed on 27 Brumaire V: P. M. Jones, ' "Agrarian Law" '.

[88] Avignon, 20 Fructidor and Bergerac, 26 Fructidor II, and Report by Perrin, 6 Frimaire III: Arch. dép. Aveyron, 8 L 16, dist. Sauveterre, and Arch. Nat., AF$_{II}$ 179, Western Bureau, pl. 1475, p. 28; Aulard, *Recueil*, vol. XVI, p. 655 and vol. XVIII, p. 349.

5. *Progressive taxation and the fair distribution of wealth*

> It is up to specific laws to equalise, so to speak, the inequalities, by the charges they impose on the rich and the relief they grant the poor.
>
> Montesquieu, *De l'esprit des lois*, 1748[1]

THE FISCAL CONSENSUS BETWEEN GIRONDINS AND MONTAGNARDS

One of the very first acts of the Constituent Assembly in 1789 was to enshrine in the Declaration of Rights the cardinal principle of fiscal justice, namely that, while all citizens were deemed equally liable to taxation, its burden should be spread between them 'in proportion to their faculties'.[2] In giving prominence to the canon of fair proportion rather than equal sacrifice, and thus opening wide the door to progressive taxation, the Constituents were simply echoing the conclusions of the leading tax reformers of their age. The economist Boisguilbert and the abbé de Saint-Pierre, intent on putting an end to 'arbitrary taxation' (*la taille arbitraire*), were among the first at the beginning of the century to have highlighted the merits of graduation; Montesquieu and Rousseau, having meditated on the sumptuary prescriptions of antiquity, considered it to be the only reliable foil against the impropriety of excessive wealth; and the chevalier de Jaucourt and Jean-Louis Graslin had persuasively argued in its favour in their bitter polemic with the physiocrats. 'The burden of taxation', Jaucourt had written, 'must

---

[1] Montesquieu, 'Comment les lois établissent l'égalité, dans la démocratie', *De l'esprit des lois*, book V, chapter 5, vol. I, p. 54.

[2] Article 17 of the 1789 Declaration of Rights, in *Les Déclarations*, ed. by Jaume, p. 15.

be assessed in accordance with the principles of distributive justice.'[3] Even Adam Smith, despite his opposition to direct forms of taxation such as poll taxes, had expressed the conviction that the subjects should contribute toward the support of government 'as nearly as possible in proportion to their respective abilities', that is in terms of 'the revenue they enjoy'.[4]

The combined strength of this corpus of opinion succeeded in surmounting the hesitations of many Constituents of differing persuasions. None contested the need to replace the unequal taxes of the old regime, which had been unjustly distributed and cruelly extorted, with moderate contributions equitably spread over all the land and its inhabitants and which would only be levied with the express consent of their elected representatives. The principle of 'no taxation without representation', which had traditionally motivated the convening of the Estates General up to and including 1614,[5] now became an argument for extending the franchise and achieving greater equality. It could be argued that political discourse à la Robespierre flowed directly from the perceived need for fairer taxation.

Although the *économiste* Dupont de Nemours was predictably in favour of a single land tax levied on farm production, others, such as the leaders of the enlightened nobility, the duc de La Roche-foucauld and his cousin Liancourt, thought that taxes on revenue were not only necessary, but constituted a 'common treasure to be apportioned' in such a way that none should be denied their 'right to subsistence'. By making 'slightly greater demands on the rich' and proposing to exempt small incomes below a predetermined threshold, they were purposefully using graduation and tax relief as a mild form of income redistribution.[6] Representatives of the third

---

[3] L. de Jaucourt, 'Impôt', in Diderot, *Encyclopédie*, vol. VIII, pp. 601–4; Fr. Hincker, 'Extinctions des impôts d'ancien régime', in Soboul, *Dictionnaire historique*, pp. 561–2; J.-P. Gross, 'Progressive Taxation and Social Justice in Eighteenth-Century France', *Past and Present* 140 (August 1993), pp. 79–126.

[4] Smith, *Wealth of Nations*, vol. II, pp. 826, 867–9.

[5] Clamageran, *Histoire de l'impôt*, vol. II, p. 179; Rousseau had explicitly reaffirmed this principle in 1755 in his article on political economy published in Diderot's *Encyclopédie*: see Rousseau, *Œuvres complètes*, vol. II, p. 290.

[6] 18 August 1790, *Arch. parl.*, vol. XVIII, *Convention*, pp. 143–6; C. Bloch, *L'assistance et l'Etat en France à la veille de la Révolution (généralités de Paris, Rouen, Alençon, Orléans, Soissons, Amiens), 1764–1790* (Paris, 1908), pp. 443–8; M. Marion, *Histoire financière de la France depuis 1715*, 6 vols. (Paris, 1914–31), vol. II, p. 196; Lemay, *Dictionnaire des Constituants*, vol. II, pp. 787, 922.

estate such as Théodore Vernier and Dominique Ramel-Nogaret, whose fiscal expertise was later to be of service to Gironde and Montagne respectively, were also convinced that different levels of wealth should command varying rates of tax and pointed to three possible thresholds in the income scale: of need (3,000 livres), comfort (6,000 livres) and affluence (12,000 livres).[7]

The new tax legislation, however, barely reflected the progressive formula: the tax on movables, based on rental values, presupposed that the cost of housing kept pace with increases in income, while the trade licence law was vaguely sumptuary in inspiration in that it granted concessions to bakers and penalised wine-merchants, inn-keepers and playing-card manufacturers. But in the absence of tax returns and reliable statistical data, these taxes, like the land tax in the absence of a land register, were a far cry from the goal of fair assessment and distribution.[8] Moreover, their introduction was painfully slow[9] and as the dismantlement of the fiscal apparatus of the *ancien régime* lingered on, they were met with a stubborn refusal to pay.

Among the supporters of Brissot at the Legislative Assembly, a consensus emerged as to the desirability of removing extreme inequalities of fortune, but without infringing or eroding property rights, and without limitations being imposed on individual freedom of enterprise: taxation within reason, but no confiscation. The Swiss-born finance minister Etienne Clavière wrote a series of articles for *La Chronique du mois* between November 1791 and March 1792 which tended to show that progressive taxation was desirable on inherited wealth, permissible on earned income, though questionable on working capital.[10] Condorcet especially, in his writings on taxation,[11] strove to strike a balance between social

---

[7] Vernier, 30 March 1790, *Arch. parl.*, vol. XII, pp. 459–68 and Ramel-Nogaret, 23 September 1790, vol. XX, pp. 70–1.

[8] The *contribution foncière* became law on 23 November 1790, the *contribution mobilière* on 13 January 1791 and the *patente* on 2 March 1791: *Arch. parl.*, vol. XX, pp. 698–712; vol. XXII, pp. 169–82; Ch. Gomel, *Histoire financière de l'Assemblée constituante*, 2 vols. (Paris, 1896–7), vol. II, p. 336.

[9] Barely a quarter of the tax rolls for the fiscal year 1792 were established by June 1793: R. Schnerb, *Les contributions directes à l'époque de la Révolution dans le département du Puy-de-Dôme* (Paris, 1933), pp. 105–85.

[10] E. Clavière, L. Mercier, A. Guy-Kersaint, J.-P. Brissot *et al.*, *La Chronique du mois, ou les Cahiers patriotiques* (Paris, November 1791–March 1792), Nos. 1–5; M. Dorigny, 'Conclusions', unpublished research summary, Sorbonne (1992), pp. 44–54.

[11] Condorcet, 'Essai sur la constitution et les fonctions des assemblées provinciales'

justice (tax allowances to cover basic subsistence) and entrepreneurial freedom (tax incentives to trade and industry). While recognising the need to curb large fortunes amassed at the expense of the poor, he wanted to protect the profit motive which in itself was not incompatible with 'equality and reason': that, for Condorcet, was the salient feature of 'republican liberty'.

Of course, Condorcet held strong egalitarian views, which sets him slightly apart from the remainder of the Gironde[12] and helps highlight the equivocal nature of the Girondin position on taxation. While Roland, shortly before his resignation as minister of the interior in January 1793, proposed to convert the *contribution mobilière* into a fully fledged *contribution progressive*, Vergniaud expressed his fear that a permanent progressive tax would result in the inexorable erosion of capital, and Brissot staunchly defended the morality of acquired wealth: why, he asked in his news-sheet *Le Patriote français*, should the man who through enterprise and thrift built up his estate be penalised and forced to relinquish it to the man who squandered his money at the gaming table or in the company of women of easy virtue?[13]

Here, the course of pure liberal individualism is clearly charted and appears to discard humanitarian concerns. But such righteous indignation may well be deceptive. On 18 March 1793, the day the Convention imposed the death penalty on anyone preaching the 'agrarian law' or attempting to undermine private property, Ramel-Nogaret proposed a complementary motion to serve, as it were, as the reverse side of the same coin, which read: 'In order to attain a more accurate proportion in the distribution of the burden each citizen has to bear according to his abilities, there shall be established a graduated and progressive tax on luxury and both landed and transferable wealth.'[14] Apart from Vergniaud, the moderates all rallied to this formula which appeared to promise the only safe and effective means of building a just democracy. Vernier lent

(1788), 'Mémoires sur la fixation de l'impôt' (1790) and 'Sur l'impôt progressif' (1793) in *Œuvres*, ed. by A. Condorcet O'Connor and M. F. Arago, 12 vols. (Paris, 1847–9), vol. VIII, pp. 355–61; vol. IX, pp. 471–83; vol. XII, pp. 625–36.

[12] Baker, *Condorcet*, pp. 308–14, 328, 491; Badinter and Badinter, *Condorcet*, pp. 541–61.

[13] Roland, 9 January 1793, Vergniaud, 4 May 1793, and Brissot, 12 August 1793: *Arch. parl.*, vol. LVI, pp. 692–3; Ch. Gomel, *Histoire financière de la Législative et de la Convention*, 2 vols. (Paris, 1902–5), vol. I, p. 450; Marion, *Histoire financière*, vol. III, p. 43.

[14] *Arch. parl.*, vol. LX, p. 292.

Ramel his eloquent support in stating that the object of taxation must be 'imperceptibly to divide and attenuate all great fortunes, to destroy inequalities, those monstrous distortions of the body politic, which devour all that surrounds them; above all, it must avoid throwing onto the poor the tribute that must principally weigh upon the rich'.[15] Vernier, on behalf of the finance committee, set about devising a graduated scale in keeping with this goal, but which would avoid 'stifling the growth of industry, activity, emulation, ambition': ambition, after all, was a passion which could serve the state while contributing to the welfare of the individual.

Such utilitarian concerns, however, did not fully meet the requirements of the radical side of the house. Robespierre's view of honourable poverty, put forward a month later, was based on the premise that the working man was entitled to the ownership of the 'fruits of his labour', and this limited ownership of material possessions entailed the notion of 'legitimate' property, guaranteed by law, designed for the poor rather than the rich, the right of further appropriation being consequently restricted 'by the obligation to respect the rights of others'. This rationale led Robespierre to endorse the principle of progressive taxation as the only democratic way to contain the excesses of possessive individualism to the benefit of the poor and thereby eradicate the intolerable extremes of opulence and deprivation. 'Eternal justice' dictated that it should be included in the amended Declaration of Rights, in these terms: 'Those citizens whose incomes do not exceed what is necessary to their subsistence shall be exempted from contributing to public expenditure; the others shall support it progressively, according to the extent of their fortune.'[16]

It is worth noting that Robespierre and his supporters concentrated their attack on the accumulation and concentration of capital, but did not propose any fixed ceiling to wealth. Progressive taxation was, in their view, to be a 'gentle and effective instrument' for correcting extreme disparities in fortune and allowing those who enjoyed a 'surplus' to pay their debt to those 'who lacked the necessities'. It was to be a fiscal revolution, but a 'mild and peaceful revolution' which would neither 'alarm property nor offend

[15] Vernier, 21 and 26 March 1793, *ibid.*, pp. 394, 398, 581.
[16] Robespierre, 24 April 1793, *Œuvres complètes*, vol. IX, p. 459–61. On Robespierre's attitude to tax exemption, see my article, 'Robespierre et l'impôt progressif', p. 285.

justice'. After all, society's obligation to the poor consisted in ensuring their wherewithal, not in demolishing wealth or striving to achieve absolute equality, which would be self-defeating. The sans-culottes, for whom they spoke, did not aspire to 'equality of fortune' but to 'equality of rights and of happiness'.[17] The rich, for their part, Danton pointed out, should realise that by shedding their surplus wealth they were warding off the threat of equal or common ownership. To pay tax was in their enlightened self-interest: 'The greater the sacrifice on their moneyed interest, the greater the safeguards on the title to their property'; and a short-term sacrifice at that, for capitalists were like sponges which could be squeezed to yield interest and then sprang back into shape.[18]

The broad consensus that therefore emerged in favour of grad-uated taxation encompassed differences of emphasis and degree, but not of kind. All those who spoke up shared the opinion that the tax reforms of the early revolutionary years had been shamefully inadequate. Moreover, it was widely felt among the provincial lawyers and administrators who made up the new governing class that the financiers and *gens d'affaires* of the *ancien régime*, the 'capitalists' whom Danton proposed to squeeze, had escaped far too lightly.[19] Not only were the very rich undertaxed, but a war subsidy was urgently needed to support the levy of troops and ensure their vital supplies. And finally, in the prevailing climate of uncertainty and fears of a complete breakdown of law and order, bold steps were needed to defuse the risk of further social unrest. It was time, wrote Robert Lindet, to link private fortunes inseparably to the public fortune, taxation having now become the preferred option, at all events the only safe and reliable way both to reduce inequality and to 'consolidate freedom and guarantee property'.[20]

[17] See Robespierre's speeches of 5 and 21 April 1791, his *Défenseur de la Constitu-tion*, No. 4 of 7 June 1792, and the 'Plan d'éducation nationale de Michel Lepeletier', 13 and 29 July 1793, in *Œuvres*, vol. IV, p. xvi; vol. VII, pp. 165, 181; and vol. X, pp. 10–42.
[18] Danton, 27 April and 8 May 1793, *Œuvres*, p. 195; F. A. Aulard, ed., *La Société des Jacobins: recueil de documents pour l'histoire du club des Jacobins de Paris*, 6 vols. (Paris, 1889–97), vol. V, p. 180; *Arch. parl.*, vol. LXIII, p. 438; L. Madelin, *Danton* (Paris, 1914), p. 132.
[19] J. F. Bosher, *French Finances, 1770–1795: From Business to Bureaucracy* (Cam-bridge, 1970), p. 253.
[20] Instruction of 7 May 1793, Aulard, *Recueil*, vol. IV, p. 41 and first *Supplément*, p. 196.

Table 6. *Tax on surplus income raised by Bo and Chabot, Castres, 26 March 1793*

Basic allowances: head of family: 600 livres; dependant: 250 livres; surplus taxed as follows:

Increments of 400 livres	Rate per livre		Tax rate per increment		Taxable income	Tax payable		Income after tax	
	s.	d.	l.	s.	l.	l.	s.	l.	s.
1st increm.									
100	4		20		100	20		80	
200	4		40		200	40		160	
400	4		80		400	80		320	
2nd increm.									
100	4	3	21	5	500	101	5	398	15
200	4	3	42	10	600	122	10	477	10
400	4	3	85.		800	165		635	
3rd increm.									
100	4	6	22	10	900	187	10	712	10
4th increm.									
100	4	9	23	15	1,300	278	15	1,021	5
5th increm.									
100	5		25		1,700	375		1,325	
25th increm.									
200	10		100		10,000	3,375		6,625	
50th increm.									
200	16	3	162	10	20,000	10,000		10,000	

Source: Arch. dép. Tarn, L 135, missions, p. 1.

PROGRESSIVE TAXATION IN THE MAKING

While the Jacobin Club in Paris launched into a passionate debate on the desirability of levelling private fortunes,[21] fiscal field trials were already under way in the French provinces. Bo and Chabot were the first to raise graduated taxes on 'surplus income' from the citizens of Castres and Rodez in late March and early April 1793 (table 6). Montpellier in the Hérault, Cambon's department, followed suit a few days later with a forced loan of 5 million livres to equip the recruits and give financial relief to their families. This example was officially recommended by Cambon to all the other departments and everywhere in France similar measures were taken or contemplated in the ensuing months. Paris levied 12

---

[21] The discussion of the war levy and forced loan flared up sporadically over two months (April–May 1793): Aulard, *Jacobins*, vol. V, pp. 149–50, 180, 189–90, 201.

Table 7. *Loan of twelve million livres levied on the rich of Paris,*
1–3 May 1793

Basic allowances: head of family: 1,500 livres; spouse: 1,000 livres; each child: 1,000 livres

Income brackets (livres)	Tax (livres)	Taxable income (livres)	Income after tax (livres)
1,000– 2,000	30	1,000	970
2,000– 3,000	50	2,500	2,450
3,000– 4,000	100	3,500	3,400
4,000– 5,000	300	4,800	4,500
5,000–10,000	1,000	8,000	7,000
10,000–15,000	2,250	10,000	7,750
15,000–20,000	5,000	15,000	10,000
20,000–30,000	10,000	25,000	15,000
30,000–40,000	16,000	36,000	20,000
40,000–50,000	20,000	48,000	28,000
above 50,000	all the surplus	50,000	30,000
		60,000	30,000
		etc.	

Sources: Ch. Gomel, *Histoire financière de la Législative et de la Convention*, 2 vols. (Paris, 1902–5), vol. I, pp. 467–8; M. Marion, *Histoire financière de la France depuis 1715*, 6 vols. (Paris, 1914–31), vol. III, p. 61.

million livres to send a body of 12,000 men to fight in the Vendée and Deux-Sèvres, the two rebel departments (table 7). Soon the Haute-Garonne was raising 6,664,000 livres, the Rhône 6 million, the Seine-et-Oise 3,500,000, the district of Melun in the Seine-et-Marne 2,886,000, the district of Montauban 1,200,000 and the Dordogne 2 million. The Meurthe, Aube, Basses-Alpes and Côtes-du-Nord raised similar amounts, with varying degrees of commitment to the progressive formula. Others, more cautious, confined themselves to paying lip-service to the decrees: Charente, Corrèze, Lot-et-Garonne.[22]

Ramel-Nogaret was now charged by the finance committee with preparing the fine details of the 'progressive contribution' and 'war subsidy', his task being to levy a tax on all 'income above what is absolutely necessary'.[23] The final outcome was to be the Forced

---

[22] L. Lévy-Schneider, *Le conventionnel Jeanbon Saint-André*, vol. I, p. 272; Aulard, *Recueil*, vol. XI, p. 662; Marion, *Histoire financière*, vol. III, p. 60; A. Troux, *La vie politique dans le département de la Meurthe*, 3 vols. (Nancy, 1936), vol. II, p. 171.

[23] 16 and 20 May 1793, *Arch. parl.*, vol. LXV, p. 117.

Table 8. *Progressive scheme of the forced loan decreed 3 September 1793*

Basic allowances: single man: 1,000 livres; wife and each child: 1,000 livres; widower with children: 1,500 livres

Increment (livres)	Rate (livres)	Taxable income (livres)	Tax payable (livres)	Income after tax (livres)
1st 1,000	100	1,000	100	900
2nd 1,000	200	2,000	300	1,700
3rd 1,000	300	3,000	600	2,400
4th 1,000	400	4,000	1,000	3,000
5th 1,000	500	5,000	1,500	3,500
6th 1,000	600	6,000	2,100	3,900
7th 1,000	700	7,000	2,800	4,200
8th 1,000	800	8,000	3,600	4,400
9th 1,000	900	9,000	4,500	4,500 ceiling
10th 1,000	1,000	10,000	5,500	4,500
12th 1,000	1,000	11,000	7,500	4,500
15th 1,000	1,000	15,000	10,500	4,500

Source: *Arch. parl.*, vol. LXXIII, pp. 351–4.

Loan of 3 September 1793, whose rates were very rigorous indeed, in keeping with the prevailing radical Jacobin mood (table 8), the higher income brackets (9,000 livres and above) being relieved of all their surplus in tax and left with a maximum income after tax of 4,500 livres. Thuriot, Chabot, Saint-André and Cambacérès had all voiced their preference for sparing 'medium fortunes' of between 3,000 and 5,000 livres per annum and making 10,000 livres the threshold of wealth, thus ensuring the tax fell only upon the 'truly rich'.[24] Those whose revenues exceeded this magic threshold were in for a hard time, or so it seemed. For in effect such drastic levelling was purely academic, the Forced Loan acting as a lever to make the rich invest in the Voluntary Loan, Cambon's pet scheme aimed at alleviating the public debt and taking as many *assignats* as possible out of circulation, and which, far from penalising the wealthy, offered the powerful incentive of actually yielding interest to the investors.[25]

[24] 22 June 1793, *Arch. parl.*, vol. LXVII, pp. 76–8.
[25] J. Jaurès, *Histoire socialiste de la Révolution française*, ed. by E. Labrousse and A. Soboul, 7 vols. (Paris, 1969–86), vol. VII, pp. 250–3; F. Bornarel, *Cambon et la Révolution française* (Paris, 1905), pp. 307–9; J.-P. Gross, 'L'emprunt forcé du 10

As Ramel pointed out, it was in any case necessary to differentiate between an emergency war loan imposed only once and a
permanent progressive income tax in peacetime which would aim at
equalising fortunes gently ('par des voies douces'). Robespierre, as
we have seen, concurred with this gradual approach: the progressive *taxe des enfants* in Michel Lepeletier's educational plan,
which Robespierre presented in person to the Convention in July,
was very mild indeed, with a single proportional rate applicable as
from 10,000 livres and remaining at a steady 10 per cent of revenue
above that level. Certainly, none among the Montagnards contra-
dicted Vernier when he declared that if the Forced Loan were to
oblige a citizen to raise cash by selling or mortgaging his estates, it
would be tantamount to a claim being laid to his property. Indeed,
Mallarmé felt it necessary to specify on behalf of the finance
committee that the Forced Loan would only apply to income from
land and industry, that is to *revenue*, but 'neither to properties nor
capital'.[26]

With these fundamental fears allayed and with the distinction
made clear between emergency and permanent taxation, the representatives in the field set about putting the new fiscal policy to the
test. Bordas and Borie thought it desirable to tax the 'bad citizens'
of Limoges 'in proportion to their fortunes', while Baudot and
Chaudron-Rousseau confined their 'revolutionary subsidy' in Montauban to those among the taxpayers already designated in the
existing tax rolls as *haut-taxés*. Roux-Fazillac, having raised a tax
on the suspects of Périgueux in 'combined proportion to their
riches and their incivism', which failed to obtain a sufficient yield,
then extended the tax also to the 'wealthy *patriots* in proportion to
their fortune'.[27]

As for the modalities, the graduation scheme generally adopted
followed an incremental scale, with every taxpayer paying the same
tax on the first slice of taxable income and the rates increasing

brumaire an II et la politique sociale des Robespierristes', in Soboul, *Actes du
Colloque Saint-Just*, pp. 74–5, 81.
26 Vernier, 20 May and Mallarmé, 22 June 1793: *Arch. parl.*, vol. LXV, p. 127 and
vol. LXVII, p. 77.
27 Limoges, 25 March 1793; Montauban, 2 October 1793; Périgueux, 10–13 Frimaire
II: P. Bordas and J. Borie, *Rapport sur le recrutement de 300,000 hommes* (Paris,
1793), Bibl. Nat., 8° Le[39] 8; Arch. dép. Haute-Vienne, L 181, missions; Tarn-et-
Garonne, L 75, dist. Montauban; Dordogne, 1 L 228, Roux-Fazillac, and 3 L 24,
dist. Bergerac, ff. 145, 149, 162; Arch. Nat., AF$_{II}$ 96, Dordogne, pl. 707, pp. 24,
28.

thereafter incrementally with each successive slice.[28] Bo and Chabot, the progressive pioneers in the Tarn and Aveyron, had granted allowances of 600 livres for the head of the family and 250 livres for each dependant, as compared to the 1,000 livres per person finally allowed by the Forced Loan. Their progressive tax only applied to 'surplus' income (*le superflu*), the first 400 livres of which were subject to a rate of 20 per cent, the rates gradually rising thereafter to a 50 per cent ceiling at the threshold of 10,000 livres. Thus, more realistically than in the case of the Forced Loan, a single man with a taxable income of 10,000 livres would pay 3,375, or roughly a third, in tax (table 6).

Saint-Just, on behalf of the Committee of Public Safety, applied the progressive principle in kind to a requisition order for grain supplies to the army: smallholders were made to contribute proportionately less per acre than holders of medium-sized holdings, who in turn were taxed less heavily than the rich farmers, with a ceiling fixed at a quarter of the yield (table 9).

During his mission with Le Bas in Alsace, Saint-Just was to raise a forced loan from the rich citizens of Strasburg, which increased on a sliding scale from 4,000 livres to a hefty 300,000 livres, the most numerous contributors being middling shop-keepers and merchants, with bankers and captains of industry paying the highest percentage.[29] In Périgord, Lakanal raised a progressive tax on the rich of Bergerac over and above their ordinary land and income contributions. It started at a fifth of the normal contribution, then went up to a quarter, then a third, and from 600 livres to exactly half. Lakanal's aim was to catch a percentage at least of unearned income and speculative invest-ments: revenue from property and capital, dividends, bank de-posits, pensions and annuities. Like Bo and Chabot, he differentiated between 'net income', that is the balance of income from land, trade or industry after deduction of all essential expenses, and 'surplus income', being the balance of net income left once basic allowances were deducted for dependants, but excluding domestic servants. The product of this progressive surtax was to be used in part as rent and tax relief for the low-income groups particularly hard-hit by inflation (table 10).

---

[28] The incremental formula was put forward by Vernier on 21 and 26 March 1793, *Arch. parl.*, vol. LX, pp. 398, 581.
[29] Gross, 'L'emprunt forcé', pp. 142–4.

Table 9. *Requisition of grain for the army proposed by Saint-Just,*
9 August 1793

Cultivated area (*arpents*)	Levy (quintals)	Assumed total yield, based on 2 quintals per *arpent* (quintals)	Crop balance (quintals)
1st bracket			
5	1	10	9
10	2	20	18
20	4	40	36
2nd bracket			
25	6	50	44
30	8	60	52
35	10	70	60
40	12	80	68
45	14	90	76
50	16	100	84
3rd bracket			
55	20	110	90
60	24	120	96
65	28	130	102
70	32	140	108
75	36	150	114
80	40 ceiling	160	120

Source: L.-A. de Saint-Just, *Rapport sur l'approvisionnement des armées, 9 août 1793* (Paris, 1793), Bibl. Nat. 8° Le[38] 393, pp. 6–7.

Vernerey in the Creuse, concerned about the rising cost of bread during the hungry gap of the winter of 1793–4, ordered the gathering of a revolutionary surtax of 600,000 livres, using two separate progressive scales, one for married taxpayers starting at 25 per cent of their standard tax liability, the other for bachelors over twenty-five years of age not serving in the forces, starting at 33 1/3 per cent (table 11).

The rates applied to the higher incomes were quite severe, since the effect was to triple the standard tax liability for a married man already owing 4,000 livres and for a single man owing 2,000 livres. At the bottom end of the scale, a 50-livre allowance ensured that the citizens most vulnerable to the high cost of subsistence would escape the tax, the aim of which was precisely to procure a ready means of subsidising the price of bread.

The progressive formula was used in inventive ways, some

Table 10. *Progressive surtax raised on the rich of Bergerac by Lakanal, 21 October 1793*

Standard tax liability (livres)	Rate (per cent)	Surtax (l. s. d.)
100	20	20
200	25	50
300	25	75
400	33⅓	133. 6. 8.
500	33⅓	166. 13. 4.
600	50	300
700	50	350
800	50	400
900	50	450
1,000	50	500
etc.		

Sources: Arch. Nat., AF$_{II}$ 96 (Dordogne), pl. 707, pp. 1–2; Arch. dép. Dordogne, 3 L 24 (dist. Bergerac), ff. 91–5; H. Labroue, *La mission du conventionnel Lakanal dans la Dordogne en l'an II (octobre 1793–août 1794)* (Paris, 1912), p. 309.

Table 11. *Progressive surtax raised on the rich of the Creuse by Vernerey, 24 Pluviôse II*

Standard tax liability (livres)	Rate (per cent)	Surtax (l. s. d.)
Heads of families		
50	25	12. 10.
100	33⅓	33. 6. 8.
200	40	80
300	50	150
500	60	300
1,000	80	800
2,000	100	2,000
4,000	200	8,000
5,000	200	10,000
etc.		
Single men over 25		
50	33⅓	16. 13. 4.
100	40	40
200	50	100
300	60	180
500	80	400
1,000	100	1,000
2,000	200	4,000
4,000	200	8,000
etc.		

Sources: Arch. Nat., AF$_{II}$ 95, Creuse, pl. 703, pp. 32–3; Arch. dép. Creuse, L 105*, missions.

unexpected. A graduated toll, in keeping with the ideas of Adam Smith, was charged on the bridge over the Dordogne at Bergerac, with pedestrians crossing free of charge, ox-carts paying the lowest rates, mounted horses and post-chaises a moderate rate, luxury carriages the highest, while heavy goods vehicles were obliged to cross at night.[30] The small Jacobin Club at Caussade, near Montauban, applied a sliding scale for members' subscriptions – 3, 6, 12, 18, 24 and 30 livres – in order to attract sans-culottes from the lower income brackets (100 to 1,000 livres).[31] Iron fire-backs were requisitioned by Romme for melting down into cannon, but exemptions were granted for those measuring one inch in thickness or under, which represented the 'basic allowance' for all households.[32] It could likewise be argued that Romme's view of food rationing, which required the whole grain of the rich man to be mixed with the poor man's siftings so that a standard loaf could be issued to all, was inspired by the same progressive philosophy, whereby each citizen was expected to contribute a share 'in proportion to his faculties'.

The unprecedented taxes raised all over France were only justified by the 'exceptional circumstances', as Vergniaud had grudgingly allowed in the debate of May 1793, in order to provide urgently needed funds in a time of war and were indeed often labelled *taxes de guerre*. The government endeavoured not very successfully to centralise the tax-recovery effort and curb what it feared might become a slide toward fiscal anarchy. But in fact the taxes levied by the *représentants* served as a test laboratory. Although none are very moderate and their degree of severity varies, the mainstream revolutionary taxes of 1793–4 follow a pattern already charted by the finance committee of the Convention.[33] Thus Vernerey's surtax, more stringent than Lakanal's, progresses rapidly to double the ordinary contribution. Bo and Chabot's removes a third of taxable income when it reaches the threshold of 'wealth' (10,000 livres) and half when it reaches the 'supertax' level of 20,000 livres. All else being equal, these are orders of magnitude (10, 20, 33, 50 per cent) comparable to scales

[30] Smith, *Wealth of Nations*, vol. II (Section v. i. c.), p. 726; Labroue, *La mission de Lakanal*, p. 476.
[31] E. Campagnac, 'L'impôt sur le revenu dans les statuts d'une société populaire en 1793', *Annales révol.* 3 (1910), pp. 242–4.
[32] Excideuil, 23 Thermidor II, Arch. Nat., AF$_{II}$ 97, Dordogne, pl. 715, p. 47; Arch. dép. Dordogne, 1 L 233, Romme, p. 22.
[33] Ramel-Nogaret, 20 May 1793, *Arch. parl.*, vol. LXV, p. 117.

of taxation not considered inappropriate in modern times.[34] They are clearly indicative of the kind of tax policy which might have been pursued after the war had the Jacobin experiment been allowed to continue.

When they arrived in Castres in March 1793, Bo and Chabot declared they were about to 'terminate the Revolution'. They and their colleagues promised the poor that they were at long last to inherit the earth and receive as their due the surplus wealth of the rich. Affluence, explained Paganel, was to be 'popularised' and the 'errors of fortune' corrected. The rich of Melun, amplified Du Bouchet with a play on words, should be administered a 'light correction': 'I have thought it fitting to remove from them part of that enormous surplus which had corrupted them in order to redirect it onto the poor sans-culottes and especially the indigent families of the brave defenders of the homeland.'[35] This was a far cry, however, from distributive justice of a fundamental kind. As Jeanbon Saint-André had written in 1792, the challenge lay not in building a society without rich or poor, but one in which there would 'no longer be rich men who are excessively rich, nor poor men who are excessively poor'.[36]

FAIR ASSESSMENT, FISCAL OBLIGATION AND EXTORTION

Those principally targeted as contributors, under the emotive label of the 'rich', comprised in fact most of the money-earning categories of citizens one would expect to find in an emerging income-tax scheme, from the upper to the lower middle and artisanal classes. At the top of the list came the *gens d'affaires*, the bankers, financiers, merchants and shipowners whose ventures and specula-

---

[34] The progressive rates laid down in the French tax laws of 1914–20 are given in L. Bocquet, *L'impôt sur le revenu cédulaire et général* (Paris, 1921), pp. 560–2; the income tax rates in France for the fiscal year 1991 comprised thirteen classes from nil, through 9.6 per cent, 24 per cent (income bracket 45,660–57,320 francs), 33.6 per cent (69,370–80,030 francs), to a top rate of 56.8 per cent (annual incomes of 246,770 francs and above): C. Bobett and J. Kesti, *European Tax Handbook, 1991* (Amsterdam, 1991), pp. 95–6.

[35] Bo and Chabot, 26 March 1793; Paganel, 3 October 1793; Du Bouchet, 15 October 1793: Arch. dép. Tarn, L 135, missions, Albi and Castres; Lot-et-Garonne, L 151 and 152, Paganel, Agen; Aulard, *Recueil*, vol. VII, pp. 422–5.

[36] Jeanbon Saint-André, *Réflexions sur l'éducation nationale* (December 1792), Bibl. Nat., 8° Le[38] 2259.

tive deals were readily denounced as uncivic ('l'égoïsme boursier', 'le vil esprit mercantile'). These were closely followed by the captains of industry, foundry- and millowners, manufacturers and businessmen, often former noblemen who had succumbed to the entrepreneurial craze under the old régime[37] and whose loyalties were now subject to scrutiny. Next came the members of the landowning bourgeoisie, whose private wealth was the product of accumulated seigneurial rents and profits from the sale of agricultural commodities, and generally belonged to the 10,000- to 20,000-livres income bracket.[38] In their wake were the long-established lawyers and feudists, the 'gens à châteaux et à parchemins', who had traditionally made a good living from the seigneurial system and its attendant legal chicaneries, and whose gold-hoarding instincts belonged to popular legend. But by far the most numerous on the tax rolls were the small merchants, wholesalers, retailers, shopkeepers and craftsmen who arguably made up the backbone of the sans-culotte class.[39]

What is particularly striking in the revolutionary tax assessments, apart from the few substantial sums demanded from the exceptionally wealthy, is the large number of small contributions expected from the less well-to-do. Thus, while the maximum sum levied by Lakanal on an individual in Bergerac was 10,000 livres, corresponding to a combined land and movables tax liability of 20,000 livres, the minimum was 50 livres, corresponding to a standard liability of 200 livres. A few merchants and shopkeepers were assessed at 4,000, 1,200 and 800 livres, but the majority were asked to pay sums of 100 or 200 livres. Monestier de la Lozère, who fixed the threshold of wealth at 10,000 livres and taxed an Aquitaine *rentier* 2,000 livres and a cattle-merchant 1,200, was usually content with levies well below 500 livres. Bo and Chabot considered a burgher from Castres or Rodez with an income of 1,500 already rich enough to be included in their tax on 'surplus wealth', while

---

[37] R. Sedillot, *La maison de Wendel de 1704 à nos jours* (Paris, 1958); G. Chaussinand-Nogaret, *La noblesse en France au XVIIIe siècle: de la Féodalité aux Lumières* (Paris, 1976), p. 127.

[38] J. Sentou, *Fortunes et groupes sociaux à Toulouse sous la Révolution (1789–1799): essai d'histoire statistique* (Toulouse, 1969); reviewed by J. Godechot, *Annales hist. Révol. fr.* 42 (1970), p. 697.

[39] While Baudot and Lacoste assessed only those traders of Montauban who were 'highly taxed' on the existing tax rolls, Saint-Just and Le Bas appear to have made no such distinction in Strasburg.

Vernerey's appeal to the 'well-to-do citizens' of the Creuse turned out to be addressed to all those who normally paid taxes of 50 livres or more.[40]

Although ostensibly aimed at penalising the very rich, the graduated levies of the Year II were in effect attempting to extract fair shares from all taxpayers in proportion to their means. In addition to the myth of a wealth tax, the myth of class warfare pales in front of the egalitarian spirit of the policy actually pursued: nobles, bourgeois and sans-culottes were all swept up into the fiscal net. Moreover, little distinction was made in practice between the 'suspect rich' and the 'civic rich' (Roux-Fazillac), or between the 'good citizens' and the 'bad' (Lakanal). All social and professional groups found themselves subject to assessment.

Whether such assessment was consistently made without discrimination is of course another matter. While abuse continued to be heaped upon the 'bourgeois aristocracy', those who 'live like nobles' or 'aspire to their status', praise was showered on civic factory-owners whose contribution to the public cause took the form of keeping their workshops turning over and their workforce busy: 'You know', Brival wrote to the committee from Limoges, 'how essential it is to protect the trades and commerce, in order that the Republic may prosper: without them, everything languishes'; and Monestier cited the example of two tobacco manufacturers from Tonneins whose entrepreneurial flair kept the local economy alive. The names of these patriotic employers are to be found on the revolutionary tax rolls side by side with those of taxpayers less noted for their public-spiritedness, such as a building contractor from Bergerac who took advantage of the demolition of the *châteaux-forts* to buy up all the reusable building materials, or a timber merchant from Lauzun who preferred to set fire to his wood rather than sell it at the maximum price.[41] It is apparent that Jacobin fiscal policy tended to mete out distributive justice without

---

[40] Bergerac, 18 Messidor II, Arch. dép. Dordogne, 3 L 56, revolutionary taxes; Dax, 5 Prairial II, Arch. dép. Lot-et-Garonne, L 530, festivals; Castres 26 and 29 March 1793, Arch. dép. Tarn, L 135, missions, pp. 1, 4; Guéret, 24 Pluviôse II, Arch. dép. Creuse, L 105*, missions.

[41] Limoges, 13 Ventôse II, Arch. Nat., AF$_{II}$ 176, Western Bureau, pl. 1445, p. 27; Aulard, *Recueil*, vol. XI, p. 518; Mont-de-Marsan, 12 Floréal II, Arch. Nat., AF$_{II}$ 194, Midi Bureau, pl. 1601, p. 25; Labroue, *La mission de Lakanal*, pp. 311, 495.

preference and its levelling effect placed all taxpayers on the same footing. This was one step toward 'fair' assessment.

Another was the presumed legality of the revolutionary taxes. Although the co-ordinated experimentation conducted by the people's representatives in the provinces between Brumaire and Thermidor II was tolerated, if not expressly endorsed, by the Assembly in Paris, and hence could be said to comply with the spirit, if not the letter, of the ancient maxim 'no taxation without representation', accusations of 'arbitrary' taxation and abuse were rife and modern financial observers such as Marcel Marion have suggested that the Terror was a period of 'fiscal anarchy'.[42] Of course, Cambon, as 'comptroller general' of the Republic's finances, felt it his duty to curb the wayward trends of the more impulsive deputies, and several decrees were passed, in Frimaire and Pluviôse, centralising the public revenue and expressly banning the raising of 'illicit' taxes or forced loans. The Committee of Public Safety included a provision in the Law of 14 Frimaire explicitly prohibiting taxes levied without an enabling decree from the Convention,[43] but to little effect.

The *représentants* themselves were careful to defend the legality of their measures. Bo, Chabot and Taillefer claimed their taxes were part and parcel of the Forced Loan and the proceeds amounted to contributions paid in advance; Laplanche claimed the tax he raised in Berry reflected the general will since it had been proclaimed in public session and endorsed by the popular societies.[44] Roux-Fazillac jealously defended his right as an elected representative to continue taxing the rich in his constituency and proclaimed his intent to double the assessment: in Nivôse, he launched an inquiry to identify those 'whose fortunes might still sustain further extraordinary taxes'.[45] While formally insisting that all sums levied should be sent to the exchequer in Paris, the government was lenient in allowing the region concerned to benefit

[42] Marion, *Histoire financière*, vol. III, pp. 145–52, 172–8, 200–6.

[43] Article 20, Section III of the Law of 14 Frimaire II, in Aulard, *Recueil*, vol. VII, p. 126; see Marion, *Histoire financière*, vol. III, pp. 172–3.

[44] Castres, 26 March, Cahors 29 September, Bourges, 4 October and Castelsarrasin, 9 October 1793: *Arch. parl.*, vol. LXV, p. 130; Aulard, *Recueil*, vol. VII, pp. 122, 221, 334; Campagnac, 'Les délégués du représentant Laplanche en mission dans le Cher', *La Révol. fr.* 44 (1903), p. 41.

[45] Périgueux, 27 Frimaire, 1 and 3 Nivôse II: Aulard, *Recueil*, vol. IX, pp. 477, 613.

directly from the funds collected and the tax measures continued unabated throughout the year.[46]

Tax returns, which alone could have established a fair proportion, were the exception rather than the rule. Charged with implementing the taxes, the local authorities ran up against the instinctive reticence of citizens to file a declaration of their assets and were obliged either to make estimates on the basis of out-of-date and very approximate tax registers, or to resort to peremptory assessments which did not go unchallenged. Maure recognised that if the 'tax on the rich' levied by his colleague Du Bouchet had in some instances proved arbitrary, this was because 'it was difficult to assess it with precision', and such taxes could not be fairly based in the absence of an 'exact knowledge of the means of the taxpayers'. As a consequence, to avoid any hint of unfairness, Maure was quick to grant reductions and exemptions. Thus citizen Robert, from Lizy-sur-Ourcq in the Seine-et-Marne, found himself the beneficiary of a complete discharge, while all he had requested was 'to be taxed in proportion to his faculties'.[47]

Lakanal, in contrast, took great pains to obtain information on the circumstances of the 'rich egoists' of the district of Bergerac from the local clubs and then sent them 'direct and personal requisitions', such as a demand for 50,000 livres to the entrepreneur Maynard, and for 10,000 livres to the merchant Loche. He personally put pen to paper and wrote to *citoyenne* Geyzand, a wealthy heiress domiciled near La Réole, urging her to pay a 'second instalment' on her 'patriotic donation' within two days in order 'not to jeopardise the public weal'. He finally required all private persons of means to fill in the following questionnaire:

1. What was your fortune in 1789?
2. What is your fortune now?
3. What pecuniary sacrifices have you made for the Revolution?
4. Have you occupied public office since 1789?
5. Of what use are you to your country?

---

[46] Thus, new taxes were raised by Lanot at Ussel in Nivôse, Vernerey at Guéret in Pluviôse, Bo at Figeac in Germinal and Monestier at Agen and Dax in Floréal, while Lakanal continued collecting money to finance the many requirements of his long mission in Bergerac up until Thermidor.

[47] Melun, 10 Germinal; Auxerre, 9 Prairial; Paris, 28 Prairial; and Sens, 29 Prairial II: Aulard, *Recueil*, vol. XII, p. 286; vol. XIII, p. 804; and vol. XIV, pp. 346, 406–7.

The answers supplied to this unusual form of tax return enabled Lakanal to raise 8,000 livres from a citizen who enjoyed a fortune of 40,000 livres and had only contributed 40 livres since 1789, and 15,000 from another with a fortune of 100,000 who had not made any sacrifice at all for the Revolution, and so on.[48] Civic conscience and moral pressure combined made personal declarations of this kind potentially lucrative to the revenue.

Lakanal's tax form clearly shows that fiscal obligation was understood not as a grudging submission to coercion, but as a civic duty. Voluntary donations were expected from all, whatever their circumstances, in this hour of need. Egoism was expected to bow to the dictates of fraternity. You paid not what you felt like giving, but what you could afford to give, i.e. your *superflu*, once and for all, in cash or in kind. The emergency of the spring and summer of 1793 generated not just bundles of *assignats*, but gifts of gold, silver and bronze coins, silver plate, salvers and soup tureens, copper kettles and humble pots and pans, which came rattling to the doorstep of the Convention from the depths of the provinces at the instigation of the *représentants* as proof of the national spirit of sacrifice. As for the taxes themselves, amounting on average to roughly a million livres per department, their recovery was long drawn out and depended on the goodwill and perseverance of the local authorities; their proceeds, in devalued paper money, rarely exceeded a quarter of the sums demanded, and at best attained a third.

Under such conditions, selfish refusal to contribute anything at all resulted in peremptory demands for payment, and off-the-cuff assessments bred arbitrary exactions. This was but one step away from harassment and extortion. The Terror was a time when men of wealth and property were liable to find themselves detained as suspects and taxation could be used as a lever. Brival, for one, deplored that citizens arrested without motive should be pressurised into bribing their gaolers, and conversely, 'it is not by making pecuniary sacrifices that a suspect can cease to be one: one cannot buy one's liberty'.[49] But freedom *could* be bought, and petty officials knew it. It is no coincidence that the deputies most renowned for their hardline fiscal policies – Laplanche in the Cher,

---

[48] Bergerac, 5–6 Prairial II, Labroue, *La mission de Lakanal*, pp. 494–6.
[49] Brive, 28 Nivôse and Limoges, 18 Pluviôse II; Arch. dép. Corrèze, L 105, missions; Arch. dép. Haute-Vienne, L 820, Jacobin club of Limoges.

Fouché in the Nièvre and Allier, Baudot in the Lot, Taillefer in the Aveyron, Chateauneuf-Randon in the Cantal – should be those who left behind them a trail of desolation wrought by the terrorist agents to whom they had quite illegally delegated the power to raise taxes. These revolutionary *commissaires-percepteurs* acted with impunity and often used force to achieve their ends.

The Law of 14 Frimaire not only prohibited the collection of revolutionary taxes, it undermined the revolutionary apparatus set up by the hardliners to carry out their policies, the so-called 'parallel hierarchies' denounced by Robespierre as a prelude to the demolition of the Hébertist movement. Little wonder that Baudot, the 'consummate Hébertist', should have loudly protested at the obstacles the new law put in the way of his activities, especially the delegation of power to subordinate agents or *hommes de liaison*.[50] These henchmen continued to gather taxes and collect silverware for several months after the recall of their masters. Surrounded by small but effective praetorian guards, remnants of the dissolved political armies, they exercised, in the words of Paganel, an 'incredible tyranny' at bayonet-point, threatening and blackmailing their victims, confiscating their cash and valuables, jewellery, buckles, pewter- and brassware, razors, scissors and tools. Paganel, Bo and Cavaignac were among the prime movers who brought these practices of oppression and extortion to a halt in the centre and south-west, suspending all 'measures of coercion relating to *taxes de guerre*', arresting the culprits and obliging them to restore their spoils to the rightful owners, but only after the harm was done, after the browbeaten citizens of Moissac, Lauzerte, Villefranche, Aubin and Aurillac had confessed their 'utter disgust with the Revolution'.[51]

'Fiscal tyranny' is obviously far from synonymous with fair taxation. At one end of the scale, civic duty calls for benevolence of the kind Paganel or Ingrand felt should occur spontaneously in

[50] E. Hamel, 'Euloge Schneider', *La Révol. fr.* 34 (1898), p. 435; Cobb, *Les armées révolutionnaires*, pp. 764–5.
[51] Moissac, 17 Frimaire; Toulouse, 21 Frimaire and 23 Nivôse; Aurillac, 4 Ventôse; Villefranche, 5–6 Ventôse; and Caussade, 15 Ventôse II: P. Paganel, *Essai historique*, vol. II, p. 188; Aulard, *Recueil*, vol. IX, p. 334; vol. X, p. 212; vol. XI, pp. 345, 357, 563; Wallon, *Les représentants du peuple*, vol. II, p. 326. Among the principal terrorist agents were Boissay and Grimaud in the Allier; Henriot, Grangier and Pauper in the Nièvre; L'Etang in the Creuse; Feyt, Dubosq and Hautefage in the Lot; Verdier and Molinier in the Aveyron: see Cobb, *Les armées révolutionnaires*, pp. 141, 245, 627–8.

civilised republican society: 'I have invited the rich and all the citizens [of Poitiers]', wrote Ingrand, 'to make for liberty and equality all the acts of devotion they require.'[52] Without much success, though, it is true. At the other end of the scale, intimidation, blackmail and extortion held sway where fragile democratic practices yielded to the abuse of power. Between the two, fair taxation occupied uneasily the middle ground. Taxes, claimed Vernerey, should be considered a 'sacred debt', 'as honourable for him who pays them as they are useful to the happiness of all'; Roux-Fazillac understood graduation as a means of persuading the recalcitrant rich to make 'the glorious sacrifice of a surplus which henceforth becomes the legacy of the poor'; and Lakanal, who promised his 'plebeian brothers' the restitution of 'the money of which they had been robbed', felt that the 'rich man is only *worthy of his political rights* if he becomes the father of the poor [my italics]'.[53] These men saw fiscal liability as stemming from a moral obligation which forged a contractual link between rich and poor: theirs was a vision of society in which a just distribution of wealth was the precondition of democracy.

Progressive taxation emerged badly dented from the transgressions of Year II. Tainted as it was by the stigma of extortion and spoliation, subsequent attempts by Vernier and Ramel under the Directory to restore its respectability and grade citizens 'according to their abilities'[54] were doomed to failure. While the Bonapartist regime opted for indirect taxes and fought shy of graduation under any guise, the fact that Babeuf's followers commandeered *l'impôt progressif* for their own ends[55] made it not just suspect, but subversive. During the age of unbridled capitalism, bourgeois opinion not surprisingly came to identify it with extreme forms of socialism. By the time Marx and Engels forged it into an instrument of class warfare and included it in the Communist Manifesto of 1848, curiously in second place after the abolition of private

---

[52] Poitiers, 14 Frimaire II: Aulard, *Recueil*, vol. IX, pp. 193–4.
[53] Bergerac, 21 October 1793; Périgueux, 4 Brumaire and 13 Frimaire II; Guéret, 12 Ventôse II: Arch. Nat., AF_{II} 95, Creuse pl. 703, p. 40; 96, Dordogne, pl. 717, p. 28; Labroue, *La mission de Lakanal*, pp. 304–9.
[54] Thus, the Loan of Year VII (6 August 1799) helped trigger the crisis which led to the coup of 18 Brumaire: Marion, *Histoire financière*, vol. III, pp. 413–15.
[55] P. Buonarroti, *Conspiration pour l'égalité dite de Babeuf*, 2 vols. (Brussels, 1828), vol. I, pp. 25–7, 81, 86; and vol. II, pp. 65–72; A. Galante Garrone, *Philippe Buonarroti et les révolutionnaires du XIXe siècle (1828–1837)*, trans. by A. Manceron and C. Manceron (Paris, 1975), pp. 61, 187–90, 271–4.

property,[56] the moderate spirit of mainstream Jacobin tax reform was quite forgotten: foolhardy indeed were those in the Second Republic who ventured to emulate their revolutionary predecessors and 'introduce into the fiscal system the principles of equity and distributive justice'.[57]

[56] *Birth of the Communist Manifesto*, ed. by D. J. Struik (New York, 1971), pp. 111, 181.

[57] This was the declared intention of Goudchaux, the finance minister of the short-lived Second Republic, whose 1849 tax bill failed to reach the statute book: E. de Parieu, *Histoire des impôts généraux sur la propriété et le revenu* (Paris, 1856), p. 306; R. Schnerb, 'Les hommes de 1848 et l'impôt', *1848 et les révolutions du XIXe siècle* 176 (1947), pp. 5–51; Gross, 'Progressive Taxation', pp. 121–6.

6. Jobs for all and to each a fair deal

> The wretchedness attending our species subordinates a man to another man: it is not inequality which is a real misfortune, but dependence.
>
> Voltaire, 'Egalité', in *Dictionnaire philosophique*, 1764[1]

FROM MENIAL SERVITUDE TO HONOURABLE POVERTY

Attitudes to poverty during the French Revolution were largely fashioned by perceptions of inequality. In advocating progressive taxation or the extension of property rights, the Jacobins assumed that transfers from the rich to the poor would make a substantial dent in poverty and narrow the distance between the two. In pooling and rationing scarce commodities, they were hoping that a different distribution system might rectify unequal consumption even without an expansion of the country's productive capacity. The 'myth' of the 'artificial dearth' (*la disette factice*), which was denounced by Gironde, Montagne and sans-culotte militants alike,[2] was proof that this was a land of plenty, with shares for everyone, and reflected a strong sense of what is fair and who has the right to enjoy what in a free and equal market economy.

The *ancien régime* differentiated between the acceptable and unacceptable faces of poverty. *Pauvreté*, on the one hand, encompassed a vast segment of the working population, those who lived on the brink of deprivation and whose main feature, as Olwen

---

[1] Voltaire, *Dictionnaire philosophique*, ed. by R. Naves and J. Benda (Paris, 1967), p. 176.
[2] Sewell, 'Sans-Culotte Rhetoric of Subsistence', p. 256.

Hufton has shown,[3] was vulnerability. Christian tradition had surrounded this category of long-suffering labouring poor with an aura of moral rectitude. *Misère*, in contrast, the state of indigence which could, in times of hardship, degenerate into absolute destitution (no food, no clothing, no shelter), was considered indecent.[4] A philosophe like Diderot was deeply revolted by the 'scenes of the most hideous wretchedness' he had witnessed on his trip to Langres and Bourbonne during the dearth of 1770.[5] What aroused his indignation, what he found truly inadmissible in a civilised society, was the failure of basic capabilities to reach certain minimally acceptable levels.[6] Provided the poor were able to sustain the delicate balance that prevented them from slipping from blessed poverty into abject destitution, and occupied their rightful place in the established order, then it followed that they were assimilated into the fabric of society and had little to fear, and that they became redeemable in its eyes.

Robespierre's conceptualisation of poverty was not 'passive' like Diderot's; he refused to resign himself to contemplating the hardships resulting from an economy governed by private ownership, but turned his attention to the question of who *commands* what, that is the question of 'entitlement relations and transfers', to use the language of modern Third World economists.[7] In referring to the assets of the working man, his 'modest wage', 'humble abode', 'rough clothes' and 'meagre savings', as a 'sacred form of ownership', Robespierre was talking in terms of entitlement, whether own-labour entitlement as in the case of a landless day labourer, or production-based entitlement, as in the case of a smallholder. 'In order to understand starvation', writes Amartya Sen, it is 'necessary to go into the structure of ownership'.[8] This was precisely Robespierre's approach, in line with that of Adam Smith, whose notion of necessities, based on 'the commodities which are indispensably necessary for the support of life' and 'whatever the custom of the

---

[3] Hufton, *The Poor*, p. 215

[4] H. C. Payne, '*Pauvreté, Misère*, and Enlightened Economics', *Studies on Voltaire and the Eighteenth Century* 154 (1976), p. 1581; and Gross, 'L'idée de la pauvreté', p. 197.

[5] Diderot, *Contes*, ed. by H. Dieckman (London, 1963), p. 90; J. Ehrard, 'Denis le Fataliste', in F. Braudel, M. Ferro, A. A. Gouber, A. Z. Manfred and R. Portal (eds.), *Au siècle des lumières* (Paris and Moscow, 1970), p. 149.

[6] Sen, *Inequality Reexamined*, p. 109.

[7] Sen, *Poverty and Famines*, pp. 45–51.   [8] *Ibid.*, pp. 1–5.

country renders it indecent for creditable people, even of the lowest order, to be without',[9] was essentially one of *minimum* ownership (ownership of food, shelter, clothing and so on).

The 'minimum share' of the primary goods which represents the 'poverty line' and gave the blessed poor their aura in the eyes of the church could do little to remedy their vulnerability. 'A poor man', Diderot had written in his *Encyclopédie*, 'with a little pride can do without relief; indigence compels him to accept.'[10] Robespierre's notion of honourable poverty went much further than 'pride', opening up the prospect of freedom from chronic indebtedness[11] and ultimately the prospect of self-reliance. If, as Condorcet had written in 1788, 'he who possesses neither property nor chattels is destined to fall into wretchedness at the slightest mishap',[12] it followed that property should be made accessible to all. The point made by Voltaire in his *Dictionnaire philosophique* was well taken: the key to human happiness was not equality, but independence. The goal of a fair share of landed interest had thus become official government policy: not the typical uneconomic holding of the subsistence farmer where liability to debt was high, as with the average sharecropper, but the self-sufficient smallholding which Saint-Just held out as the only sure foundation of individual prosperity.[13] 'Honourable poverty' is therefore not a value judgement or a moral view of poverty; if it were, it would then 'like beauty, lie in the eye of the beholder'.[14] However vague or arbitrary a notion it might appear, for Robespierre and his companions it was very much a matter of economic fact, a clearly perceived threshold based on the standards and conventions of their time, different no doubt from those described by Adam Smith as prevailing in England or Scotland, but clearly discernible to Arthur Young on his travels

---

[9] A. Smith, 'Taxes upon Consumable Commodities', in Book V of *Wealth of Nations*, vol. II (Section v. ii. j), p. 869.

[10] D. Diderot, 'Indigence', in vol. VIII of the *Encyclopédie* (1765): *Œuvres complètes*, ed. by J. Assézat and M. Tourneux, 20 vols. (Paris, 1875–7), vol. XIII, p. 428.

[11] Hufton, *The Poor*, pp. 54–8.

[12] Condorcet, 'Essai sur la constitution et les fonctions des assemblées provinciales' (1788), in *Œuvres*, vol. VIII, p. 453, cited by Hufton, *The Poor*, p. 19.

[13] Report of 23 Ventôse II, in Saint-Just, *Discours et rapports*, p. 165.

[14] M. Orshansky, 'How Poverty is Measured', *Monthly Labour Review* (1969), cited by Sen, *Poverty and Famines*, p. 17.

through France and which he encapsulated in his description of the small hill farms of Béarn.[15]

Economic independence of this kind was of course a distant dream to the mass of labouring poor. A more basic form of ownership recognised by eighteenth-century French trades as essential to their welfare was the manual worker's entitlement to enjoy the fruits of his own labour.[16] Jacobinism was particularly sensitive to sans-culotte aspirations in this regard. As Jean Bart shrewdly points out, where Condorcet and the Girondins defined ownership in their draft declarations of rights as relying on the concept of profit and entrepreneurship ('every man is master in disposing as he likes of his properties, his capital, his income and his industry'), the Montagnard version came down firmly on the side of the working man by replacing the word 'capital' with 'the fruits of his labour'.[17] Gilbert Romme, as we have seen, had forcefully expressed the view that 'every man who works is really a man of property ... His arms are his capital.'[18]

Since ownership was considered a natural right, this line of reasoning was not without consequence for the state. It was felt in Jacobin circles that government policy could and should influence the labour market and the pattern of entitlement transfers. Thus article 21 of the Montagnard Declaration of 24 June 1793 reads as follows: 'Poor relief is a sacred debt. Society owes their subsistence to unfortunate citizens in adversity, either by procuring them work or by ensuring the means of existence to those who are unable to work.'[19] Provision of jobs or social benefits for the unemployed – the alternatives were equally daunting. Man's right to work entailed the corollary that work should be freely available. Diderot in the *Encyclopédie* had held out a fertile prospect of 'untilled land to clear, colonies to settle, factories to support, public works to prosecute',[20] more than justifying the dynamic relief schemes of the 1770s. But if jobs now became scarce or raw materials ran short, it

---

[15] Young, *Travels in France and Italy*, p. 52.
[16] See M. Sonenscher, *Work and Wages: Natural Law, Politics and the Eighteenth-Century French Trades* (Cambridge, 1989).
[17] Article 18 of Condorcet's text and article 16 of the final draft: J. Bart, 'Statut de la propriété, question agraire: usages collectifs et exploitation individuelle', in J.-P. Jessenne *et al.*, *Robespierre*, pp. 253–62.
[18] G. Romme, report of 17 April 1793, Bibl. Nat., 8° Le[38] 2274; Galante Garrone, *Gilbert Romme*, pp. 299–300.
[19] *Les Déclarations*, ed. by Jaume, p. 301.
[20] Diderot, 'Hôpital', in *Encyclopédie*, viii (1765), *Œuvres*, vol. XV, p. 141.

followed that the government could no longer evade its responsibility to create the opportunities and supply the tools and wherewithal. Romme, for example, was to assume this responsibility without flinching by instituting a voucher system enabling farmers, blacksmiths and cartwrights to obtain iron from their local foundry, at the regulation price, for the making of ploughshares and other essential implements. Such support measures to agriculture were an integral part of the interventionist economy of Year II, while a year later, as Denis Woronoff confirms, the unbridled Thermidorian free-for-all obliged farmers to revert to 'commercial sources of supply'.[21]

Although the public works initiatives of 1790–1 had failed to resolve some basic conceptual dilemmas (their impact on private-sector labour markets, for example, or how to set wages), this was no longer an urgent concern in 1793, since the war alleviated unemployment and even caused labour shortages in some regions: public works remained on the agenda but held a low priority and by the time the economy collapsed in 1795, the state was 'bankrupt of funds, plans, and will'.[22] Nevertheless, the *travaux de secours* and *ateliers de secours* decreed on 28 June 1793 at the instigation of the Convention's welfare committee, whose rapporteur was Jean-Baptiste Bo, were bold attempts to launch a nationwide employment programme for the chronically or seasonally unemployed, the idle or *oisifs*, especially those of middle age who were not subject to military service. Bo appears quite sensitive to the call for an egalitarian division of public works, which was a fundamental demand of the sans-culottes in their occupations as independent small producers.[23] In the provinces, the revolutionary progressive taxes levied on the wealthy enabled such schemes, for a brief spell at least, to get off the ground. Highway repairs, bridge-building and the dredging of waterways to enhance navigation were activities favoured by the representatives.[24] Cottage industries were also encouraged and where the unemployed possessed special skills, efforts were made to supply them with materials and the tools of

---

[21] D. Woronoff, *L'industrie sidérurgique en France pendant la Révolution et l'Empire* (Paris, 1984), p. 416.
[22] Woloch, *New Regime*, p. 247.   [23] Burstin, 'Problems of Work', p. 276.
[24] Roux-Fazillac in Charente, Lakanal in Dordogne, Monestier de la Lozère in Landes and Lot-et-Garonne.

their trade and piece-rates were agreed for the purchase of their products.[25]

Albert Mathiez accused Lakanal of using his road-mending project in Périgord to reinstitute the hated *corvées*, thus undermining the pioneer reforms undertaken by Turgot in neighbouring Limousin thirty years previously.[26] To do justice to Lakanal, he was a keen reader of Rousseau and followed to the letter the advice given by the master in his draft constitution for Corsica, even to the extent of rolling up his sleeves and wielding a spade himself.[27] Rousseau, of course, in recommending the *corvée*, had expressly differentiated between labour service and forced labour. Lakanal, in Périgord, imposed the unpaid labour service on the bourgeois members of society alone as a form of civic duty, while he made sure the poor sans-culottes were paid the going rate for the time spent shovelling gravel and filling in potholes.

Mathiez, nevertheless, makes a useful point in drawing attention to the deceptive affinity between the social remedies prescribed by the Revolution and those of the *ancien régime*. Unquestionably, the language used is so often redolent of the paternalism of the monarchy, with its emphasis on the virtues of toil and sweat and the blessed nature of the labouring and deserving poor. In the same vein, 'idleness', wrote both Brival and Roux-Fazillac, echoing an ancient adage, 'is the mother of all the vices'.[28] In what way are the *ateliers de secours* workshops recommended by Bo any different from the *ateliers de charité* of the 1770s? These had been aimed at putting the poor to work in state-funded enterprises, normally road-mending or textile-working, according to the three-tier system favoured by Turgot in Limousin and Necker during his tenure of the controller-generalship. Bo, who was from Rouergue, an area of small farms where the *ateliers de charité* had given the best results by providing a stopgap during the crop year,[29] was firmly in favour of remedies of this kind to seasonal unemployment.

[25] Roux-Fazillac, Angoulême, 18 September 1793, Arch. dép. Charente, L 1962, missions, and L 1239, dist. Confolens.

[26] A. Mathiez, review of H. Labroue, *La mission de Lakanal*.

[27] Rousseau, 'Projet de constitution pour la Corse' in *Œuvres complètes*, vol. III, pp. 508–15.

[28] Limoges, 18 Pluviôse, and Tulle, 4 Fructidor II: Arch. dép. Haute-Vienne, L 820, Jacobin club of Limoges, and Corrèze, L 258B, Tulle arms factory, f° 623.

[29] Hufton, *The Poor*, pp. 183, 191.

In his Vendémiaire report on the 'extinction of mendicity',[30] Bo harps on about the subversive nature of unemployment and divides the 'idle' into three traditional categories, handed down from the Middle Ages: the *pauvres honteux*[31] who were intermittently out of work and whom Hufton calls 'a privileged élite among the poor', because they had a regular roof above their heads, clean clothes and 'moral values acceptable to the rest of society'; the inveterate vagabonds (*vagabonds de race*) who were thought to eschew gainful employment because they were work-shy; and the lawless vagrants (*gens sans aveu*) whose addiction to work could only be expected from prolonged repression in the workhouse. This recalls the *hôpital général* of the classical age and Vincent de Paul's policy of internment graphically described by Michel Foucault, and symptomatic of the 'basic dualism' inherent in the Revolution's attitudes to formal poor relief.[32]

The prospects for change would appear dim indeed were it not for some very real practical reforms cloaked at times in conventional discourse. First and foremost among these is the notion of a 'fair day's wages for a fair day's work', which Thomas Carlyle was subsequently to recognise as fundamental to labour legislation.[33] Using guarded language, Bo in Vendémiaire put forward the idea that those who benefited from the work schemes should not only receive a wage covering their basic subsistence needs, but might also have access to a provident fund to cover illness or prepare for their retirement. Roux-Fazillac, who was organising public works in the Charente at this time, understood fair retribution to include a minimum subsistence wage, provision for sickness and accident benefits, and credits set aside for old age. Subsumed in this approach is the principle that the worker is entitled to put aside some 'savings' in cash or kind for a rainy day: such was the bonus accruing from the sales of ecclesiastical ornaments which Vernerey

---

[30] J.-B. Bo, *Rapport sur l'extinction de la mendicité, fait au nom du Comité des secours publics* (Paris, 21 vendémiaire an II), Bibl. Nat., 8° Le³⁸ 499, pp. 1–39; Woloch, *New Regime*, p. 247; cf. M. Mollat, *Les pauvres au Moyen-Age: étude sociale* (Paris, 1978), pp. 158, 198, 296–9; Burstin, 'Problems of Work', pp. 288–90.

[31] Mollat, *Les pauvres*, pp. 215–16.

[32] M. Foucault, *Histoire de la folie à l'âge classique* (Paris, 1972; 2nd edn, Paris, 1977); Hufton, *The Poor*, pp. 3, 139–42; see also A. Forrest, *The French Revolution and the Poor* (Oxford, 1981), pp. 76 and 99–115.

[33] T. Carlyle, 'Past and Present' (1843), *The Works of Thomas Carlyle*, 30 vols. (1896–9), vol. X, pp. 14–23.

added to the basic pay of the building workers occupied in transforming the church of Aubusson into a Temple of Reason, or the 'salary supplement' in the form of 'non-precious' building materials from the *châteaux-forts* demolition programme which Brival awarded the casual labourers of Limousin for the repair of their cottages.[34] This notion of a fair reward for services rendered, over and above the subsistence wage, is of fundamental significance in the new thinking of Year II.

The formal abolition of slavery in the colonies was preceded by the abolition of that other form of menial servitude, namely domestic service, proposed by Saint-Just in these terms: no more masters and servants among citizens, but 'an equal and sacred undertaking between the man who works and he who pays him'.[35] This new definition of a contract of employment as an economic relationship between equal partners was formally enacted in the 1793 Constitution which gave the vote to domestic servants, while the Declaration of Rights stipulated: 'Every man may commit his services, his time; but he may not sell himself nor may he be sold; his person is not an alienable property. The law recognises no domesticity; there can only exist an undertaking of care and recognition between the man who works and the one who employs him.'[36] During his visits to the provincial cities of Aurillac, Montauban and Castres, Bo was careful to explain to his listeners the scope of this revolutionary change in social relations. Comparing domestic service to slavery, he declared it to be contrary to nature: no citizen was allowed to 'buy another' and likewise, no poor man could be obliged to 'sell himself'. 'It is high time', he went on, 'to erase this demarcation between the citizen who enjoys and he who labours: the Constitution endows them with the same political existence and we are bound by morality to do so.' Henceforth, a servant was a citizen like any other, whose labour and time were for hire, 'as a labourer hires himself out by the clock, as men of property put their advice up for sale'.[37]

---

[34] Aubusson, 6 and 22 Ventôse, Arch. Nat., AF$_{II}$ 95, Creuse, pl. 703, p. 52; Limoges, 12 Ventôse II, Arch. dép. Haute-Vienne, L 106, missions, Brival.

[35] 'Essai de constitution' (proposed 24 April 1793), part I, chapter 3, Article III, in Saint-Just, *Œuvres complètes*, ed. by Ch. Vellay, 2 vols. (Paris, 1908), vol. I, p. 435.

[36] Article XVIII, Declaration of 24 June 1793, in *Les Déclarations*, ed. by Jaume, p. 301.

[37] Bo, speech of 13 Pluviôse, 17 Ventôse and 8 Floréal II, Bibl. Nat., 8° Lb^{40} 2504.

The word 'wages' in French (*gages*), traditionally confined to the earnings of domestic servants and deemed to belong to the age of privilege, was now banned from usage and replaced by the respectable word *salaire*, and Sganarelle's anguished cry in the final scene of Molière's *Dom Juan* consequently was doomed to oblivion.[38] The term 'salary' generated all the connotations of a fair reward for a contract of work, based on mutual respect between employer and employee, and comprising recognition of the quality of the work done and the value attributed to it, akin to the 'fees' charged by the self-employed or members of the liberal professions such as the lawyers who made up the backbone of the new political class. Semantics clearly have their importance in this context.

As the programme of public works indicates, the money provided by the revolutionary taxes opened up a new vista of systematic job creation and the possibility of a labour market which would not exclusively be determined by the law of supply and demand. The affirmation of the right to work imposed on the state the ominous contractual obligation to provide it, and the notion of a contract of employment between equals generated the recognition of a fair salary for services rendered. In these circumstances, unemployment could no longer be attributed to chance, or bad luck, or, as in the past, to a vice harboured by the individual whose own fault it was thought to be and whose amendment required a spell in a house of correction, a presupposition intrinsic in the use of the terms 'idle' and 'idleness'. A sense of collective responsibility was beginning to permeate economic and social relationships and the transition from menial servitude to honourable poverty made it necessary to overcome the psychological barrier that separated idleness (*oisiveté*) from unemployment (*chômage*).

THE ELITE WORKFORCE: THE SUBSISTENCE WAGE AND FRINGE BENEFITS

With a major war in progress, full employment in the essential defence industries (mining, iron and steel, armaments, tanneries) was not hard to achieve. Indeed, in those areas of France where

---

[38] As his master is delivered to the flames at the end of the play, Sganarelle, the archetypal *ancien régime* manservant, complains that his many years of loyal domestic service have gone unrewarded: *Dom Juan ou le Festin de pierre* (1665) act V, scene vii.

smelting, casting and gun-making were the tradition, in the arms factories of Charleville, Saint-Etienne, Tulle and Moulins, the rhetoric had it that all able-bodied men and their families were mobilised in the war effort. They made up an 'army of the interior' and their cities and villages were transformed into 'a vast workshop' echoing with the clanging of metal: 'Republicans of all ages, old men, women (at Tulle, women make bayonets), children, arm yourselves with hammers and files: let everywhere the furnaces be lit, let everywhere the anvils start to sound!'[39] Elsewhere, as at Bergerac and Montauban, new arsenals were being built from scratch or industrial plant converted from non-economic use. The depressed textile mills on the banks of the Tarn were turned into an unlikely bronze cannon foundry whose furnaces would melt down church bells and Jeanbon Saint-André wrote optimistically that 'our fullers and our machines for friezing cloth offer us ready-made facilities for hollowing out gun barrels'.[40]

In practice, amateurish improvisation was a risky business and the foundrymen and gunsmiths in the armaments industry were highly trained workers whose skills were jealously protected by their craft unions. Although subjected to harsh conditions with continuous shifts of twelve hours a day for nine days out of ten, they formed the elite of the French workforce and were fully aware of their economic importance. While these vital industries were placed for a time under close government supervision, they remained, as Denis Woronoff has shown,[41] in private hands and proved far from docile, especially in respect of the price and income legislation. It soon became clear that the concept of a pay ceiling, the *maximum des salaires* decreed on 29 September 1793, representing the rate prevailing in 1790 augmented by 50 per cent, could not for long be contained in the case of this very special category of worker. Haim Burstin confirms that the maximum wage was never enforced where war production was concerned.[42]

---

[39] Proclamations of 4 Prairial (Périgueux), 13 Thermidor (Tulle) and 2 Fructidor II (Excideuil), by Romme and Roux-Fazillac: Arch. dép. Charente, L 68[1], Romme; Corrèze, L 260, Tulle arms factory; Dordogne, 1 L 233, Romme.

[40] Montauban, 15 May 1793, L. Lévy-Schneider, 'Quelques recherches', *La Révol. fr.* 24 (1893), p. 417; C. Richard, *Le Comité de salut public et les fabrications de guerre sous la Terreur* (Paris, 1921), p. 243.

[41] On the various conditions governing the relations between the factories placed *en régie* and the client state, see Woronoff, *L'industrie sidérurgique*, pp. 387–8.

[42] Burstin, 'Problems of Work', p. 280.

The energetic *représentants* who were sent to the arms factories
for periods of six months or more to establish government control
over military procurement and ensure vital requirements were
met[43] were generally prepared to lend a friendly ear to grievances
from the shop-floor: professionals like the forge-master Legendre,
overseer of the Capucins armouries in Paris, or the Saint-Etienne
gunsmith Noël Pointe, who was in control of the production of
rifles and munitions at Moulins and Guérigny, or the newly
promoted 'ironside' general Roux-Fazillac who effectively took
over as managing director of the small-arms factory at Tulle.
Others, such as Romme, who was placed in charge of the naval gun
arsenal at Ruelle, or Lakanal, who started up a new rifle-manufac-
turing plant from scratch at Bergerac, were socially committed
idealists whose knowledge of metallurgy and manufacturing techniques was faulty, but who surrounded themselves with experts and
were prepared to undergo a crash apprenticeship 'à la Pierre le
Grand'.[44] They quickly came face to face with corporatist solidarity
and a grim determination on the part of the metal-workers to
'desert' or lay down their tools if their rightful claims were not met.
Although the Le Chapelier law of 1791 prohibited collective action
by workers,[45] there were ways of making grievances felt short of
organising a fully fledged strike. Similarly, the absence of workers'
associations did not prevent them from voicing their demands
stridently in the popular societies, as the records of the Jacobin club
in Tulle, published by Victor Forot, make clear.

The provision of a basic subsistence salary, enshrined in the new
Declaration of Rights as a social obligation, inevitably generated in
the hierarchy of skilled trades the notion of a minimum rather than
a maximum wage. A typical craftsman in a rifle shop traditionally
opted for piece-work, his remuneration covering both his labour
and the raw material which he supplied himself. Thus, a gun-barrel
maker would be paid the cost of eleven ounces of iron for the tube,

<hr/>

[43] Petitjean in the Isère and Mont-Blanc; Massieu in the Ardennes; Lambert in the Haute-Marne; Legendre in the Nièvre; Deydier in the Eure and Orne; Ferry in the Cher and Indre; Romme in the south-west; Noël Pointe in the Nièvre and Allier: Woronoff, *L'industrie sidérurgique*, p. 47.
[44] Lakanal, Bergerac, 10 Ventôse II, Arch. Nat., AF$_{II}$ 262, Committee of Public Safety, pl. 2212, p. 42; Aulard, *Recueil*, XI, p. 465; Richard, *Le Comité de salut public*, pp. 141–3; see also J.-P. Gross, 'Le projet de l'an II: promotion ouvrière et formation professionnelle', *Annales hist. Révol. fr.* 300 (April–June 1995), pp. 209–21.
[45] Burstin, 'Problems of Work', pp. 277–8, 284–5.

while bayonet-grinders would supply one and a half pounds of iron and seven ounces of steel for the blade. The labour comprised two parts: on the one hand, the cost of subsistence, and on the other, the quality of the workmanship, validated in the corporatist system by the time of service spent as an apprentice and journeyman before rising to master of the craft.

Since the subsistence portion was supposed to cover at least the cost of basic foodstuffs and since prices kept rising and the value of the *assignats* falling, it was decided in Ventôse to abandon cash payment for the subsistence portion of workers' pay and deliver them instead a ration of two pounds of bread per day, deducted from their wages at the controlled price. The instigator of the *salaire de subsistance*, paid in kind and not in paper money, was Romme, who made it the stable and guaranteed part of foundry-men's pay in the arsenals of Ruelle and Abzac, equal for all irrespective of trade or grade. Grain-stores were established to this end within the foundry premises and although with the approach of the 'hungry gap' Romme was obliged to reduce the daily bread ration to a pound and a half, he supplemented it with two ounces of dried beans and a pint of wine, and on the fifth and tenth days of the decade, a meat ration instead of beans. The miners and forge-workers supplying the cannon-foundries received in addition to their bread ration regular distributions of rice and lard. The foundry grain-stores were also used to 'appease the worries' of workmen's families who were entitled to food rations every other day. 'I have ensured the subsistence of those who work in the foundries', wrote Romme, 'but I would only have imperfectly achieved my aim if the wives and children of these good citizens were to go without bread.'[46]

The *salaire de subsistance* was in keeping with the unskilled worker's natural preference for the security of a daily wage as opposed to piece-work rates.[47] However, the portion of earnings corresponding to the craftsmanship of the worker was the subject of tough collective bargaining and the concessions which were made to the trades underline the importance the Jacobins attached

---

[46] Resolutions of 15, 19, 26 and 27 Ventôse, 11 Germinal, 3 and 28 Floréal, 4 and 22 Prairial and 7 Messidor II: Arch. dép. Charente, L 67, Romme, L 1239, dist. Confolens; L 1473[1], dist. La Rochefoucauld; L 1962, Romme; and Dordogne, 1 L 233, Romme. See also Richard, *Le Comité de salut public*, pp. 302, 305.
[47] Burstin, 'Problems of Work', p. 278.

both to the quality of the end-product and to a fair reward for skilled workmanship. The *corporations* monopolised the acquisition and transfer of technical know-how under the apprenticeship system and the horizontal structure, together with guild solidarity, ensured that there was a clear demarcation between each trade. 'All the workers in the same shop', wrote Romme, 'are responsible one to the other for the activities and the success of the work they carry out in common.'[48] Nevertheless, the series of pay awards agreed by Roux-Fazillac at the firearms factory of Tulle reflect very clearly both the meritocratic criterion of fair reward and the principle of job comparability. While the gun-barrel smiths were able to negotiate a piece-rate of nearly 9 livres, the fitters were able to achieve 7 livres, i.e. the same rate as the locksmiths in the gunlock shop, on the grounds that 'it takes the same time to assemble a rifle as it does to file a lock-plate' (table 12).

As for the executive grades, the factory management board being made up of skilled master craftsmen who stood to earn more doing piece-work than being promoted inspector or controller, Roux-Fazillac felt it only right to establish a salary scale based on merit and commensurate with their talents and attainments: an annual salary of 3,000 livres for the post of chief inspector, 2,400 for assistant inspector and 2,000 for controller or shop manager (table 13). Since allowances were authorised by legislation, he likewise granted monthly bonuses to master craftsmen for the successful training of their apprentices and pecuniary awards to the apprentices themselves on qualification. This in effect added an extra 65 livres per month to the pay packet of a master gunsmith and 20 livres to that of a newly qualified journeyman (table 14). The list of the first workers at Tulle to benefit from these new measures in Thermidor totals more than 150 names. Similar rewards for good workmanship and regular attendance were posted on the notice-board by Lakanal at the arms factory of Bergerac.[49]

These cash handouts in the form of allowances and bonuses as a reward for merit over and above regular salary awards and guaranteed subsistence pay were clearly intended to circumvent, if not undermine, the policy of income controls. Retirement pensions awarded on the basis of length of service (table 15) have also to be

[48] Grèzes, 11 Messidor II, Arch. Nat., AF$_{II}$ 97, Dordogne, pl. 715, pp. 13–18; Richard, *Le Comité de salut public*, pp. 309–10.
[49] Bergerac, 15 Messidor II, Arch. dép. Lot, L 13, Lakanal.

Table 12. *Tulle small-arms factory: piece-rates awarded to journeymen, 1792–1794*

Trade	Piece	19 August 1792 (l. s. d.)	16 April 1793 (l. s. d.)	12 Pluviôse II (l. s. d.)
Gun-barrel maker	barrel	4 . 6.	6. 5. 6.	8. 19. 6.
Locksmith	lock-plate	3. 14. 2.	4. 6.	7.
Fitter	rifle	—	4. 6.	7.

Sources: Arch. Nat., AF$_{II}$ 95, Corrèze, pl. 694, p. 3; Arch. mun. Tulle, 1 D 2, municipal register, f° 122.

Table 13. *Tulle small-arms factory: salary scale for managers, foremen and executive grades, Floréal II*

Grade	Annual salary in livres
Chief inspector	3,000
Assistant inspector	2,400
Controller (rifles, barrels, plates)	2,000
Reviser (barrels, stocks, plates)	1,800
Storekeeper	1,200
Secretary	1,200

Sources: Arch. dép. Corrèze, L 258 B, Tulle arms factory, f° 775; Arch. mun. Tulle, 1 D 2, municipal register, f° 127.

Table 14. *Tulle small-arms factory: allowances awarded to master craftsmen and apprentices qualifying as journeymen, Floréal–Fructidor II*

Trade and grade	Justification	Allowance
Master gun-barrel maker	training an apprentice	65 livres per month
Master locksmith	training an apprentice	45 livres per month
Master-polisher	training an apprentice	45 livres per month
Master-fitter	training an apprentice	45 livres per month
Apprentice locksmith	completion of his model	20 livres
Apprentice (all trades)	bonus	15 livres

Sources: Arch. dép. Corrèze, L 258 A, Tulle arms factory, ff. 18–250, and L 258 B, ff. 51–104; L 259, ff. 367–768.

Table 15. *Tulle small-arms factory: retirement pensions awarded in Prairial II*

Retirement age	Years of service	Trade and grade	Annual pension
50	30	master-fitter	250 livres
—	35	master locksmith	300 livres

Sources: Arch. dép. Corrèze, L 258 A, Tulle arms factory, f° 181, and L 258 B, f° 55.

taken into consideration. Evidently justified in the eyes of the Montagnards by the key role they attributed to the workers in the armaments industry, the meritocratic criterion nonetheless gave rise to a substantial inflationary package, to which must be added a number of quite significant fringe benefits.

The distribution of coke and firewood and the provision of free lodging close to the workshop and medical care when industrial injuries were sustained were already benefits enjoyed by metal workers under the *ancien régime*. Denis Woronoff describes the practice of keeping the furnaces continuously alight, which made it necessary for the foundrymen to live on or close to the premises, while part of the fuel was naturally diverted to heating in winter and forge-masters were attentive to the need to minimise occupational hazards and nurse the sick or injured. This was traditionally understood as a 'moral obligation' on the employer's part.[50]

The Jacobin programme of free housing and health care for workers in the armaments industry clearly needs to be considered in this context rather than trumpeted as a 'daring' and 'unique' innovation in the history of social legislation.[51] Nevertheless, on account of the massive recruitment drive generated by the creation of new factories and the expansion of existing facilities to meet the increase in production, innovative measures did indeed prove necessary. Thus Lakanal organised free meals and free accommodation in the émigré houses of Bergerac for the many gunsmiths, locksmiths, silversmiths and edge-tool makers he recruited for his

[50] Woronoff, *L'industrie sidérurgique*, pp. 182–5.
[51] Such is the interpretation propounded by both Camille Richard and Alessandro Galante Garrone: Richard, *Le Comité de salut public*, p. 308; Galante Garrone, *Gilbert Romme*, p. 345.

new factory in all the neighbouring departments of south-western France, while Roux-Fazillac opened the houses of the suspect detainees of Tulle to the Marchois stonemasons who migrated south to help in building the new workshops on the banks of the Corrèze. He turned a former convent into a 'workers' barracks' and thus established a model for the industrial *cités ouvrières* of the next century. He ensured these workers were paid a travel and installation allowance prior to starting work.[52]

Firearm workers in Tulle who were laid off on account of sickness or injury as from the end of Prairial were paid allowances 'in proportion to their position and service', while all the foundrymen, coalminers, quarry-workers, wood-cutters and haulage workers involved in service for the naval arsenals were able to benefit from a sophisticated social insurance scheme instituted by Romme on 19 Fructidor. This scheme provided each worker with free medical care 'at the expense of the Republic'; the continuation of full pay for the duration of his sick leave; the undertaking, in cases of permanent disability or death, to ensure his family's subsistence, his children's education and the farming of his land; and automatic entitlement to servicemen's welfare benefits.[53] Occupational health care was thus understood as a collective responsibility and the welfare of the workers and their families considered a necessary input to be integrated into the economics of production.

The influx of new and unskilled manpower into the armaments industry and the emergence of new technologies, especially in the field of steel-manufacturing, resulted in a number of training initiatives being taken in addition to the standard apprenticeship schemes; these likewise added to the cost of production. Courses were run by master craftsmen sent from Paris and Tulle to Bergerac to help turn the blacksmiths and edge-tool makers into gunsmiths and each workshop, according to Lakanal, strove to become a training unit, or in the new modish jargon, *une école normale.*[54]

[52] Labroue, *La mission de Lakanal*, pp. 415–20; Richard, *Le Comité de salut public*, pp. 125, 708.
[53] Gar-dor-Isle (Abzac), 19 Fructidor II, Arch. dép. Charente, L 68¹, Romme; Richard, *Le Comité de salut public*, pp. 308, 708; Galante Garrone, *Gilbert Romme*, p. 345.
[54] Bergerac, 15 Messidor II, in *Procès-verbaux du Comité d'instruction publique de la Convention nationale*, ed. by J. Guillaume, 6 vols. (Paris, 1890–1907), vol. IV, p. 833.

Experts from the Ardennes helped improve casting techniques at
the arsenal in Ruelle and gave tuition to suitably gifted young
workers who 'looked forward to a good salary' at the end of their
course.[55] The small steelworks at Miremont in Périgord ran state-
of-the-art steel-making courses of six months' duration under the
guidance of German steel-workers from Nassau, who were paid a
fee of 150 livres for each pupil successfully trained, while the
trainees were awarded a lump sum of 100 livres on qualification.[56]

Such incentives added to the wage bill. All in all, skilled manpower in the essential defence industries had become a very
expensive commodity. The *maximum des salaires* was left far
behind in the inflationary spiral and the notion of remuneration
itself was substantially enlarged to encompass not only basic
subsistence, but performance-related allowances, training incentives, fringe benefits and medical insurance. While short-term
funding was secured by peremptory demands made to the war and
navy departments and extraordinary taxes raised on the rich
citizens of the vicinity, this did not prevent the real cost of the end
product rising dramatically, notwithstanding the depreciation of
the *assignat*. The price of a complete rifle, for example, set at 31
livres 10 sols in February 1788 and maintained at this level
throughout 1793, had increased, a year later, in Pluviôse II, to 60
livres, or almost double.[57]

Intent on achieving greater productivity but also on taking up
the industrial challenges of their age, the Jacobin leaders were
pursuing a labour policy that neglected neither the quality of the
work nor the welfare of the workers. In their view, the long term
outweighed the short term. Industrialisation and technology were
on the march and they considered it essential that the élite craft
corporations should be involved in the process of change. To that
end, fair remuneration and a fair share of the profits appeared only
natural. To these sons of the Enlightenment, living in an age in
which slavery and menial servitude had just been 'abolished' but

[55] Ruelle, 1 and 13 Floréal, and 4 Prairial II, in Richard, *Le Comité de salut public*,
p. 303.
[56] Resolution of Romme and Roux-Fazillac, 2 Fructidor II, Arch. Nat., AF$_{II}$ 97,
Dordogne, pl. 718, pp. 2–5; Woronoff, *L'industrie sidérurgique*, pp. 355–8, 364.
[57] G. Mathieu (ed.), *Documents inédits pour servir à l'histoire de l'industrie, du
commerce et de l'agriculture en Bas-Limousin à la fin du XVIIIe siècle et au début
du XIXe siècle: la manufacture d'armes de Tulle* (Paris, 1913), pp. 59–77; Richard,
Le Comité de salut public, p. 123.

one in which capitalist exploitation was only just beginning, economic development and social progress appeared closely wedded and at times virtually indistinguishable.

THE MINIMUM SHARE AND THE WELFARE STATE

In no other area of political reform was so much promised and so little actually delivered as in the field of social security. Decree after decree proclaimed the eradication of mendicity and the end of chronic deprivation, and ever larger appropriations were earmarked with seemingly reckless abandon for poor relief (well over 200 million livres between November 1792 and 9 Thermidor), while the pages of the *Archives parlementaires* abound with innumerable pathetic examples of parliamentary largesse[58] – all to no lasting effect. Dwindling resources due to currency erosion and fiscal shortcomings, diversion of funds resulting from the urgent requirements and contingencies of war, recalcitrance or inertia on the part of the local administrators, and above all shortage of time effectively undermined the promise of a millennium. The events of Thermidor heralded the return to *laissez-faire* economics and the progressive dismantling of the centrally funded Jacobin welfare system, relentlessly pursued during the Directory years. Although Alan Forrest expresses his astonishment that 'so much was achieved in such unpromising conditions',[59] the upheavals of the Revolution were intrinsically inimical to the single most crucial prerequisite of success in an enterprise of this kind, namely sustainability.

We have, of course, accustomed ourselves to judge the action of the Montagnards not on their achievements but, more questionably, on their intentions. It may indeed be taxing credulity to suggest that we should take these men at their word and share in their illusions, and few would deny that the sheer euphoria of millenarist sentiment proves indigestible at times. Nevertheless, Forrest considers that 'the ideal espoused by the Revolution' should not be belittled,[60] and it may be profitable to give the

---

[58] For example, a recorded minute for 15 Floréal II reads: 'To Claude Petit, seventy-three years of age, and to his blind wife, aged seventy-five, a provisional relief of 150 livres each', *Arch. parl.*, vol. XC, p. 173.

[59] Forrest, *French Revolution and the Poor*, p. 176.   [60] *Ibid.*, p. 171.

deputies the benefit of the doubt, if only because the advantage gained is that of being able to watch the revolutionary dream unfolding through their eyes. The sincerity of their personal commitment, at least, appears above suspicion. Each without hesitation shouldered the 'sacred debt' of society toward the poor as a 'pressing and urgent duty'; to delay in doing so, Roux-Fazillac maintained, was to 'become guilty of crimes'. Frenchmen in general, claimed Bo, were undergoing a 'popular awakening' in the 'practice of social virtues: it is by doing good that one becomes good'. 'Let us love and help our brothers in need', wrote Lakanal, 'let us show respect to old age in misfortune: that is the true religion.'[61] Brival and Romme, for their part, practised what they preached and throughout their term as members of the Convention donated part of their deputies' salary each month to the poor, each earning himself in the process the title 'ami des pauvres'.[62]

Enlightenment philanthropy tended to be more demonstrative and emotional than Christian charity. Thus, Ingrand amidst the poor of Guéret, and Laplanche among the wailing orphans of Bourges, cannot retain their 'tears of tenderness', and Lakanal's Gascon sensibility is worthy of the finest bourgeois drama: he positively shudders at the idea that the selfishness of the rich can condemn 'the father to crime, the mother to prostitution and the children to shame and wretchedness'.[63] To Lakanal, these risks are very real, for failure to assist the destitute may 'force them to seize the dagger of crime'.[64] On a more threatening register still, the delegates of Taillefer in the Aveyron warn that poverty may seek to avenge itself for the patronising 'munificence of the mighty' who in the age of privilege 'humiliated and insulted it'.

Inasmuch as revenue from taxes was now looked upon as a 'common treasure' to be shared, revolutionary *bienfaisance* was at a far remove from old regime charity. The difference, already recognised by the Constituent Assembly, was not one of degree, but one

61 Bergerac, 4 Brumaire; Périgueux, 26 Frimaire; Aurillac, 13 Pluviôse II: Arch. dép. Dordogne, 1 L 228, Roux-Fazillac; Tarn, L 136, Bo, p. 4; Labroue, *La mission de Lakanal*, p. 253.
62 See Romme's letter to his wife, 10 Prairial III, in Brunel and Goujon, *Les martyrs de prairial*, p. 367; on Brival, A. Kuscinski, *Dictionnaire des conventionnels*, p. 93.
63 Guéret, 27 September; Bourges, 6 October 1793; Bergerac, 21 Pluviôse II: Arch. dép. Creuse, L 734*, Jacobin club of Guéret; Arch. Nat., AF$_{II}$ 169, Western Bureau, pl. 1389, pp. 13–19; Labroue, *La mission de Lakanal*, pp. 193–5.
64 Bergerac, 30 Vendémiaire and 4 Brumaire II, Arch. dép. Dordogne, 3 L 24, dist. Bergerac, f° 98.

Table 16. *Welfare legislation passed by the Convention, 1792–Thermidor II*

Date	Category of relief	Total in livres (where applicable)
26–7 November 1792	volunteers' families	2 million
20 February 1793	those in adversity	—
19 March 1793	welfare guidelines	—
4 May 1793	servicemen's families	10 million
4 June 1793	war widows	—
8 June 1793	blind and disabled	—
18 June 1793	relatives of Vendée victims	—
28 June 1793	home relief to indigents	—
August 1793	victims of disasters .	6 million
18 August 1793	servicemen's families	—
19 August 1793	orphans	—
27 August 1793	servicemen's families	—
27 August 1793	crop loss by farmers	15 million
15 September 1793	servicemen's families	5 million
13 October 1793	court acquittals	—
15 October 1793	extinction of mendicity	—
28 Brumaire II	servicemen's families	—
1 Frimaire II	servicemen's families	—
5 Nivôse II	war widows	—
9 Nivôse II	war widows and children	—
4 Pluviôse II	destitute (protection from pawnbrokers)	—
13 Pluviôse II	those most in need	10 million
21 Pluviôse II	servicemen's families	—
8–13 Ventôse II	Ventôse decrees	—
13 Ventôse II	citizens in dire need	—
22 Floréal II	national welfare scheme	17 million
13 Prairial II	servicemen's families	100 million
22 Messidor II	blind and disabled	—
23 Messidor II	hospital properties	—

Sources: Arch. parl., vols. LII to XCIII; Ph. Sagnac, *La législation civile de la Révolution française (1789–1804): essai d'histoire sociale* (Paris, 1898); C. Bloch, *L'assistance et l'Etat en France à la veille de la Révolution (généralités de Paris, Rouen, Alençon, Orléans, Soissons, Amiens), 1764–1790* (Paris, 1908); L. Petitcolas, *La législation sociale de la Révolution: législation ouvrière et législation d'assistance (1789–1799)* (Paris, 1909).

of kind. La Rochefoucauld-Liancourt, speaking on behalf of the committee on mendicity, had said that 'charity' was no longer an 'arbitrary blessing' but a legislative responsibility and a social obligation to be included in the Rights of Man.[65] Thus, under the republican regime, waifs and strays (*enfants abandonnés*) became national property (*enfants de la patrie*). This was more than a semantic change motivated by the belief in the virtues of regulation. As Jeanbon Saint-André declared in 1793, 'the Republic is the mother of all citizens without distinction: she must give a shelter to the unfortunate who have none'; all 'must hold hands: the poor need to live'.[66] We have seen to what good effect the leitmotiv of the 'large family' could be used as a rallying cry in times of common need, and Paganel and Lakanal exploited it to the full, portraying the *patrie* as a 'common mother' whose 'elder sons', the poor, could not be left to starve. Lequinio reminded his colleagues that the 'fathers' of the *grande famille* were in fact the legislators themselves.[67]

That this was not empty rhetoric was evident during the few crucial months of the 1794 campaign, when poor servicemen's families actually received their allowances and the relief agencies regularly handed out bread rations to the needy. In the course of his mission to the heartland, Roux-Fazillac expressed the view that this was a sphere where the very credibility of the Revolution was at stake: posterity would judge it by the manner in which the laws granting social benefits were strictly applied. And Romme prefaced his resolution on health care for the foundrymen and their families with the statement that it is to 'console or destroy adversity that republican virtues need to be practised with that fidelity, that promptness, that fraternal piety which belong to the reign of equality'.[68] They were using Jacobin discourse to describe the emergence of a new and as yet ill-defined notion: the welfare state. Notwithstanding the enormity of the task and the transitory nature of the millennium, they could not be found wanting.

While welfare was a universal concept from which no deserving

---

[65] C. Bloch, *L'assistance et l'Etat*, pp. 430, 449–50; H. Sée, 'Les conceptions économiques et sociales'; Hufton, *The Poor*, pp. 3–4.

[66] Letters of 20 February and 8 June 1793, *Arch. parl.*, vol. LXVI, p. 164; L. Lévy-Schneider, 'Quelques recherches', *La Révol. fr.* 29 (1895), p. 76.

[67] Speech of 29 November 1792, *Arch. parl.*, vol. LIII, p. 659.

[68] Périgueux, 13 Frimaire, and Gar-dor-Isle (Abzac), 19 Fructidor II: Arch. Nat., AF$_{II}$ 96, Dordogne, pl. 707, p. 28; Arch. dép. Charente, L 68^1, Romme.

person should be excluded, society's 'sacred debt' in the revised Declaration of Rights was in fact highly selective and confined to those in dire need who were incapable of working. This was in keeping with the humanitarian ethos expressed on the eve of Revolution by the participants in the essay contest of Châlons-sur-Marne,[69] and reflected in the ideas put to the Constituent Assembly by Bernard d'Héry and the founders of revolutionary *bienfaisance*, who wished only to guarantee the bare subsistence of their fellow citizens and little beyond that margin of survival.[70] Moreover, it was realised that no single safety net could hope to ensure the same measure of relief overnight for all the needy, and in selecting their priorities the Montagnard Convention naturally came down in favour of the next of kin of those serving in the forces. In the space of eighteen months, the sums decreed on paper in support of soldiers' and sailors' dependants take us from the parsimony of the *ancien régime* to the liberality of modern times, albeit within strictly defined limits and with a clearly defined aim in view: given the widespread resistance to military service and distrust of the army prevalent in French rural society,[71] the welfare policy was understood as a necessary and intrinsic part of the war effort.

Maignet, speaking in November 1792 on behalf of the Comité des secours, specified that benefits should only be made available to dependants who were unable to work and had no means of support other than the volunteer's earnings, for example an invalid father, a disabled wife or a small child, and that relief should be proportional to need and should not exceed what was 'strictly necessary'.[72] However, the military recruitment drives of the spring and summer of 1793 resulted in a relaxation of the conditions of entitlement and a substantial increase in the number of potential beneficiaries and by the middle of Year II the scale of benefits had almost tripled (tables 17–18).

---

[69] J. Spurlock, 'Essays in Reform on the Eve of Revolution: The Public Essay Contests of the Academy of Châlons-sur-Marne', *Studies on Voltaire and the Eighteenth Century* 191 (1980), p. 885.

[70] Pierre Bernard d'Héry represented the Yonne department at the Legislative Assembly, where as a member of the Comité des secours publics he presented his report on the destruction of mendicity on 13 June 1792; he was to be denounced by Maure as a royalist during the Terror: see Woloch, *New Regime*, pp. 244–5.

[71] Forrest, *French Revolution and the Poor*, p. 162.

[72] Report of 26 November 1792, *Arch. parl.*, vol. LIII, pp. 594–5.

Table 17. *Annual allowances for servicemen's families (in livres)*

Beneficiary	26 November 1792	4 May 1793	21 Pluviôse II
Child under 12	25/40[a]	50	100
Spouse	60	100	100
Parent over 60	40/60[b]	100	100
Orphaned child	—	50	100

Notes: [a] 40 livres for a child aged eight or under; 25 livres for a child aged eight to twelve.
[b] 40 livres for a parent aged sixty to seventy; 60 livres for a parent aged over seventy.
Sources: Decrees of 26 November 1792, 4 May 1793, 5 Nivôse and 21 Pluviôse II: *Arch. parl.*, vol. LIII, p. 595; vol. LXIV, pp. 124–6; vol. LXXXIV, pp. 502–7.

Table 18. *Maximum entitlements for deceased servicemen's families*

Beneficiary	4 May 1793	4 June 1793	5 Nivôse– 21 Pluviôse	13 Prairial
War widow	240 l.	1,000 l. pension	1,500 l. plus bonus	1,500 l. plus double bonus
Child under 12	160 l.	—	mother's benefit÷2	mother's pension and benefit÷2
Father/mother	240 l.	—	600 l.	+ 1 year's benefit
Other relative	—	—	150 l.	+ 1 year's benefit

Sources: Decrees of 26 November 1792, 4 May 1793, 5 Nivôse, 21 Pluviôse and 13 Prairial II: *Arch. parl.*, vol. LXIV, pp. 124–6; vol. LXVI, pp. 27–8; vol. LXXXII, p. 299; vol. LXXXIV, pp. 129, 502–7; and vol. XCI, p. 209.

Thus, a soldier's wife with two small children aged seven and twelve was entitled to an annual allowance of 125 livres in November 1792, 200 livres in May 1793 and 300 livres in Pluviôse II, while a venerable war widow saw her entitlements increase five- or six-fold, excluding bonuses and regardless of her husband's rank. The fact that the equality of civic virtue now overshadowed the traditional weight of rank[73] reflects both the rising tide of egalitarian expectations and the determination on the part of the Convention to ensure substantial aid really reached all the soldiers' families without exception. Jeanbon Saint-André and Roger Ducos were instrumental in obtaining these increases following appeals

[73] Woloch, 'Contraction and Expansion of Democratic Space', p. 318.

Table 19. *Additional annual benefits granted by Pinet, Paganel, Roux-Fazillac, Tallien and Lakanal, 7 September 1793–8 Brumaire II*

Beneficiary	Bachelor	Father of two children	Father of three children
Each volunteer from a single family after the first	10 l.	20 l.	30 l.
Parent over 60	extra 50 l.		
All beneficiaries of decree of 4 May	extra 48/60/96 l. according to class		
Orphaned child whose mother is still alive	extra 50/100 l. according to age		
Invalided soldier	full pension		

Sources: Arch. Nat., AF$_{II}$ 169, Western Bureau, pl. 1386, p. 38; Arch. dep. Dordogne, 3 L 24, dist. Bergerac, f° 8; Lot-et-Garonne, L 151 and 447, missions.

from their colleagues in the field that larger sums be granted war widows with young children and families with several sons serving in the ranks (table 19). They spoke to Robespierre who was himself involved in preparing amendments to the legislation.[74] Robespierre was sensitive to the need to simplify the bureaucracy of welfare administration and overcome red tape and the 'coolness' (*froideur*) of local officials. Lakanal felt that 'public notoriety' should suffice as proof of identity when claims were made and Roux-Fazillac was adamant in thinking that nothing should prevent claimants obtaining the benefits to which they were entitled, and however obscure the legislation might appear, 'it should always be interpreted in their favour'.[75]

Refreshing as this admonition may have appeared to an age as yet unaccustomed to state-funded social security, treasury funds were slow in materialising and the only source of ready cash was from the proceeds of the revolutionary taxes. Laplanche in the Cher, Guimberteau in the Indre-et-Loire and Roux-Fazillac in the Dordogne all stated their intention of making advance payments to servicemen's families in this way. Between October 1793 and

[74] Decree of 5 Nivôse II, *Arch. parl.*, vol. LXXXII, p. 299; Mathiez, 'Le carnet de Robespierre', p. 4.
[75] Périgueux, 10 September 1793 and Bergerac, 8 Brumaire II, Arch. dép. Dordogne, 4 L 45, dist. Excideuil, f° 8; and 3 L 24, dist. Bergerac, ff. 65, 102.

Thermidor II, some 65,000 livres were paid out in allowances to families in the Corrèze, 185,000 to those in the Dordogne and 24,000 to those of the district of Montauban in the Lot.[76] During those few crucial months that led up to the victories of the French forces, money was therefore available and benefits were received, and as Jean-Paul Bertaud has shown, this fact had a tangible impact on the valour of the combatants on the battlefield.[77]

In raising the first progressive tax on the wealthy citizens of Castres, Bo and Chabot had stipulated that the contributions were primarily destined for servicemen's families and only 'what was left over' for the relief of the 'indigent class'. Romme took the district of Angoulême to task for intercepting a shipment of grain on its way to the foundries and diverting it to the local poorhouse.[78] No deviation from this order of priorities, which might have compromised the war effort, was ever entertained. It is hardly surprising, therefore, that a six-month delay occurred between the landmark law providing cash payments for outdoor relief (28 June 1793) and the decision to earmark nationwide credits for that purpose (13 Pluviôse). As Roux-Fazillac remarked, 'it's much easier to make a good decree than to get it executed'.[79] Turning his back on the slow legislative process, he began work in the Charente. Then, determined to rid his home department, the Dordogne, of chronic poverty once and for all, and confident that revolutionary taxes would yield more than enough for his purpose, Roux together with Lakanal organised an ambitious crash welfare programme, the main thrust of which favoured not the *hôpitaux*, where the urban destitute were traditionally confined, but outdoor relief schemes

---

[76] Arch. Nat., AF$_{II}$ 95, Corrèze, pl. 694, pp. 5, 26; 116, Lot, pl. 877, p. 25; Arch. dép. Dordogne, 1 L 228, Roux-Fazillac; 3 L 24, dist. Bergerac, f° 117; 8 L 131, poor relief; Tarn-et-Garonne, L 75*, representatives, f° 9; Labroue, *La mission de Lakanal*, p. 328. See also G. Thuillier, 'Les secours aux parents des défenseurs de la patrie (1792–1796): orientation de recherche', in *Actes du 113e Congrès national des sociétés savantes, Strasbourg, 1988: Colloque sur la sécurité sociale* (Paris, 1989), pp. 459–89.

[77] J.-P. Bertaud, *La Révolution armée: les soldats-citoyens et la Révolution française* (Paris, 1979); see also A. Mathiez, *La victoire de l'an II* (Paris, 1918), p. 203, and A. Forrest, *Conscripts and Deserters: The Army and French Society During the Revolution and Empire* (Oxford, 1989), pp. 31–4.

[78] Castres, 26 March 1793 and Tonneins, 7 Messidor II: Arch. dép. Tarn, L 135, missions, p. 1; Charente, L 67, Romme.

[79] Périgueux, 19 Frimaire II, Aulard, *Recueil*, vol. IX, p. 291–4; Woloch, *New Regime*, pp. 248–9.

geared to the needs of the rural poor. They replaced the *dépôts de mendicité*, which Bernard d'Héry had considered disorderly and lethal, with the newly decreed *agences de secours*, on the basis of one such home relief agency per *canton*, and organised charity workshops and local distributions of food and clothing.[80] An initial cash injection of 225,000 livres was followed by further levies, as Roux and Lakanal obstinately refused to channel any funds from their taxes to the treasury in Paris, which they claimed would have amounted to a 'betrayal' of the poor.[81]

Roux-Fazillac's and Lakanal's example was emulated by Romme, who followed in their wake and organised the 'bread of equality' rationing scheme as the winter receded and resources became scarce; by Paganel, in the Aveyron and the Tarn, whose 'family grain-store' programme aimed to supply 50 pounds of flour per head every month and thus give 'confidence to the indigent by giving him a joint share in the food of the rich', while branches from trees felled for the arsenals were converted into logs and faggots for free distribution to the needy.[82] Monestier de la Lozère, in the Lot-et-Garonne, ensured free rations of flour were distributed among the poor not only to the infirm, the elderly and children too small to work, but also to the able-bodied poor 'in sufficient quantity to enable them to procure work'.[83] Vernerey's tax on the rich of the Creuse, levied in Pluviôse at a time when such taxes had become 'illegal', was motivated by the necessity to subsidise the cost of bread for the poor who otherwise would have had to pay for their loaf of bread 10 sols a pound. When summoned to transfer the funds raised to the treasury, he did so only after having subtracted the amount required for further welfare distributions.[84]

---

[80] Thus, in this part of France at least, for a short while, the decrees of 19 March and 28 June 1793 did not remain 'dead letters' until their annulment in Frimaire Year V: Forrest, *French Revolution and the Poor*, p. 82; see also Woloch, *New Regime*, pp. 246–7.

[81] Angoulême, 18 September and 12 October 1793, Arch. dép. Charente, L 1962, missions, and L 1239, dist. Confolens; Périgueux and Bergerac, Frimaire–Nivôse II: Arch. Nat., AF$_{II}$ 96, Dordogne; Arch. dép. Dordogne, 1 L 228, Roux-Fazillac, and 3 L 24, dist. Bergerac, Arch. mun. Périgueux, D/2 and D/4; Labroue, *La mission de Lakanal*, pp. 321–5.

[82] Rodez, 1 and 12 Ventôse II, Arch. dép. Aveyron, 1 L 183, Paganel, and 2 L 18, dist. Aubin.

[83] Marmande, 1 Ventôse II, Arch. Nat., AF$_{II}$ 117, Lot-et-Garonne, pl. 885, p. 14; Arch. dép. Lot-et-Garonne, L 148, Monestier (de la Lozère).

[84] Guéret, 24 Pluviôse, and Aubusson and Evaux, 2 Germinal II: Arch. Nat., AF$_{II}$ 95, Creuse, pl. 703, pp. 32–3, 51–2; Arch. dép. Creuse, L 105, Vernerey.

In contrast to energetic local assistance of this kind, the comprehensive relief law introduced by Barère in response to rising aspirations, with the title *Livre de la Bienfaisance Nationale*,[85] was a grand centralised scheme which the Convention intended to implement immediately. Limited in the first instance to the 'forgotten' country poor and only to those who through old age, widowhood, infirmity or pregnancy were deprived of income and prevented from working, the number of beneficiaries on paper was restricted to 400 for each department where the rural population exceeded 100,000 souls.[86] While in the poorer districts all over France (Creuse, Aveyron, Mayenne, Orne, Hérault, Pas-de-Calais) the application forms were promptly filled in and dispatched together with subsidiary lists of deserving claimants falling outside the regulation quota, elsewhere, as in the districts of Brive (Corrèze) and Gaillac (Tarn), the hundreds of blank forms received were never completed and remain in the archives as a silent testimony to the indifference or scepticism of the local officials.[87] Nevertheless, as Woloch has demonstrated, funds were soon flowing and the pensions on the *Grand Livre* began to reach the most deserving recipients.[88]

While the true benefit of welfare lies both in its active implementation and in its continuity, dynamic and imaginative altruism of the kind practised by the deputies-on-mission tended to peter out after their departure from the scene. Even if their pledges to eradicate the scourge of chronic poverty tend to have a hollow ring, one would have expected the cash handouts and subsidised bread rations to have lingered on in the collective memory of the rural population. But barely a month after the fall of Robespierre, notwithstanding the valiant efforts of Roux-Fazillac, Lakanal and Romme, the Thermidorian Pellissier was reporting the 'distressing inexecution' of poor relief legislation in the Dordogne, a department which 'appeared to have been forgotten until now'! Happily, at Boussac in the Creuse, Cledel reported in contrast that well-to-do citizens were in the habit of providing bread for the poor at

[85] Forrest, *French Revolution and the Poor*, pp. 82–3.
[86] 'Livre de la bienfaisance nationale', 22 Floréal II, *Arch. parl.*, vol. XC, pp. 250–6.
[87] Arch. dép. Creuse, L 297, dist. Aubusson, 1 Brumaire III; Aveyron, 1 L 1948, poor relief, 5–12 Messidor II, and 10 L 121, dist. Villefranche, 22 Floréal II; Corrèze, L 321, dist. Brive; and Tarn, L 918, dist. Gaillac, 22 Floréal II.
[88] Woloch, *New Regime*, p. 252.

'below cost-price', which seems to suggest that Vernerey's brand of *bienfaisance* had borne fruit, for a while at least.[89]

SHARES IN KIND, SYMBOLIC EXTRAS AND HEALTH CARE

Fifty-pound rations of flour, bundles of logs and faggots, small allotments payable in relief benefit vouchers, roof tiles from the seigneurial manor and worn clothes and bed-linen from bourgeois households made up a steady if unequal flow of material assistance channelled through the *agences de secours*. Such objects, on account of their very basic character (*de première nécessité*), lend to the process of equal distribution a singular graphic relevance. Staple food, a vegetable garden, shelter, heating and clothing are things that no one should be without. It was thus decreed that goods and chattels such as articles of clothing and kitchen utensils deposited at the municipal pawnbroker's with a value of less than 20 livres could henceforward be retrieved without redemption.[90] Churches were stripped not only of silver chalices but also of ecclesiastical vestments. 'Throughout the history of the catholic church', Brival explained to the Limousins, 'whatever it made use of belonged to the poor.' While most of the woollen garments and linen were sent to the army, Vernerey gave instructions that the silk robes taken from the churches of the Creuse should be stripped of their gold braid and then distributed to the poor young women and girls of each commune renowned for their civic virtues.[91]

Here we move imperceptibly from the realm of strict equality and fair shares (a loaf of bread or a blanket) toward that of equality of opportunity. Poor young women and chaste young girls dressed in white were given an important part to play in the republican ceremonies of the Jacobin period. The fine fabrics from the sacristies that Vernerey offered them have a symbolic value that transcends their material worth and points not just to moral and spiritual purification, but to social promotion. Thus *silk* (rather

[89] 12 and 16 Fructidor, and 11 Vendémiaire II, Aulard, *Recueil*, vol. XVI, pp. 405, 655; vol. XVII, p. 189; and vol. XX, pp. 309, 600.
[90] 4 Pluviôse II, *Arch. parl.*, vol. LXXXIII, p. 580; on the *monts-de-piété*, Woloch, *New Regime*, pp. 285–9.
[91] Tulle, 13 Nivôse and Aubusson, 6 Ventôse II: Arch. Nat., AF$_{II}$ 95, Creuse, pl. 703, p. 39; and 171, Western Bureau, pl. 1403, pp. 12–13 and 1404, p. 3; Wallon, *Les représentants du peuple*, vol. II, p. 156.

than wool or flax) placed in the hands of a penniless waif lifts her from the gutter and the rags to which she is accustomed and gives her the illusion of riches, attenuates the class barrier and opens up the prospect of bourgeoisification.

Social mobility made accessible to the disinherited is a central theme of Jacobin thinking, to be found in most of the articles of the 1793 Declaration of Rights, a text which affirms men's equality before the law, the search for the common good, but also the need for social advancement. While the requirement to eat a bread of equality entailed for the urban rich a process of downward levelling, the distribution of precious fabrics, dowries and marriage trousseaux to the rural poor tended in the other direction, upward, and within reach of a *petit-bourgeois* status. Clearly, such a transition was long-term and assistance to that end was limited to the lucky few. Dowries, linen and utensils represented an important commodity bundle a girl could contribute to her new household economy. A celebrated passage in Montesquieu's *De l'esprit des lois*, reproduced word for word by the chevalier de Jaucourt in his article on natural equality in the *Encyclopédie*, describes how the dowry was used in ancient Greece as a means of redistributing wealth from the rich man to the poor man's daughter.[92] Although Montesquieu expressed doubts as to the feasibility of such a scheme and Jaucourt felt it would be 'madness' to want to introduce the practice in a modern republic, both Laplanche in Berry and Lagasquié in Rouergue, among others, were attracted by the symbolic relevance of such a transfer within the context of revolutionary taxation.

As Laplanche bestowed his civic blessing on the chosen young Berrichon maiden who had promised to give birth to many 'little republicans', or as the betrothed couple in the 'Triumph of the Poor' in the Aveyron village received their trousseau and 600 livres dowry 'at the expense of the rich', or as the provincial club of Carcassonne settled dowries on a handful of 'politically suitable young people',[93] there may have been an awareness among the

---

[92] From a passage in Aristotle's *Politics*, book II, chapter 7: Montesquieu, *De l'esprit des lois*, book V, chapter 6, vol. I, p. 53; L. de Jaucourt, 'Egalité naturelle', in *Textes choisis de l'Encyclopédie*, ed. by A. Soboul (Paris, 1962), p. 87.

[93] Bourges, 30 September 1793, Aulard, *Recueil*, vol. VII, p. 144; and Rodez, 23 Brumaire II, in Caron, 'La Commission civile révolutionnaire', pp. 345–8; C. Petit, 'Le triomphe du pauvre: les pauvres contre les riches à l'époque

onlookers that 'poor relief', with all its derogatory connotations, need not be degrading or niggardly, but can at times be uplifting, confer 'well-being' rather than 'welfare' and in association with the honours of a civic award, operate an improvement not just in terms of material wherewithal, but in the quality of life itself.

While Dupont de Nemours and Brissot tended to attribute to the individual the responsibility though not the fault for his or her physical or material distress,[94] Romme and Roux-Fazillac, as we have seen, favoured collective responsibility for workers who fell ill or suffered industrial injuries. Jacobin interventionism generated a very gradual shift from the notion of private misfortune, and consequent home care bestowed by the next of kin, to the ultimate prospect of a national health service providing hospital beds and therapeutic skills to the community. Medical history and social security prior to the development of the welfare state have become an important and growing area of historical research in recent years,[95] and I shall therefore confine myself here to indicating a few areas where Jacobin policy reflected emerging concepts of collective sanitary care.

According to the conventional wisdom, the sick, the disabled and the aged were best cared for in the bosom of the family, and the Revolution did not question this tradition. Thus, the Comité de Mendicité of the Constituent Assembly recommended *assistance à domicile* as a general rule of thumb, and the Convention, in both its Girondin and Montagnard components, continued to advocate it. Nevertheless, the decree of 28 June 1793, while extolling the virtues of family care, planned to appoint peripatetic medical officers and

révolutionnaire à travers une fête rouergate', *Annales du Midi* 90 (1978), pp. 141–54; Higonnet, ' "Harmonization of the Spheres" ', p. 123.

[94] P. S. Dupont de Nemours, *Idées sur les secours à donner aux pauvres malades dans une grande ville* (Philadelphia and Paris, 1786), pp. 10–11; J.-P. Brissot de Warville, *Théorie des lois criminelles*, 2 vols. (Paris, 1781), vol. I, p. 261; Bloch, *L'assistance et l'Etat en France*, pp. 436–40; Foucault, *Histoire de la folie à l'âge classique*, 2nd edn, p. 432.

[95] C. Jones, *Charity and Bienfaisance: The Treatment of the Poor in the Montpellier Region, 1740–1815* (Cambridge, 1982); C. Jones, *The Charitable Imperative: Hospitals and Nursing in the Ancien Régime and Revolutionary France* (London, 1989); J. Barry and C. Jones, *Medicine and Charity Before the Welfare State* (London and New York, 1991); D. Weiner, *The Citizen-Patient in Revolutionary and Imperial Paris* (Baltimore, 1993); and J. Valette (ed.), proceedings of the 'Colloque sur l'histoire de la sécurité sociale', published yearly in *Actes du Congrès national des sociétés savantes.*

district nurses to visit the sickly poor in their homes, midwives to supply their services free of charge to large families and local apothecaries to administer essential drugs and carry out smallpox inoculations on children.

One of the effects of dechristianisation was the forced secularisation of all nursing staff. Thus, nuns such as the *sœurs grises* employed in the poorhouses and *dépôts de mendicité* were dismissed and replaced by civilian nurses, preferentially mothers accustomed to child care. Roux-Fazillac established lay committees in the Charente to supervise outdoor relief composed exclusively of female citizens with children of their own, whose experience of motherhood, that most republican of virtues, would tangibly supersede the sterility of religious life and enhance the quality of sanitary care. Paganel blamed the 'harsh and tyrannical' attitudes of sisters for all the deficiencies of the institutions inherited from the *ancien régime*.[96] Old maids gave way to nursing mothers busily breastfeeding their children in keeping with the teachings of Rousseau: this, to Lakanal, amounted to 'an institutional revolution', while Roux-Fazillac allocated priority poor relief to those mothers of Tulle who voluntarily breast-fed their offspring.[97] Incentives were likewise given to wet-nurses, especially 'those of a robust complexion', to offer their services to the *enfants de la patrie* and thus contribute to the 'propagation of humankind'.[98]

The Jacobin vision of a centralised hospital service closely tied to the prosperity of the state was a far cry from reality. The secularised public hospitals were given an extended mandate in the field of therapy and convalescent care which they were mostly ill equipped to fulfil. The *hôpital général*, the institution established by Vincent de Paul with the aim of eradicating or hiding from view the more offensive manifestations of begging and destitution,[99] was still confined to its penitentiary role as an asylum for paupers, prostitutes, invalids and madmen. All cities of more than 5,000 inhabi-

---

[96] Roux-Fazillac, Angoulême, 18 September 1793 and 8 Brumaire II; Périgueux, 13 Brumaire II: Arch. dép. Charente, L 500*, missions, L 1239, dist. Confolens, and L 1962, missions; Arch. Nat., AF$_{II}$ 170, Western Bureau, pl. 1394, p. 44; Aulard, *Recueil*, vol. VIII, p. 210; Paganel, *Essai historique*, vol. II, pp. 46–52.

[97] Lakanal, Report of 29 Fructidor II, Bibl. Nat., 8° Le^{38} 945; Roux-Fazillac, Tulle, 25 Messidor II, Arch. Nat., AF$_{II}$ 95, Corrèze, pl. 696, p. 13.

[98] Arch. dép. Dordogne, 8 L 145, dist. Périgueux, welfare; see Forrest, *French Revolution and the Poor*, pp. 129–32.

[99] Hufton, *The Poor*, pp. 139–59; Woloch, *New Regime*, pp. 239–40.

tants had such a foundation by 1750 and their cramped and insalubrious conditions continued to provoke dismay among philanthropists during the Revolution. The proposed new institutions, such as the *maisons de secours* for wounded servicemen, the *maisons d'accouchement* or maternity homes, the *hospices* for old people and unmarried mothers or the *maisons de santé* for treating venereal diseases, were deprived of any funding and never saw the light of day. The deputies' efforts were therefore mainly concentrated on improving the existing poorhouses and military hospitals, such as those of Limoges, Poitiers (specialising in the treatment of scabies) and Bergerac, an important transit point for military personnel, by augmenting the facilities, increasing the number of beds and providing bedding and blankets. Down-filled mattresses and covers were confiscated from church seminaries and émigré households for use by the *hôpital général* or the *hôtel-dieu*.[100]

Dechristianisation served the hospitals well all over France as abbeys and monasteries were added to existing facilities. Limoges was not alone in being offered the prospect of a 'new Jerusalem at a bargain price'.[101] In Bergerac, the convent of the Ladies of the Faith was given over to use as a military annexe, while the principal hospital in Périgueux was transferred lock, stock and barrel to new and more spacious and hygienic premises in the former religious community of Sainte-Claire. Jeanbon Saint-André, Elie Lacoste and Roux-Fazillac supervised the conversion of the former monastic buildings into wards and extended the sizeable orchard and vegetable plots by adding a botanical garden for raising medicinal herbs. While patients were expected to contribute 13 sols per month for a hospital bed, sums of money from the revolutionary taxes were provided for essential refurbishment and maintenance work and these varied from 50,000 livres in the case of the *hôpital général* at Bourges to 10,000 livres for the district poorhouses of the Dordogne and 1,000 livres for converting a vicarage into a cottage-hospital at Eymet near Bergerac. At Sainte-Claire in Périgueux, rules of hygiene were strictly enforced, patients barred from

---

[100] Laplanche in Bourges, 6 October 1793, Arch. Nat., AF$_{II}$ 169, Western Bureau, pl. 1389, pp. 13–19; Wallon, *Les représentants du peuple*, vol. II, p. 116; Brival and Lanot, Tulle, 27 Vendémiaire II; Arch. Nat., AF$_{II}$ 95, Corrèze, pl. 694, p. 12; Brival and Ingrand, Poitiers, 24 Ventôse II, Arch. Nat., AF$_{II}$ 176, Western Bureau, pl. 1448, pp. 25–36; Aulard, *Recueil*, vol. XI, p. 703; Forrest, *French Revolution and the Poor*, p. 67.

[101] Forrest, *French Revolution and the Poor*, p. 49.

sleeping more than one to a bed and the more sturdy encouraged to take some exercise in the gardens and help with the weeding.[102]

Although these measures are far removed from modern concepts of a hospital service with high standards of medical care and nursing and a high turnover of patients, there is a perceptible shift in attitudes away from the concept of hopeless long-term internment toward better sanitation and more effective cures. The Montagnards clearly made a conscientious effort to transform the image of the overcrowded asylum into that of a hygienic institution where healing might become the rule. As Thérésia Cabarrus (Madame Tallien) put it to the citizens of Bordeaux in a widely disseminated speech, it was their common wish that hospitals should cease to be 'horrible tombs' and become instead 'temples dedicated to humanity'.[103] Pupils of both sexes in the primary schools established by Lakanal and Roux-Fazillac were expected to pay regular visits to the refurbished poorhouses in order to console their unfortunate inmates but also to learn the basic rules of sanitation.

While the *dépôts de mendicité* were frequently used as prisons to house prisoners of war and deserters, so too many former monastic buildings were turned into detention centres where ordinary suspects were held under the Terror in conditions conducive to ill health. Significantly, measures were taken to ensure tolerable conditions of internment for the sick, frail and infirm, and special treatment given to pregnant women and nursing mothers. A number of deputies, including Brival, Paganel, Vernerey, Monestier de la Lozère and Chaudron-Rousseau, were in favour of releasing the sick and sending them home for proper care, if necessary under house arrest or supervision by the local authorities. Others were more wary, fearing that suspects were likely to sham illness or disability in order to obtain their freedom. Thus, Roux-Fazillac established infirmaries within the precincts of the Corrèze gaols and organised regular visits by medical officers whose services were chargeable to the detainees, although Romme ensured that poor relief was made available to the needy prisoners of the Charente

[102] J.-P. Gross, 'La protection sociale en l'an II', in Valette (ed.), *Actes du 114e Congrès national des sociétés savantes, Paris, 1989: Colloque sur l'histoire de la sécurité sociale*, ed. by J. Valette (Paris, 1990), pp. 168–9.

[103] T. Cabarrus-Fontenay, Bordeaux, 25 Germinal, and Monestier de la Lozère, Agen, 2 Floréal II: Arch. dép. Lot-et-Garonne, L 148, missions; see Barry and Jones, *Medicine and Charity*.

and Dordogne, especially the aged and infirm who required treatment.[104]

The provision of medical assistance and welfare benefits within prison walls adds an unexpected humanitarian dimension to the otherwise callous treatment of victims of the Terror. By recognising the suspects' need for medical care the government's representatives were paradoxically showing compassion toward those who had been thrown into gaol without due process of law under the terrorist legislation, and thereby attenuating their exclusion by treating them 'fairly' despite the hardship they were forced to endure. Humanitarian concerns transcended judicial rigour and egalitarianism dictated that none should be denied the right to physical well-being, irrespective of their political affiliation. In an age prior to the advent of social protection and a public health service, and at a time when the rights of man were often openly flouted, the affirmation of the right to health care implied recognition of the ethical need to give every human life an equal value.

[104] Paganel, *Essai historique*, vol. II, pp. 46–52; Arch. dép. Lot-et-Garonne, L 151, missions, p. 11; Brival, Tulle, 5 and 28 Nivôse and Poitiers, 23 Pluviôse II: Arch. Nat., AF$_{II}$ 175^{B}, Western Bureau, pl. 1438, p. 34; Corrèze, L 105, detainees; Roux-Fazillac, Tulle, 21 Pluviôse and 21 Germinal; Romme, Périgueux, 20 Floréal II: Arch. Nat., AF$_{II}$ 95, Corrèze, pl. 696, p. 12; Arch. dép. Charente, L 68^{1}, Romme, and L 1962, missions.

7. A place at school and a time for rejoicing

Lycurgus claimed that children belonged not individually to their fathers, but to the state.

Lycurgus established meals at which all the citizens ate together a common fare ordained by law ... The most exquisite of all their dishes was the one they called the *black broth*.

André Dacier, 'Lycurgue', in Plutarch's *Lives*, 1721[1]

Learning was a basic requirement common to all men. The 'bread of reason', as Danton called it, was a vital commodity to be distributed to every child in the family, and which the Montagnards in their Declaration of Rights vowed to 'put within the reach of all citizens'. It was, in the words of Condorcet, a collective debt which 'society owes equally to all its members'.[2] Understood as a fundamental human and social right, it followed that its provision should be made by the state free of charge: 'Equal rights would have been consecrated in vain', wrote Roux-Fazillac, 'if all the citizens without distinction were not able to acquire the same knowledge.' But it was also understood to be an individual obligation and hence compulsory in nature: Lakanal ruled that those deprived families who did not bother to send their children to school would not be entitled to welfare payments.[3]

Isser Woloch has recently described how in 1793 the idea of

---

[1] *Les vies des hommes illustres de Plutarque*, trans. by A. Dacier, 3rd edn, 10 vols. (Amsterdam, 1735), vol. I, pp. 224, 230–4, 241.

[2] Danton's speech of 7 Frimaire II, in *Œuvres*, p. 229; article 23 of Condorcet's draft declaration, *Les Déclarations*, ed. by Jaume, p. 242; Badinter and Badinter, *Condorcet*, pp. 445–50.

[3] Lakanal, Bergerac, 3 Brumaire, and Roux-Fazillac, Périgueux, 19 Frimaire II: Arch. Nat., AF$_{II}$ 171, Western Bureau, pl. 1400, p. 28; Arch. dép. Dordogne, 1 L

universal public education came to be catapulted to a central position in republican ideology,[4] and I shall therefore confine myself here to a brief account of some of the fascinating pioneering experiments carried out during the Jacobin period. Although meticulously prepared, most of these proved to be of short duration; they were limited to a few provincial cities, to the exclusion of the rural areas; and obviously their originality can only properly be assessed in the broader context of what came before and after, the church-run elementary schools (*petites écoles*) already on offer under the monarchy, the mixed schooling promoted as from 1795, which marked a retreat from the principle of universal and free primary education, the Guizot law of 1833 and the ultimate establishment throughout France of the modern *école communale* (the rural version of which has now become a fragile and endangered species).

The Comité d'instruction publique, under the distinguished leadership of Condorcet, Sieyès and Grégoire, had been charged by the Legislative Assembly and the Convention to elaborate a detailed plan for the organisation of a national education system. Among those with a philosophical bent whom it harnessed to this task were Romme, who had joined the committee at its inception in October 1791, Roux-Fazillac and Lequinio who became members in October 1792, Lakanal who was co-opted in February 1793 and Jeanbon Saint-André in July of that year.

While a subject such as education inevitably gave rise to many divergent views, most were in favour of establishing primary schools where the first notions of grammar, arithmetic and civics would be taught. In this they did not differ fundamentally from Adam Smith who considered that 'for a very small expense, the public can facilitate, can encourage and can even impose upon almost the whole body of the people the necessity of acquiring those most essential parts of education', namely the ability 'to read, write and account'.[5] Controversy centred on the degree of public involvement and whether the schools should be state-funded and state-run. Grégoire did 'not want to force anybody', Danton's

---

232, missions, and 3 L 24, dist. Bergerac, f° 97; Aulard, *Recueil*, vol. IX, p. 291 and second *Supplément*, p. 148; Labroue, *La mission de Lakanal*, pp. 219–22, 230.

[4] Woloch, *New Regime*, pp. 177–81.

[5] Smith, *Wealth of Nations*, vol. II, book V, part 3, article II (section v. i. f.), pp. 758–88.

preferences fluctuated between the private and the public sector, and Romme tended to favour an optional scheme with free schools allowed to compete with state schools. Egalitarians like Saint-André felt strongly that schooling should be compulsory so that all republican children would follow exactly the same syllabus according to a 'uniform mode'.[6] Only by such contact on the school bench could equality and fraternity develop among the young of differing social backgrounds and the spartan ideal of devotion to and identification with one's country become a reality: 'I too am a father', Danton declared, 'but my son does not belong to me, he belongs to the republic'; and in defending the country's right to raise its children, Robespierre was to warn against the pride and prejudices of families and the dangers of what he ominously called 'domestic federalism'.[7] In fact, the debate took a dramatic turn at the very moment Girondins and Montagnards were locked in the terminal stages of their deadly conflict, with the newly formed Committee of Public Safety intervening on 30 May 1793 and effectively usurping the prerogatives of the education committee by decreeing that the prompt organisation of the primary schools was a matter of 'national salvation', a term Roux-Fazillac was henceforward to use whenever referring in public to education.[8]

With the disappearance of the Gironde as a political force, a tacit consensus emerged from the brainstorming process, exemplified by the affinities of the draft education bills now put before the assembly. Even though the legislation had not by any means run its full course, the main features of Lakanal's draft plan put forward on behalf of the education committee on 26 June bear a striking resemblance to the guidelines decreed on 30 May and the Lepeletier *Plan d'éducation nationale* presented to the Convention by Robespierre on 13 and 29 July. The broadly agreed provisions included the establishment of free primary schools nationwide on the basis of one school in every community of between 600 and

---

[6] Saint-André, 3 October 1792, in L. Lévy-Schneider, 'Quelques recherches', *La Révol. fr.* 29 (1895), p. 65; cf. Romme, project of 20 December 1792, in *Procès-verbaux du Comité d'instruction*, vol. I, pp. xxv–vi, and vol. II, pp. xxv, xlv, lxxx, pp. 679–88, 718–21; Galante Garrone, *Gilbert Romme*, pp. 278, 294; Woloch, *New Regime*, p. 179.

[7] Woloch, *New Regime*, p. 179; Hunt, 'Male Virtue and Republican Motherhood', p. 200.

[8] Decree of 30 May 1793, *Arch. parl.*, vol. LXXV, *Convention*, p. 313; Roux-Fazillac, Angoulême, 24 September 1793, in Aulard, *Recueil*, second *Supplément*, p. 148.

1,000 souls (the population of a large commune, canton or urban *section*), in which all children 'without distinction and without exception' would be brought up together at the taxpayers' expense, boys from the ages of five to twelve and girls from the ages of five to eleven, in separate classrooms for each sex, with the school-teachers, both male and female, receiving the same salary throughout the Republic.[9]

Although Lakanal's plan for free and compulsory elementary education has been dubbed the *plan de la Plaine* as opposed to the genuine *plan de la Montagne* of Lepeletier or the Bouquier version railroaded through the Convention a few months later,[10] in fact Lakanal was one of the members of the six-man commission proposed by Robespierre, including Robespierre himself, which thrashed out most of the outstanding contentious issues. While Grégoire and Coupé de l'Oise dissented, the majority of the commission, enlarged on 15 September to include Saint-Just, Rühl, Saint-André, Laignelot, Bo and Romme, voiced their agreement. So by this date there existed a clear-cut Montagnard or Robes-pierrist community of thinking on elementary education. This is of significance because Lakanal and Roux-Fazillac, working in close association, were the first to put the newly forged scheme to the test in the provinces, before it even reached the statute book, with the Dordogne and Corrèze departments being chosen as the principal pedagogical field laboratories.

THE EDUCATIONAL FIELD TRIALS OF BERGERAC, PÉRIGUEUX AND TULLE

Leaving Romme in Paris to put the finishing touches to the primary-school bill, Lakanal and Roux-Fazillac made their way southward in order to 'prepare through education the happiness of the advancing generations'. Lakanal surprised the revolutionary

[9] Decree of 30 May 1793, *Arch. parl.*, vol. LXXV, p. 313; Lakanal's Plan of 26 June 1793 in *Procès-verbaux du Comité d'instruction*, vol. I, pp. xlvii–ix, liii; 'Plan de Michel Lepeletier', in *Œuvres de Maximilien Robespierre*, vol. X, pp. 10–42; *Une éducation pour la démocratie: textes et projets de l'époque révolutionnaire*, ed. by B. Baczko (Paris, 1982); Woloch, *New Regime*, p. 178.

[10] Even the so-called 'reactionary' plan of Daunou in Brumaire IV contains many 'Robespierrist' elements: M. Gontard, *L'enseignement primaire en France de la Révolution à la loi Guizot (1789–1833): des petites écoles de la monarchie d'ancien régime aux écoles primaires de la monarchie bourgeoise* (Paris, 1959), pp. 104–6, 151; Woloch, *New Regime*, pp. 180–3, 193.

committee and *société populaire* of Bergerac on his arrival by declaring that learning being a universal need, the wealthier citizens of the city were required to pay a progressive tax to finance the establishment of four primary schools, each comprising sections for boys and girls. This was in keeping with Lepeletier's recommendation that a common fund be set up to which 'the poor would pay very little, the rich nearly everything', in effect a minimum of 30 sols for a contributor at the bottom of the tax ladder and a maximum of 100 livres per 1,000 livres of income for the well-to-do taxpayer: 'but once the fund has been formed, it is then divided equally between all, with everyone deriving the same advantage, namely the education of their children'.[11]

Although the choice of four schools for each of the *sections* of Bergerac cannot be considered a startling innovation, since they corresponded to the four *régences* already established in the city under the *ancien régime*,[12] the spirit of the enterprise was undoubtedly secular and modern. The teaching staff were chosen among the members of the *société*, in three cases man-and-wife teams assisted by their own children.[13] Lakanal's claim that the vocation of *instituteur* was 'sublime' and that he himself planned to fill such a post once his job as a deputy was done may well have served as an incentive, together with the promise of a salary of 1,200 livres per annum each for both male and female teachers. To offer this kind of annual salary to a humble elementary schoolteacher was a novelty (which was later to wear off under the impact of inflation).[14] Indeed, within a month to the day of his resolution being published, four émigré houses had been converted to classrooms, school benches delivered, partitions erected to divide the boys from the girls, the progressive tax had been levied and the teachers were

---

[11] 'Plan de Michel Lepeletier', *Œuvres de Robespierre*, vol. X, p. 26; Lakanal, resolutions of 21–4 October 1793, Arch. dép. Dordogne, 3 L 24, dist. Bergerac, ff. 91, 95, 97; Labroue, *La mission de Lakanal*, p. 219; Woloch, *New Regime*, pp. 178–9.

[12] B. Butel and G. Mandon, 'Alphabétisation et scolarisation en Aquitaine au XVIIIe siècle et au début du XIXe siècle', in Fr. Furet et J. Ozouf (eds.), *Lire et écrire: l'alphabétisation des Français de Calvin à Jules Ferry* (Paris, 1977), p. 12.

[13] For the Egalité *section*, Niolle and his wife aided by her daughter; for the Droits de l'homme *section*, Bourson and his wife aided by their two children; for the République *section*, Granger and citizeness Poussou-Dupeyron aided by her daughter Annette; and for the Union *section*, Pouvereau and his wife with the latter's sister.

[14] Woloch, *New Regime*, pp. 182, 190.

receiving their first month's pay, and the *représentant* adorned with
his tricolour sash and accompanied by the constituted authorities
set forth on a tour of the city to inspect the classes with due pomp
and ceremony. And the treasurer's records show that the initial
fund was substantial enough to allow regular monthly payments to
be made to the teachers at least until Germinal, after which further
levies became necessary.[15]

Roux-Fazillac took the long road from Angoulême to Périgueux
via Bergerac in order to compare notes with Lakanal, and on his
arrival in the *chef-lieu* of the Dordogne issued a proclamation
announcing that a new milestone of the Revolution had been
reached and that 'insurrection', necessary to recover freedom,
would henceforth be superseded by 'instruction', necessary to
preserve it. Of the five primary schools established in Périgueux,
two were housed in émigré homes and three in former monastic
buildings. The teachers were appointed by the *représentant* in
person among citizens recommended by the Jacobin club.[16] Salaries
were fixed at 1,200 livres for the schoolmasters and 1,000 livres for
the mistresses, the first quarter being paid in advance together with
a bonus of ten days' pay to cover installation costs. By early
Nivôse, the classes were operational and the teachers having to
cope with a 'full house'.[17]

Roux-Fazillac's transfer to the Corrèze in early Pluviôse resulted
in similar action being taken in Tulle 'for the public good', with
four schools being organised in émigré houses, the large number of
children in the city justifying the appointment of two teachers per
classroom in each of the boys' and girls' sections.[18] Teaching had
begun in earnest by the end of Germinal in all the establishments
and by Thermidor the number of girls receiving primary schooling

[15] Arch. dép. Dordogne, 1 L 378, constituted authorities, f° 264 and 3 L 56, revolutionary taxes, ff. 407–13; Arch. mun. Bergerac, M 1, mun. delib., 7–10 Pluviôse II; Labroue, *La mission de Lakanal*, p. 225.

[16] Brunet and his wife, Charles Foulhioux and his wife, Espic and citizeness Tonaux, Antoine Bardon and his elder daughter, and Warconsin aided by the daughter of Lemoine.

[17] Périgueux, 16–20 Frimaire II, Arch. Nat., AF$_{II}$ 171, Western Bureau, pl. 1400, pp. 14, 28 and pl. 1403, p. 16; Arch. mun. Périgueux, D/3, mun. register, vol. I, at 22 Frimaire II, and D/4, vol. II, f° 116; Labroue, *La mission de Lakanal*, p. 227.

[18] The schoolmasters appointed were Baron and Borie for the Unité *section*, Marin and Laval for the Sans-Culottes *section*, Gendre and Besle for the Montagne *section*, Dulignan and Sarget for the Centre *section*. The mistresses likewise numbered eight: Chavain and Tramont, Rigault and Jarrige, Vidalin and Pamphille, Roussel and Rossignol.

Table 20. *Girls aged six to eighteen attending primary school in Tulle, Year II*

Month	Section Centre	Section Montagne	Section Sans-Culottes	Section Unité	Total
Floréal	74	143	90	118	425
Thermidor	117	124	101	87	429

Source: Arch. mun. Tulle, 1 R 3, IE DEP 272/236 (register opened 28 Prairial II).

had reached 429, with class sizes varying from thirty-seven to as many as seventy-two girl pupils per teacher. While most of the girls were aged between six and thirteen, in the Montagne class, for example, which numbered 124 girls, many of the pupils listed were well into their teens, with some even as old as seventeen or eighteen years of age. Clearly, a sizeable proportion of the younger female generation of Tulle were eager to learn and to take advantage of the tuition being offered (table 20).

Teachers were now paid on a per capita basis in accordance with the provisions of the new Bouquier decree passed on 29 Frimaire, the entitlement for schoolmistresses being one and a quarter livres per pupil per month, or 15 livres per year. Between Thermidor II and Brumaire IV, the schoolmistresses of Tulle were regularly receiving 83l. 6s. 8d. per month, totalling 1,000 livres per annum.[19] Lakanal, the champion of equal pay, had by now resigned himself to a reduction of 200 livres in female salaries as compared to those initially awarded in Bergerac.[20] By all accounts, in these three provincial cities, primary education had been set in motion and funds made available through local taxes to ensure a fair measure of continuity over several years. Above all, a sound democratic basis had been established, enabling children of all backgrounds to attend school.

THE GUARDIANS OF EQUALITY: *INSTITUTEURS* AND *INSTITUTRICES*

The ideal Jacobin schoolmaster or *instituteur* was expected to display astounding versatility and possess a wide range of virtues

[19] Tulle, 15 Pluviôse and 30 Ventôse II, Arch. mun. Tulle, 1 D 2, commune, IE DEP 272/55, ff. 125, 135; and 1 R 3, girls schools' register, IE DEP 272/236, 28 Prairial II seq.; G. Mathieu (ed.), *Notes et documents sur l'instruction publique en Corrèze pendant la Révolution* (Paris, 1912), pp. 1–87.
[20] Cf. Lakanal's law of 27 Brumaire III, Woloch, *New Regime*, p. 182.

that few could hope to attain. The job profile was that of a cultured man of letters, unassuming and frugal in his habits and close to nature, approachable yet commanding respect, a model citizen and a persuasive orator, a *pater familias* devoted to other people's children, a philosopher and a sportsman, a mathematician and an agronomist, a *Socrate rustique* and a secular *vicaire savoyard* rolled into one. His qualifications would include experience of farming, industry and commerce, and mastery of a craft which he could pass on to the young. He was expected to be a republican since an important part of his job consisted in teaching civics not just to his class but to the community at large.[21] Married status was an essential prerequisite – no doubt as a foil to the celibate clerics who until now had dominated education, had fallen victim to the anti-religious movement and were currently unemployed – but also because Rousseau the educationalist had recommended to the Poles that schoolteachers should be 'tous mariés'.[22] In addition, Romme and Roux-Fazillac both considered it desirable to place the school beneath the tutelage of a committee of 'enlightened fathers' who could guarantee its independence from sectarian pressures and inject into the educational process the social dimension necessary to integrate it into the community.

As for the schoolmistress or *institutrice*, her task was understood as a natural extension of the educational mission of motherhood. The decree on elementary textbooks included a course on 'the preservation of children' and their 'physical and moral upbringing' from pregnancy, through birth and infancy to school age.[23] Thérésia Cabarrus's speech on education, which was widely disseminated in the south-west by Pierre Monestier, emphasises the pre-school role of the mother in instilling into her offspring a sense of 'duty, principle and method' to serve as 'the thermometer of happiness' in later life. A young mother's experience tending the elderly and sick in the *hôpital* would also serve her well in preparing her for the teacher's profession. As for intellectual skills, although

---

[21] Condorcet, 20 April 1792; Lanthenas and Romme, December 1792; Lakanal, 26 June 1793: in *Procès-verbaux du Comité d'instruction*, vol. I, p. xlii and vol. V, pp. 661–4; Labroue, *La mission de Lakanal*, p. 237.

[22] J.-J. Rousseau, 'Considérations sur le gouvernement de Pologne', in *Œuvres complètes*, vol. III, p. 534.

[23] Decree of 9 Pluviôse II, *Procès-verbaux du Comité d'instruction*, vol. III, p. li.

reading and writing were prerequisites for women teachers, arithmetic, according to Lakanal, was not. This was a male preserve, understood as belonging to the realm of 'enlightenment' and enlightened men (*lumières*), whereas women's corresponding asset was 'morality'. 'Who can teach modesty [*pudeur*]', asked Thérésia Cabarrus, 'if not the voice of a woman?'[24]

Although the model teacher was evidently an elusive animal, Roux-Fazillac was lucky in running one to ground in Bordeaux and bringing him to Périgueux: Charles Foulhioux, a professional journalist from Lyons with a cosmopolitan experience as correspondent for the *Courrier de l'Europe*, the *Gazette d'Utrecht* and the *Révolutions de Paris*. Foulhioux's wife, who accompanied him as schoolmistress, had been employed as tutor to the children of Bordelais shipowners. Clearly, appointing these heavyweights as primary-school teachers in the provincial outback was a case of overkill. But Roux-Fazillac was intent on exploiting Foulhioux's very considerable literary talents in his community role preaching the republican catechism to the people of Périgueux in the converted cathedral on *décadi*.[25] This Foulhioux accomplished to perfection for a couple of months until other concerns and ambitions took him and his wife to Paris, leaving their small flock for others to tend.

A more fitting example of a man suited to the job is that of Jean Broussard from Challignac in the district of Barbézieux (Charente), whose qualifications included the 'three Rs' and in addition some practical knowledge of geometry and land surveying (*arpentage*), while his wife Jeanne could teach reading, writing and the 'first four rules of arithmetic'.[26] Proficiency of this high standard was exceptional and in some instances candidates' spelling, for example, left much to be desired.[27] The speed with which appointments were

[24] Th. Cabarrus-Fontenay, 'Discours sur l'éducation', Bordeaux, 10 Nivôse II and circular of 25 Germinal II; and Monestier de la Lozère, Agen, 2 Floréal II: Arch. Nat., AF$_{II}$ 117, Lot-et-Garonne, pl. 887, p. 1.

[25] Ch. Foulhioux, 'Instruction morale et civique', Périgueux, 10 Nivôse II, Arch. Nat., AF$_{II}$ 171, Western Bureau, pl. 1406, p. 20; see also Caron, 'Recherches biographiques: Foulhioux'.

[26] Aulard, 'La commune de Challignac', p. 551.

[27] As in the case of Jeanne Pareau whose job application on behalf of herself and her friend Anne Ribault reads: 'Si j'écris aux singulier cé que joublioient d'avoir une colegue [sic]': Arch. dép. Haute-Vienne, L 534–5, primary schools, at 13 Prairial II; cf. Woloch, *New Regime*, p. 188.

made and the lack of teacher-training facilities exposed the experiment to the risk of failure. 'Training', wrote Saint-André, 'is the secret of education', while Romme expressed the fear that in the absence of colleges of education, their scheme was liable to degenerate into 'organised charlatanism'.[28]

This risk was probably keenly felt by the teachers themselves as they launched into their calling with no formal syllabus nor any textbooks, apart from copies of the Declaration of Rights and the Constitution helpfully supplied by the municipality. In addition to the core subjects, Lakanal decreed that 'social responsibility' should be taught, but no religion, since the schools were entirely secular. Boys would practise military drill once every ten days under the supervision of an officer of the National Guard, while the girls would be occupied with useful handiwork. Regular visits would be made by pupils of both sexes to the poorhouses and the elderly in their homes.[29]

Textbooks and teaching aids were in the pipeline, of course. Both Romme and Fabre d'Eglantine intended that the republican calendar should be used in schools to contribute to a better understanding of agricultural techniques, as a simplified farmers' almanac, in addition to which Romme the mathematician somewhat optimistically considered it to be a brilliant practical application of the new decimal system.[30] His *Annuaire du cultivateur*, completed before his departure on mission (though only published a year later), is a simplified encyclopedia of botany, agriculture and animal husbandry, with a table of weights and measures, admirably suited in his view to elementary education.[31] Thibaudeau, Léonard Bourdon and abbé Grégoire were working on a potted record of contemporary feats of arms with the title 'Tableau des actions

[28] *Procès-verbaux du Comité d'instruction*, vol. III, p. li and vol. IV, p. xxvi; Labroue, *La mission de Lakanal*, p. 59; Gontard, *L'enseignement primaire en France*, p. 140.

[29] Lakanal, resolution of 24 October 1793.

[30] Reports of 5 October 1793 and 3 Brumaire II: *Arch. parl.*, vol. LXXVI, p. 120 and vol. LXXVIII, pp. 496–507; A. C. Thibaudeau, *Mémoires sur la Convention et le Directoire*, 2 vols. (Paris, 1824), vol. I, p. 79. See P. Crépel, 'Gilbert Romme et les mathématiques', and M. Frœschlé, 'A propos du calendrier républicain: Romme et l'astronomie', in Ehrard (ed.), 'Gilbert Romme: actes du colloque de Riom (19–20 mai 1995)', in *Annales hist. Révol. fr.* 304 (April–June 1996), pp. 207, 303.

[31] G. Romme, *Annuaire du cultivateur* (Paris, Year III), Bibl. Nat., S 20896; cf. *Vocabulaire des poids et mesures* and *Instruction sur le calcul décimal* (Years II and III) in Aulard, *Recueil*, vol. XXIII, p. 609.

héroïques' for mass circulation by the education committee. While waiting for the distribution of these textbooks, Lakanal spent much of his time in Bergerac sifting through émigré and congregational book collections in search of works on history, travel, anatomy, botany, mineralogy, chemistry and zoology, which he had placed on shelves in the newly created municipal library to serve as reference material for his teaching staff and other interested citizens. He appointed Antoine Lemaire, a political journalist known locally as the 'ami du *Père Duchesne*', to the post of chief librarian.[32]

The state primary school which emerged from these experiments, in the limited urban context of three small provincial cities, was as representative as can be of the republican institution of the future. It was called upon to fulfil a dual role. On the one hand, it would serve as an egalitarian levelling mechanism thanks to which social classes would be mingled as rich and poor children sat side by side on the schoolbench, in accordance with the goal set by Saint-André: 'confondre les classes par l'éducation'.[33] In the state school envisioned by Lepeletier and Robespierre, the children would be 'received equally, brought up equally from the surplus wealth of the rich, fed equally, dressed equally'.[34] On the other hand, since elementary school was also a springboard to adult occupations, it held up the prospect of a really fair democracy in which not only would 'careers be opened to talent' as in 1789 (article 6 of the Declaration of Rights), but true equality of opportunity would be assured, since the same fund of basic knowledge would be available to all. To the abolition of privilege, the Revolution was now adding, in theory at least, the eradication of ignorance.

FURTHER EDUCATION AND AGRICULTURAL EXTENSION

While Romme in Paris supervised the installation of a decimal chronometer in the chamber of the assembly, Bo on his peregrinations through the *massif central* encouraged local officials to place clocks in the dismantled towers of their churches so that the

---

[32] C. Perroud, 'Le Père Duchêne à Bergerac', *La Révol. fr.* 41 (1904), pp. 288, 459.
[33] Jeanbon Saint-André, *Réflexions sur l'éducation nationale*, Paris, 20 December 1792, Bibl. Nat., 8° Le[38] 2259.
[34] *Œuvres de Maximilien Robespierre*, vol. X, p. 27.

190   *A place at school and a time for rejoicing*

country folk could learn to tell the time.[35] Roux-Fazillac and
Lakanal both obtained modern streetlamps for the illumination of
the main thoroughfares of Périgueux and Bergerac.[36] In a figurative
sense also these prophets of enlightenment would have liked to lift
the veil of ignorance and extend the progress of human knowledge
to the tiniest cottage in the remotest valley. A short cycle of
elementary education confined to the towns evidently fell far short
of this ambition.

Civic lectures in the Temple of Reason on *décadi* were only a
small part of adult education. In the complete absence of formal
training facilities, the dissemination of practical information and
new technologies had to be conducted by other means: on the
factory floor, for example, in the case of the key workers of the
steel and armaments industry. But no extension service, of the kind
recommended by abbé Rozier and abbé Grégoire,[37] yet existed to
disseminate the agronomic improvements of the age to the farmer
in the field. The press made a concerted effort to 'give a clear idea
to our country brethren of the simplest and most economical means
of hastening the progress of agriculture': the *Journal d'agriculture*[38]
and the *Feuille villageoise*[39] led the field, with Lequinio's *Ecole des
laboureurs*[40] and now Romme's own *Annuaire du cultivateur* vying
with each other to publicise Parmentier's alternatives to bread or
the advantages of forage crops and sown pasture (*prairies artifi-
cielles*). At the local level, news-sheets such as the *Journal d'instruction populaire* sponsored by Lakanal contained articles on crop

[35] Romme, 15 Brumaire II, in A. Mathiez, 'Robespierre et la déchristianisation', *Annales révol.* 2 (1909), p. 327; Bo, Cahors, 24 Ventôse II, Arch. dép. Lot, L 12, missions.

[36] Périgueux, 3 Nivôse and Bergerac, 16 Pluviôse II, Arch. mun. Périgueux, D/4, mun. register, vol. II, f° 123; Arch. dép. Dordogne, 1 L 232, missions, p. 6, and 3 L 24, dist. Bergerac, f° 182. On streetlighting, see A. P. Herlaut, *L'éclairage de Paris à l'époque révolutionnaire* (Paris, 1932).

[37] F. Rozier, *Cours complet d'agriculture théorique, pratique, économique et de médecine rurale et vétérinaire ... ou Dictionnaire universel d'agriculture*, first 8 vols. (Paris, 1781–9), vol. VI (2nd edn 1793), pp. 1–23; and H. Grégoire, *Œuvres*, ed. by A. Soboul, facs. edn, 14 vols. (Paris and Liechtenstein, 1977), vol. II, pp. 71–95.

[38] *Procès-verbaux des Comités d'agriculture et de commerce de la Constituante, de la Législative et de la Convention*, ed. by F. Gerbaux and C. Schmidt, 4 vols. (Paris, 1906–10), vol. III, p. 159.

[39] To which Romme was an early contributor: Galante Garrone, *Gilbert Romme*, pp. 264–5; see also M. Edelstein, *La Feuille villageoise: communication et modernisation dans les régions rurales pendant la Révolution* (Paris, 1977).

[40] *Procès-verbaux du Comité d'instruction*, vol. I, p. xxiii.

protection and weevil control, and didactic dialogues modelled on Hirzel,[41] while Publicola Pedon's *Journal de la Haute-Vienne* devoted an entire column of its Floréal and Prairial issues to the cultivation of root and tuber crops.[42] But the readership of such articles was limited to the literate landowners and mainly urban classes frequenting the political clubs.

Paganel was one of the first to organise agricultural shows and competitions in the districts of the Tarn for the promotion of pulses and root crops. Sums of up to 400 livres were awarded as prizes to 'the first farmer who during the month of May (old style, we have to use it since they are not yet familiar with the other) shall present the first crop of carrots, turnips or potatoes harvested from his plot'.[43] Several deputies with agricultural inclinations approached the farmers directly in the hope of improving their techniques, but most were attentive to local farming practice. Thus, Féraud accompanied the peasants of the Hautes Pyrénées to their fields to watch them pick wild chicory to serve as a substitute crop when grain was scarce. Monestier encouraged the sowing of *blé d'Espagne* (buckwheat) in the Agenais because it was tradition-ally used as a forage crop and enabled rye and barley to be kept till maturity as food rather than fodder.[44] Romme, who favoured human contacts on the village square, cross-examined a farmer returning from the fields with a cartload of corn containing two sheaves 'with green ears'. On learning that the peasants of Périgord were in the habit of cutting green stems of rye to give to their cattle, he issued a prohibition order threatening to deprive persistent offenders of their 'right to cultivate': no grain crop destined for human consumption, he claimed, should ever be cut before maturity. But Romme's interventionism ran up against ingrained cropping practices and the farming community's in-herent resistance to change, and he was obliged to make an

---

[41] *Journal d'instruction populaire*, Sarlat (Messidor II), Bibl. Nat., 8° Lc[11] 930 bis; cf. H. C. Hirzel, *Le Socrate rustique, ou description de la conduite économique et morale d'un paysan philosophe*, trans. by Frey des Landres (Zurich, 1762).

[42] Arch. dép. Haute-Vienne, L 818, *Journal du département de la Haute-Vienne*; C. Leymarie, 'Le Journal de la Haute-Vienne (1793)', *Le Bibliophile limousin* (July–October 1901).

[43] Albi, 10 Pluviôse II, Arch. Nat., AF$_{II}$ 175, Western Bureau, pl. 1434, p. 39; Aulard, *Recueil*, vol. X, p. 527.

[44] Aulard, *Recueil*, vol. XII, p. 630 and vol. XIII, p. 37.

exception in the case of grain legumes, such as vetch, traditionally grown as forage crops.[45]

Lakanal briefly achieved one of his ambitions by establishing a *maison d'économie rurale*, or agricultural centre and model farm, in the district of Bergerac, where farmers could come and see 'new agronomic discoveries tested', examine and compare new varieties of beans and fruit, collect batches of improved seed supplied by the Muséum in Paris and receive tuition in botany and mechanisation. With the assistance of the scientist Daubenton, he secured the services of a first-rate horticulturalist named Poiteau who directed the centre for nearly two years until his salary ceased to be paid and he was obliged to pack his bags and return to Paris.[46]

Here at least was visible proof that science could be popularised and progress was not a vain word. Lanot made the observation in the Corrèze that the 'man of nature', the ordinary peasant, was always fond of 'talking agriculture' and Bo was of the opinion that even the most 'crassly ignorant' of countrymen were keen to learn and better their lot, rather than remain forever slaves of archaic farming systems.[47] Agricultural extension was understood as an integral part of education, which promised to all those who worked on the land the distant but tangible reward of emancipation and economic development, namely the opportunity to achieve self-sufficiency. 'Training citizens', declared Lakanal, quoting Rousseau, 'is not something done in a day', and Roux-Fazillac admitted that 'the effects will be slow'.[48] Even though it was a long haul, the democratic and utilitarian rewards of education would be of benefit to all, children and adults, without exclusion. The important thing was to have made a start.

---

[45] Périgueux, 19 Germinal, 2, 17, and 27 Floréal II: Arch. Nat., AF_{II} 172, Western Bureau, pl. 1413, p. 11; 178, Western Bureau, pl. 1463, pp. 19–22; Arch. dép. Dordogne, 3 L 25, dist. Bergerac, ff. 106, 146; 1 L 233, Romme.

[46] *Procès-verbaux du Comité d'instruction*, vol. II, p. 456; Labroue, *La mission de Lakanal*, pp. 259–64.

[47] Lanot, Tulle, 30 Nivôse II; Bo, Saint-Flour, 29 Pluviôse and Martel, 1 Germinal II: Arch. Nat., AF_{II} 171, Western Bureau, pl. 1407, p. 45; 175^B, Western Bureau, pl. 1441, p. 4; and 177, Western Bureau, pl. 1450, p. 3; Aulard, *Recueil*, vol. X, p. 325; vol. XI, p. 238; and vol. XII, p. 96.

[48] 'Former des citoyens n'est pas l'affaire d'un jour': Rousseau, 'Economie politique' (*Encyclopédie*, vol. V), in *Œuvres complètes*, vol. II, p. 285; Lakanal, Bergerac, 3 Brumaire II; Roux-Fazillac, Périgueux, 27 Frimaire II.

THE JACOBIN FESTIVAL, A 'SCHOOL FOR ADULTS'

Sieyès, who took Condorcet's place at the education committee after the fall of the Gironde, considered revolutionary festivals to be a means of civic education as important as the primary schools, and Paganel called the fête *l'école des adultes*.[49] Through the wide repertory of genres identified by Mona Ozouf and Michel Vovelle,[50] the Jacobin celebrations of Year II faithfully mimic the political climate of the day: the solemn burning of the relics of feudalism, the lugubrious ceremonies of remembrance for the fallen martyrs of the Republic (Lepeletier, martyr of liberty, Marat, martyr of equality, but also Chalier, Gasparin, the young Bara), the vilification of those guilty of treason (bonfires of the effigies of Vergniaud, Brissot and Gorsas), the colourful but alarming improvisations of the short-lived period of dechristianisation, mainly sacrilegious anti-Catholic masquerades, the staid and dreary official rites in honour of Reason and the Supreme Being, the smaller civic gatherings around the patriotic altar or the liberty tree. While most are obviously theatrical representations of recent history and the new social order (the overthrow of the *ancien régime*, the triumph of liberty over tyranny, the exercise of civil and political rights, the practice of republican virtues), some have a lot to say in symbolic terms about the Terror, mainly in its anarchical mode, and to these deviations I shall return.[51]

A significant number of festivities, however, fall into a different category altogether, that of the family feast, involving the active participation of the local community, and are often orchestrated by the deputies themselves, who take a prominent part, in a deliberate effort to entertain, win over public support, validate the new fraternal lifestyle and cultivate the idea of a common happiness. Didactically, they turn away from the past and the conflictual present and offer a simulation of the society of tomorrow. These feasts are carefully scripted and deserve close scrutiny.

The family gathering clearly reflects the family ethos discussed in

[49] Paganel, *Essai historique*, vol. II, p. 117.
[50] Ozouf, *La fête révolutionnaire*, pp. 99–124; M. Vovelle, *Les métamorphoses de la fête en Provence de 1750 à 1820* (Paris, 1976).
[51] Ozouf, *La fête révolutionnaire*, and L. Hunt, *Politics, Culture and Class in the French Revolution* (Berkeley, 1984).

chapter 2 and is often built around the theme of 'fair shares for all'. Thus, the welfare celebrations organised in Guéret by Ingrand under the title *fête de la bienfaisance* in late September 1793 combined the traditional harvest festival with a glorified soup kitchen à la Vincent de Paul. Twenty quintals of flour were supplied by the district, the bread ovens were requisitioned for the day and freshly baked loaves were distributed at every street corner. In the moving pageant, the local dignitaries were accompanied by farmers brought in from the fields in their working clothes, while the people's representative gave his hand to the poorest woman and the oldest woman of the city, each surrounded by her offspring. All held hands and the procession to the town hall was likened to a 'human chain'.[52] Likewise in Périgueux, where youth was awarded the full honours: boys and girls from the newly opened primary schools, including a sprinkling of *enfants de la patrie*, the waifs and strays of old, erstwhile 'victims of egoism and unconcern', mingled together with a batch of newlyweds, and at the end of the unruly procession came Roux-Fazillac steering a team of oxen and plough amid joyous country folk, all heading for a better future.[53]

To be an 'egoist' is to declare oneself 'an enemy of our common mother, *la patrie*', wrote Lakanal in his resolution declaring war on 'sordid self-interest' and appealing for the peaceful settlement of all unresolved lawsuits by arbitration, thus ostensibly putting an end to centuries of chicanery and taking the wind from the sails of the legal profession, that breed of 'public vampires' who 'bleed the poor'. To celebrate this court-case amnesty between landlords and tenants and reward his brothers of the Dordogne for burying their hatchets, Lakanal convened a festival of Friendship, where all drank from the same public fountain and sang a hymn to the end of litigation.[54] Akin to the *fête de l'amitié*, the *fête du travail* was also aimed at reconciliation. This, however, was a far from leisurely affair – road-mending seldom is. All the citizens of the department were invited to rise at dawn, grab their spades and shovels and man the public highways. When the starter's musket sounded, echoed from post to post, the hard day's repair work began, with the representative in person rolling up his sleeves to set an example,

---

[52] Arch. dép. Creuse, L 734, Jacobin club of Guéret, 29 September 1793.
[53] Arch. mun. Périgueux, D/4, mun. register, 8 and 20 Nivôse II, 2 vols., vol. II, pp. 117–22.
[54] Labroue, *La mission de Lakanal*, pp. 193–5.

faithful as ever to the teaching of Jean-Jacques.[55] Backbreaking though such public gatherings were and while all shared equally in the common task, pushing wheelbarrows and spreading gravel, the bourgeois supplied his muscle power free of charge and the ordinary working man was paid a day's wages for his contribution, as was only fair. And when the day's labour was done, food and wine were served to all and fiddlers were invited to enhance the rejoicing: a family picnic by the roadside to the sound of music.[56]

The important feature of collective festivities of this kind was the image of a 'happy family' at work and at play, an image inherited, as we have seen, from the *fête de la fédération* celebrations of 14 July 1790 on the Champ de Mars in Paris. A short while after this 'model festival', imbued with the family spirit, the Constituent Assembly had recommended arbitration to settle amicably all disputes between fellow citizens and, to that end, the setting up of 'family tribunals' and 'peace and reconciliation bureaus', an idea taken up again in the 1793 Constitution which provided for the appointment of public arbitrators who would act as mediators or 'ombudsmen' of sorts.[57]

Brival observed that there were too many feasts to celebrate and the 'republican calendar would prove too short to contain them all'.[58] The important feature of the family festival is that it spills over from the public holiday into the daily routine, endows toil, not just play, with a civic and festive air, and aims at republicanising workaday life. All that relates to the joint effort, sharing, sacrifice, the common endeavour is now permeated with a sense of exhilaration, heightened by the common experience of the call to arms and the *levée en masse*. Thus, the national mobilisation of 1793–4 required every able-bodied man, woman and child to rally round and 'lend a hand', an iterative theme to be found in Romme's proclamation to the inhabitants of the south-west in Prairial Year II, with its vivid imagery of the republican family whose members

---

[55] Rousseau, 'Projet de constitution pour la Corse', *Œuvres complètes*, vol. III, p. 508.

[56] Bergerac, 8 and 28 Pluviôse and 6 Ventôse II: Arch. Nat., AF$_{II}$ 96, Dordogne, pl. 706, pp. 3–12; Arch. dép. Dordogne, 1 L 232, Lakanal, p. 18; Labroue, *La mission de Lakanal*, pp. 291, 515.

[57] Decree of 16 August 1790 and articles 85 and 95 of the Montagnard Constitution; cf. decrees of 10 Frimaire, 17 Nivôse and 6 Germinal II, prescribing arbitration rather than court proceedings.

[58] Tulle, 10 Nivôse II, Arch. Nat., AF$_{II}$ 171, Western Bureau, pl. 1407, p. 18.

are called upon to serve the *patrie* each according to his or her means.[59]

Whether it be Romme urging all members of the close-knit community to shoulder their share of the common burden, or Brival calling on every man on *décadi* to attack a Limousin *château-fort* and contribute a stone to the republican altarpiece, or Bo gathering together the citizens of the Albigeois on their rest-day to help bring in the harvest and fill the public grain-store with newly threshed corn, or Ingrand leading the poor women of Guéret in a human chain to share in the ritual distribution of loaves, or Roux-Fazillac accompanying his schoolchildren toward the land of plenty, or Lakanal reconciling sharecropper and landlord in a show of brotherly love – all these demonstrations and allegories hammer home the same message: if everyone receives a fair share, he and she must in return give their due to the community, for fair distribution within the bosom of the family requires that all should receive according to their needs and all should give according to their abilities. It also suggests that the interests of the wider family/ community must have the edge over our narrow interests as individuals and that this priority can be brought about amicably and without friction if fairness prevails.

Foremost among the representations of Jacobin concord was the civic banquet. Not the 'vertical' paternalistic public meal of the *ancien régime*, at which the far end of the table was reserved for those who through shortage of funds were allowed to bring their own food, while the leftovers were unceremoniously meted out to the destitute when the meal was over,[60] but the 'horizontal' banquet of the new era at which all the guests partook of the same fare and were truly equals. A good social mix was not easy to achieve, however. The citizens of Toulouse segregated themselves at separate tables and Paganel was shocked to see the 'black broth' of the spartan sans-culottes, the *brouet noir* recommended by Lycurgus, Phocion and Mably,[61] 'eclipsed' by the delicate dishes of the rich and the flickering candles of the poor obscured by the 'dazzling brightness' of the bourgeois lanterns, at what was meant

[59] See p. 54 in this volume.
[60] Such as the old-style banquet held at Digne in 1790 to celebrate the return of abbé Gassendi: Vovelle, *Les métamorphoses de la fête*, p. 190.
[61] Plutarch, *Vies des hommes illustres*, vol. I, p. 241, and vol. VI, p. 342; G. Bonnot de Mably, *Entretiens de Phocion sur le rapport de la morale et de la politique* (Paris, 1792), p. 106.

to be a general reconciliation after the Federalist insurrection of the summer.[62] Conversely, the egalitarian meal organised by Cavaignac and Dartigoeyte at Auch degenerated into a drunken mêlée at which militant atheists took advantage of the chaos to indulge in an iconoclastic romp.[63]

The imperfect celebrations of Toulouse and Auch underline the precariousness of communal feasts, since the first is a demonstration of inequality and class division and the second one of equality and intolerance, but neither reveals much fraternity. Transgressions or *dérapages* of this kind were not infrequent. Thus, at Tulle, the mustachioed leaders of the 'black band' of dechristianisers put on a short play with a guillotine prior to a civic banquet, during which the guests were promised 'plenty of free meat', and Taillefer intervened to put a stop to an 'odious piece of entertainment' in which young recruits were made to march up and down in front of a scaffold. But Taillefer himself obliged wealthy landlords at Gourdon to dance around a bonfire disguised as kings and cardinals. At the feasts of Cahors and Villefranche-de-Rouergue, stage-managed by the physician Lagasquié, the colleague and friend of Marat, the world was turned upside down as in the carnivals of old and the poor were waited on by the rich who were forced to stand behind them, since 'the former etiquette prevented the valet from sitting at the table of the master'.[64]

The perpetrators of the 'triumph of the poor', as the name of this feast suggests, celebrated not the end of but the reversal of privilege, the revenge of poverty on affluence and the humiliation of the well-to-do. By making men of property quake in their boots, they restored inequality under a different guise, exacerbated social friction and gave to the political antagonism between Gironde and Montagne the dimension of a class struggle, which was manifestly far removed from reality. Camille Desmoulins's *Vieux Cordelier*

---

[62] Toulouse, 29 Vendémiaire and 5 Brumaire II, Arch. Nat., AF$_{II}$ 185, Midi Bureau, pl. 1530, p. 16, and pl. 1531, p. 26; Aulard, *Recueil*, vol. VII, p. 531 and vol. VIII, p. 49.

[63] Auch, 3 Frimaire II, *Moniteur*, 30 November 1793; Aulard, *Recueil*, vol. VII, p. 662.

[64] Report by Chauvin, Germinal III, Bibl. Nat., 8° Le^{39} 245, p. 61; Taillefer, *Ma réponse aux épisodes de Fréron* (20 Pluviôse III), Bibl. Nat., 8° Lb^{41} 1616; Wallon, *Les représentants du peuple*, vol. II, p. 326; Caron, 'La commission civile révolutionnaire'; Cobb, *Les armées révolutionnaires*, pp. 624–33; Petit, 'Le triomphe du pauvre'; cf. E. Le Roy Ladurie, *Le carnaval de Romans: de la Chandeleur au mercredi des Cendres, 1579–1580* (Paris, 1979), pp. 240–53.

took the *Père Duchesne* to task precisely for this kind of rabble-rousing provocation by definition inimical to the liberal ideal of the 'brotherhood of man'.[65]

Banquets need not be divisive, however, as the majority of Jacobin *fêtes* demonstrate. All citizens without distinction, male and female, young and old, could sit around the same table side by side in what amounted to a 'true communion' of equals, as the atheist Lequinio described it in Saintes, the aim being to 'raise the poor man to the full stature of his dignity ... suppress in the rich man the slightest feeling of superiority', and instil in 'both their hearts the gentle feeling of sincere fraternity which alone can make the happiness of humankind'.[66] The fare might be frugal and Lacedaemonian, as at the Feast of Reason at Challignac, thus underlining the personal sacrifice implicit in consumer collectivism, symbolised by the chaste Marie, elected goddess for the occasion; or more self-indulgent, as at Bergerac, where ham and sausage were plentiful and the wine flowed freely, and where the assembled citizens, as they respectfully listened to Lakanal's long speech, ogled the 'very beautiful' citizeness Mounet whose sensual incarnation of Reason made them forget the bread of equality for a while.[67]

Jeanbon Saint-André set great store by the value of competitive sport and on public holidays athletic competitions were frequently organised to occupy the young and energetic.[68] What activity, indeed, is more entertaining and more conducive to fair play, more liberal, equal and fraternal, than the practice of sport? And when, after the games and the communal meal, the musicians struck up a jig, few could resist the temptation to join in the dancing, that most democratic of pastimes. As elegant bourgeoises gave their arm to roughneck sans-culottes and all were caught up in the fun of the occasion, Roux-Fazillac and Vernerey looked contentedly on at the mass of equal citizens milling around in the public square, merged into a 'single family':[69] the *bal populaire* taking on the role of

[65] *Le Vieux Cordelier*, No. 5, in Desmoulins, *Œuvres*, vol. X, p. 309.

[66] Saintes, 1 Nivôse II, Arch. dép. Charente, L 67, missions.

[67] Aulard, 'La commune de Challignac', p. 550; Labroue, *La mission de Lakanal*, p. 289; Galante Garrone, *Gilbert Romme*, p. 344.

[68] Jeanbon Saint-André, *Réflexions sur l'éducation nationale* and report of 20 December 1792, Bibl. Nat., 8° Le[38] 2127, p. 17.

[69] Périgueux, 19 Frimaire and 3 Nivôse II and Guéret, 25 Pluviôse II: Aulard, *Recueil*, vol. IX, p. 291 and vol. XI, p. 128.

ultimate catalyst, bringing the republican dream to life and demonstrating its viability.

Whether it be in the shared exertion of collective road-mending, or the shared rest when the day's job is done, in the well-worn clichés of civic speeches or the fair play of athletic contests, in the communion of a country picnic or the social mix and merry-making of the folk-dance, the Jacobin festival during its brief lease of life wove a network of sociability and nursed fraternal reflexes. Paganel records that public gatherings became a common feature of the provinces in the following years and the popularity of the *jour de fête* contributed in no small way to the establishment of a republican way of life.[70] It could be claimed that the spirit which it fostered, in some parts of France at least, has left its mark to this day.

[70] Paganel, *Essai historique*, vol. II, p. 117.

Conclusion

> The love of democracy is the love of equality. The love of democracy is also the love of frugality. Since it promises to each the same happiness and the same benefits, each should find in it the same pleasures and harbour the same aspirations, something which can only be expected from general frugality.
>
> Montesquieu, *De l'esprit des lois*, 1748[1]

The civic feast helps draw the threads of our story together. When the fraternal rejoicings are over, however, and the fond illusions dispelled, we return inevitably to the harsh realities of the Terror, which it has not been my purpose to evade. Rather it has been to show that the egalitarian agenda of the Jacobin phase of revolution was not fatally locked within an inevitable spiral of violence or bound to generate a police-state mentality, but that some imaginative political initiatives, often taken quite independently from the centre, were bent on achieving social harmony by peaceful and lawful means and in some instances actually succeeded in doing so. If such is the case, the shared meal, the dancing and the laughter, and the image of the common happiness they convey, need not induce scepticism, but carry political credibility. Fraternity, the pale secular ersatz of the Christian 'love thy neighbour', considered desirable on public holidays, but apparently inessential and ineffectual the rest of the time, may after all be capable of exerting an enduring influence on the pattern of human behaviour and thus be of relevance to the social contract.

Plato in his Socratic *Dialogues* puts forward a view of human relations governed by two very basic and conflicting urges which

[1] Montesquieu, 'Ce que c'est que l'amour de la république dans la démocratie', *De l'esprit des lois*, book V, chapter 3, vol. I, p. 49.

appear set on a collision course: the lust for power and the thirst for justice.[2] If the lust for power is dominant and its exercise carried out for its own sake or in virtue of the principle that might is right, then it more than justifies the historian's concern with rhetoric and the supposed primacy of political motivation. If, however, the thirst for justice asserts itself and provides a sufficient moral counter-weight to the sheer wielding of power, then the economic disparities embedded in the social fabric will come to the fore and tangible remedial action will have to be sought that has immediate relevance to the lives of ordinary citizens. Such action too deserves to be studied and evaluated objectively, and need not, in the context of the French Revolution, automatically be linked to the Terror's perceived significance as 'a programme for moral and social regeneration'.

Inasmuch as politics as we understand them today are not so much concerned with abstract concepts of liberty and equality as with material needs and the means to satisfy them (food, jobs, housing, schools, stable prices, taxation and so on), then Jacobin egalitarianism in practice was concerned with the very stuff of politics. It happened that the politicians themselves, involved as they were in the day-to-day management of community affairs, tended to be carried away by the novel habit of interventionism and the heady prospect of a new Jerusalem, and individual liberties were sometimes flouted or given a rough ride, but they could not for long be ignored: the emphasis placed on human rights and active participation in the democratic process saw to that.

Jacques Godechot, who tended to shun strictly ideological explanations of historical events, nevertheless criticised the Jacobin model of democracy for breeding intolerance and for attaching more importance to civic duties and social obligations than to individual rights. The 1793 constitution, in his view, tends to 'subordinate individual liberties to the exercise of democracy, and not democracy to liberties'.[3] While Godechot's criticism is well founded, it leaves aside the consideration that this undeniable theoretical flaw, reflected in political practice, was more than matched by a conscious effort to achieve greater fairness. By introducing the notion of 'sharing', the Jacobins projected a vision of the common good in which no one would be the loser. Sharing,

---

[2] Plato, *Gorgias*, ed. by M. Canto (Paris, 1987), pp. 17–31, 42–5, 59–97.
[3] Godechot, *Les institutions de France*, p. 250.

as we have seen, entails a measure of compromise and sacrifice, or 'frugality' as Montesquieu would have said. It suggests a fair rather than an equal apportionment between all members of the same family, men and women, young and old, strong and weak, which is to the disadvantage of none individually and to the advantage of all collectively. It underscores the reasonableness of the vision of democracy introduced by the Enlightenment and helps explain its continuity.

Revolutionary experience confirms that fair shares for all can be achieved, if the circumstances are right, by appealing to people's sense of equity and relying on their sociability. It need not require a dose of 'restrictionist economics' of the kind once denounced by Talmon, resulting in state interference at the expense of individualism, 'the state acting as the chief regulator with the purpose of enforcing ascetic austerity'.[4] It is of interest in this respect that a number of historians on both sides of the Atlantic are today calling into question readings of the Terror such as those proposed by François Furet and Mona Ozouf in their *Dictionnaire critique*, which continue to dwell on the totalitarian potential and latent illiberalism of the French Revolution at the expense of its democratic and egalitarian achievements. To quote Isser Woloch, 'by implicitly and even explicitly invoking the concept of totalitarianism to encompass the Terror's thrust, such histories preclude almost by definition any serious consideration of democratic initiatives in 1793–4'.[5] Florence Gauthier's close monitoring of human rights in the revolutionary context indicates that while the Terror was a period of repression, it was simultaneously a period of emancipation which saw the birth of 'anti-repressive liberties' and furthered the development of self-determination and the abolition of slavery.[6] Lynn Hunt, for her part, considers that the question of gender, in the context of family policy, shows the Jacobins to have been 'confirmed liberals' in their 'defence of individual rights'; their determination to foster a community consensus did not preclude the pursuit of policies that 'seem much less communitarian than individualistic', the Terror 'did not eliminate that individualism',

---

[4] Talmon, *Origins of Totalitarian Democracy*, pp. 61–2, 160–4.
[5] Woloch, 'Contraction and Expansion of Democratic Space', p. 309.
[6] Gauthier, *Triomphe et mort du droit naturel*.

and it is therefore 'hard to see the Jacobin revolution as unabashedly proto-totalitarian'.[7]

The example of women's rights is indeed significant: they were far from neglected under Jacobin rule, as is borne out by the inheritance legislation allowing daughters as well as sons to claim an equal share of their father's estate, by the enactment granting humble milkmaids a say in the sharing-out of the commons, and by the opportunity given all the girls in the small provincial city of Tulle to attend school and to learn to read and write. In many other areas too, Jacobin egalitarianism in practice followed a course which was destined to complement, rather than undermine, the liberal, individualist programme of the Revolution. It is understandable that when the page was turned after Thermidor, few were prepared to give credit in this respect where credit was due. Even the repentant, though not reluctant, terrorist Bertrand Barère, who as mouthpiece of the Montagne had put forward much of its radical social legislation and who in later life was converted to utilitarianism and became an unconditional admirer of Jeremy Bentham,[8] glosses over in his memoirs the important body of evidence which bears witness to this complementarity and which might have helped redeem his former colleagues in the eyes of later generations.

The men whose activities we have surveyed all would have agreed that once the social precondition for happiness is met – namely that all citizens without exception are able to enjoy their rights equally – there is no reason why liberty in all its forms should not flourish. Although, during the eventful months of the Terror, they were brought face to face with the risks of the arbitrary exercise of power, they rarely if ever sought expediency at the expense of legality. Indeed, as we saw in chapter 2, they exercised moderation and preached reconciliation and rehabilitation. By defending the 'right to err', they recognised the need for toleration and were implicitly advocating a pluralistic form of society. The real problem lies elsewhere: in the manner in which equality is promoted, in the extent to which some are prepared to use coercive force to impose it, but also in the stubborn refusal of hardened self-seekers to

---

[7] Hunt, 'Male Virtue and Republican Motherhood', pp. 204–7.

[8] B. Barère, *Mémoires*, ed. by H. Carnot and P. J. David d'Angers, 4 vols. (Paris, 1842–4), vol. II, pp. 239–40; see L. Gershoy, *Bertrand Barère: A Reluctant Terrorist* (Princeton, 1962).

entertain the demands of social justice, or in the reluctant acquiescence of those who have something to lose and may be prepared to call on the Riot Act to defend their interests.

With the collapse of Jacobin illusions after Thermidor, 'sordid self-interest', to use Lakanal's expression, once again reared its ugly head and as the gilded youth jostled for power, justice was relegated to a secondary role. It was then, in the words of Philippe Buonarroti, that the 'egoists' seized the initiative, turned their backs on 'virtue', which alone could have ensured the rule of law, and ushered in a new era of privilege, with the Constitution of Year III consecrating the victory of the 'aristocracy of wealth'.[9] This trend was confirmed under the Directory and the Bonapartist regimes, in which Marcel David detects few signs of fraternity at work.[10] Society in France, as elsewhere in Europe, was now set on a competitive and confrontational course, breeding further inequalities and class distinctions, and blurring the legitimacy of communal obligations.

Thomas Carlyle, seeking to identify the causes of the Chartist unrest in England, was to make the point that 'it is the feeling of injustice that is insupportable to all men': to the question 'Is this fair?' the periodic answer 'No, it is not fair!' generates the need for rectification, if necessary by direct action.[11] In pinpointing thus the psychological mechanism that can trigger a strike or even a revolution, Carlyle was unconsciously echoing Robespierre, the liberal humanist, who in December 1792, after four and a half years of revolutionary experience, expressed the conviction that 'the source of order is justice' and Saint-Just who a year later came to the same conclusion: 'I know only what is just and unjust.'[12] They and their companions had tried but failed to achieve a durable social order based on justice understood as fairness. The challenges today are not dissimilar. Modern post-revolutionary history teaches us that uncontrolled individualism only helps the strong at the expense of the weak, but conversely that collectivism imposed by constraint

---

[9] Cited by M. Dommanget, 'Les Egaux et la Constitution de 1793', in *Sur Babeuf et la conjuration des Egaux* (Paris, 1970), pp. 174–203.

[10] M. David, 'La fraternité au temps du dénigrement (1800–1814)', *Annales hist. Révol. fr.* 295 (January–March 1994), pp. 1–18.

[11] T. Carlyle, 'Chartism' (1839), chapters 5 and 7, in *Critical and Miscellaneous Essays*, 4 vols. (London, 1899), vol. IV, pp. 118–204.

[12] Robespierre, 2 December 1792, *Œuvres complètes*, vol. IX, p. 109; Saint-Just, preamble to his 'Republican Institutions', *Frammenti sulle istituzione*, p. 35.

tends to achieve social justice at the expense of individual freedom. The singular merit of the short-lived Jacobin episode is to have shown us that these two tendencies are not necessarily contradictory, that liberty and equality can coexist in the presence of fraternity, that in a society governed by moral principles there must necessarily be limits to what one may undertake for one's personal advantage or on behalf of the people. It has demonstrated compellingly that the right to existence must be given precedence over the right to self-fulfilment. And in setting aside the notion of class antagonism and putting forward a sociable view of human relations, it has given us a glimpse of what a fair society might one day be like.

Bibliography

MANUSCRIPT SOURCES

Note: Abbreviations used given in square brackets.

ARCHIVES NATIONALES, PARIS [ARCH. NAT.]

Sub-series AF$_{II}$ containing the correspondence between the deputies-on-mission, the Convention and the Committee of Public Safety and including texts of resolutions and proclamations.

Départements

Aveyron	AF$_{II}$ 89,	pl. 655–6	(Bo, Chabot, March 1793–Prairial II)
	89,	pl. 657–8	(Paganel, October 1793–Pluviôse II)
	89,	pl. 659–60	(Taillefer, October 1793–Frimaire II)
Charente	AF$_{II}$ 93,	pl. 685	(Roux-Fazillac, September 1793–Frimaire II)
	93,	pl. 686	(Romme, Ventôse–Prairial II)
Cher	AF$_{II}$ 93,	pl. 691	(Laplanche, September–October 1793)
Corrèze	AF$_{II}$ 95,	pl. 694	(Brival, Lanot, Borie, Bordas, August 1793–Ventôse II)
	95,	pl. 695–6	(Roux-Fazillac, Pluviôse–Fructidor II)
Creuse	AF$_{II}$ 95,	pl. 703	(Ingrand, Monestier, Petitjean, Vernerey, March 1793–Floréal II)
Dordogne	AF$_{II}$ 96,	pl. 704	(Baudot, Cavaignac, Pinet, Lakanal, Boussion, July 1793–Prairial III)
	96,	pl. 705	(Lacoste, Saint-André, Garrau, Ysabeau, Monestier du Puy-de-Dôme, Pinet, April 1793–Fructidor II)
	96,	pl. 706–10	(Lakanal, Frimaire–Fructidor II)
	96,	pl. 711	(Lakanal, Paganel, Pinet, Tallien, July 1793–Nivôse II)

		97,	pl. 713–15	(Romme, Germinal–Fructidor II)
		97,	pl. 716–17	(Roux-Fazillac, Septemb̂er 1793–Pluviôse II)
		97,	pl. 718	(Roux-Fazillac, Romme, Fructidor II; Taillefer, September 1793–Brumaire II; Tallien, Pluviôse–Ventôse II)
Haute-Garonne	AF$_{II}$	104,	pl. 780	(Paganel, October 1793–Pluviôse II)
Gers	AF$_{II}$	106,	pl. 787–91	(Dartigoeyte, March 1793–Germinal II)
Gironde	AF$_{II}$	107,	pl. 795	(Mathieu, Treilhard, June 1793; Romme, Thermidor–Fructidor II)
		107,	pl. 796–8	(Tallien, Ysabeau, September 1793–Ventôse II)
Landes	AF$_{II}$	113,	pl. 847–9	(Monestier de la Lozère, Pluviôse II–Vendémiaire III)
Lot	AF$_{II}$	116,	pl. 875–6	(Bo, Nivôse–Prairial II)
		116,	pl. 877	(Baudot, Pinet, Cavaignac, Ysabeau, August 1793–Floréal II)
		116,	pl. 878	(Saint-André, Lacoste, March–May 1793; Lakanal, Messidor II)
		116,	pl. 879	(Paganel, Vendémiaire–Pluviôse II)
		116,	pl. 880	(Treilhard, Mathieu, July 1793; Taillefer, Pinet, Monestier du Puy-de-Dôme, September 1793–Brumaire II)
Lot-et-Garonne	AF$_{II}$	117,	pl. 881	(Tallien, Ysabeau, Garrau, Paganel, Lakanal Leyris, Chaudron-Roussau, March 1793 Brumaire II)
		117,	pl. 882–4	(Paganel, Tallien, September 1793)
		117,	pl. 885–6	(Monestier de la Lozère, Pluviôse–Germinal II)
		117,	pl. 887	(Thérésia Cabarrus-Fontenay, Floréal II)
		117,	pl. 888	(Monestier du Puy-de-Dôme, Pinet, October 1793–Pluviôse II)
Tarn	AF$_{II}$	143^{B},	pl. 1142	(Bo, Chabot, Baudot, March 1793–Prairial II)
		143^{B},	pl. 1143	(Bouillerot, Mallarmé, Year III)
		143^{B},	pl. 1144	(Paganel, Brumaire–Ventôse II)
Vienne	AF$_{II}$	146^{A},	pl. 1168	(Ingrand, Brival, Pluviôse–Ventôse II)
		146^{A},	pl. 1169	(Ingrand, Frimaire–Floréal II)
Haute-Vienne	AF$_{II}$	146^{A},	pl. 1170	(Baudot, July–October 1793; Brival, Lanot, September 1793–Ventôse II)
		146^{A},	pl. 1171	(Bordas, Borie, March–April 1793; Lanot, Frimaire–Ventôse II)

Circumscriptions

Western Bureau

AF$_{II}$ 167 (March 1793)   168 (May 1793)   169 (September 1793)
170 (Brumaire II)   171 (Frimaire II)   172 (Pluviôse II)
173 (Messidor II)   174 (Year III)   175 (Year III)
175^A (Pluviôse II)   175^B (Pluviôse II) 176 (Ventôse II)
177 (Germinal II)   178 (Floréal II)   179 (Messidor–Fructidor II)
180 (Vendémiaire II)

Midi Bureau

AF$_{II}$ 182–97   (1793–Year II inclusive)

DEPARTMENTAL ARCHIVES [ARCH. DÉP.]

Aveyron	1L 178	(Mission of Bo and Chabot, March–May 1793)
	1L 180	(Missions of Fabre, Leyris, Bonnet, 1793–Year II)
	1L 181	(Mission of Bo, Year II)
	1L 353	(Correspondence with Châteauneuf-Randon, Frimaire Prairial II)
	1L 354	(Correspondence with Musset, Chazal, Bo, Paganel, Jean de Bry, Goupilleau, 1793–Year IV)
	1L 938	(Resolutions by Bo concerning grain supplies, Year II)
	1L 989	(Grain supplies, 1793–Year II)
	1L 1384	(Revolutionary taxes on suspects, 1793)
	1L 1385	(Forced Loan of 3 September 1793)
	1L 1386–7	(Revolutionary taxes and levies, Year II)
	1L 1948	(Poor relief, *Livre de la bienfaisance nationale*, Year II)
	1L 1952	(Welfare claims from needy mothers and widows, Year II)
	2L 8*	(District of Aubin: missions, Floréal II–Fructidor III)
	2L 12*	(District of Aubin: missions, Years II–III)
	2L 18	(District of Aubin: correspondence, Years II–III)
	5L 158	(District of Rodez: missions)
	5L 230	(District of Rodez: education, 1791–Year III)
	8L 16	(District of Sauveterre: missions, 1793–Year III)
	10L 15	(District of Villefranche-de-Rouergue: Taillefer, Year II)

	10L 121*	(District of Villefranche: *Livre de la bienfaisance nationale*, Year II)
	10L 124	(District of Villefranche: commons, 1794–1808)
Charente	L 67	(Missions of Bernard de Saintes, Guimberteau, Lequinio, Ingrand, Goupilleau, Bonnet, Fabre, Romme, Guezno and Topsent)
	L 68[1]	(Missions of Romme and others, 1793–Year II)
	L 68[2]	(Correspondence with Romme concerning grain supplies, Ventôse II)
	L 500*	(Correspondence with Roux-Fazillac, Harmand, Tallien and Ysabeau, Year II)
	L 1239	(District of Confolens: resolutions by Roux-Fazillac, Romme, Bordas, May 1793–Prairial III)
	L 1473[1]	(District of La Rochefoucauld: resolutions by Romme, Lequinio, Tallien, Topsent, Guezno, Pluviôse–Germinal II)
	L 1962	(Missions to the Charente by Romme, Roux-Fazillac, Legendre, Bordas, 1793 and Years II–III)
	L 1963	(Resolutions and proclamations, September 1793–Fructidor III)
Corrèze	L 96	(Missions, 1793–Year IV: changes in personnel)
	L 97	(Missions, 1793–Year IV: unrest)
	L 98	(Missions, 1793–Year IV: grain supplies)
	L 99	(Missions, 1793–Year IV: departmental administration)
	L 100	(Missions, 1793–Year IV: military affairs)
	L 101	(Missions, 1793–Year IV: Tulle arms factory)
	L 102	(Missions, 1793–Year IV: public works)
	L 103	(Missions, 1793–Year IV: judicial matters)
	L 104	(Missions, 1793–Year IV: poor relief)
	L 105	(Missions, 1793–Year IV: detainees)
	L 258–9	(Tulle arms factory: Roux-Fazillac, Year II)
	L 260*	(Tulle arms factory: correspondence, Thermidor II–Messidor III)
	L 263–4	(Welfare, *ateliers de charité*, road-mending, 1791–Year VII)
	L 273	(Education, September 1790–Floréal VIII)
	L 318	(District of Brive: education, 1792–Year VIII)
	L 321	(District of Brive: welfare, 1790–Year IV)
	L 322*	(District of Brive: soldiers' welfare payments, 1791–3)

	L 334*	(District of Tulle: correspondence with Lanot and Roux-Fazillac, Year II)
	L 760	(Jacobin club of Brive, Year III)
	L 779*–80	(Jacobin club of Treignac: measures by Lanot)
Creuse	L 105*	(Missions of Goupilleau, Ingrand, Monestier du Puy-de-Dôme, Petitjean, Vernerey, Chauvin, Cledel)
	L 146	(National festivals and ceremonies, 1793–Year IX)
	L 232	(Primary education, Year II)
	L 297	(District of Aubusson: welfare decree of 22 Floréal II)
	L 417	(District of Evaux: recruitment of stonemasons for the Tulle arms factory by Roux-Fazillac, Year II)
	L 551	(District of Felletin: welfare payments, Year II)
	L 557*	(District of Guéret: waifs and strays, January 1793–Brumaire II)
	L 733*	(Jacobin club of Guéret, March–April 1793)
	L 734*	(Jacobin club of Guéret, September 1793–Nivôse II)
	L 744	(Reports by members of the Committee of Public Safety in Paris)
Dordogne	1L 225	(Mission of Lacoste and Saint-André, 1793)
	1L 226	(Mission of Treilhard and Mathieu, June 1793)
	1L 227	(Missions of deputies to Agen, summer of 1793)
	1L 228	(Mission of Roux-Fazillac, October 1793–Nivôse II)
	1L 231	(Mission of Paganel, Year II)
	1L 232	(Mission of Lakanal, Year II)
	1L 233	(Mission of Romme, Year II)
	1L 237	(Mission of Chauvier, Year III)
	1L 304–5	(Missions: correspondence, October 1792–Brumaire IV)
	1L 306	(Missions: correspondence, Prairial II–Year IV)
	1L 594–7	(Education, 1791–Year VII)
	1L 665–7	(Welfare, taxation, 1792–Year VIII)
	2L 93	(District of Belvès: Forced Loan, 1793–Year II)
	2L 125	(District of Belvès: soldiers' welfare benefits, Years II–III)
	2L 133	(District of Belvès: education, Years II–IV)
	2L 157	(District of Belvès: welfare, decree of 22 Floréal II)

	3L 24–5	(District of Bergerac: missions, 1792–Year III)
	3L 56	(District of Bergerac: revolutionary taxes, Year II)
	4L 32*	(District of Excideuil: missions, correspondence, Pluviôse II–Prairial III)
	4L 45*	(District of Excideuil: resolutions by Romme and others, September 1793–Fructidor II)
	4L 214	(District of Excideuil: primary schools, 1793–Year IV)
	5L 124	(District of Montignac: primary schools, Years II–III)
	7L 52	(District of Nontron: revolutionary taxes by Lakanal and Roux-Fazillac, Year II)
	8L 130–1*	(District of Périgueux: soldiers' welfare, 1792–Year II)
	8L 137	(District of Périgueux: primary schools, Years II–III)
	8L 145	(District of Périgueux: poor relief, hospitals, 1791–Year II)
	13L 12	(Jacobin club of Périgueux)
Lot	L 2	(Council deliberations, December 1792–Frimaire Year II)
	L 10–11	(Missions to the Pyrenees Armies; requisitions)
	L 12–13	(Missions of Baudot, Chaudron-Roussau, Taillefer, Bo, July 1793–Ventôse II)
	L 14	(Proclamations, Year II)
	L 73–4	(Missions of Delbrel, Paganel, Pinet; correspondence, 1793–Year III)
	L 79	(District of Lauzerte: unrest, 1790–Year III)
	L 416	(District of Prayssac: suspects, Year II)
	L 417–19	(District of Puy-l'Evêque: certificates of civism)
Lot-et-Garonne	L 147	Missions of Tallien, Ysabeau, Treilhard, September 1793–Year III)
	L 148	(Mission of Monestier de la Lozère, Germinal–Prairial II)
	L 149–52	(Missions of Paganel and Garrau, March 1793–Year II)
	L 283	(Missions of Paganel and Monestier de la Lozère, 1793–Year II)
	L 292	(Missions of Treilhard, Mathieu and Monestier, 1793–Year II)
	L 293	(Demolition of *châteaux-forts*, abolition of seigneurial rents, 1793–Year II)
	L 300	(Mission of Paganel to Agen, 1793–Year II)
	L 313	(Mission of Monestier de la Lozère, Prairial II)
	L 317	(Mission of Monestier, Pluviôse–Floréal II)

	L 500–1	(Primary schools, 1793–Year VII)
	L 530	(Cult of Reason festival, 20 Frimaire II)
	L 531	(Welfare, decrees of 28 June 1793 and 22 Floréal II)
	L 534	(Agen hospitals: measures by Paganel)
Tarn	L 130–2	(Missions, 30 March 1793–22 Brumaire III)
	L 135–6	(Missions, 26 March 1793–11 Brumaire III)
	L 705*	(District of Albi: missions, Ventôse II–Year IV)
	L 815*	(District of Castres: missions, Frimaire II–Pluviôse III)
	L 855*	(District of Gaillac: missions, Brumaire II–Year IV)
	L 975	(District of Lavaur: missions, September 1793–Messidor III)
	L 1513–14	(Jacobin club of Albi, correspondence, Year II)
	L 1531–5	(Jacobin club of Castres, correspondence, 1793–Year III)
	L 1571	(Jacobin club of Puycelci, correspondence, Year II)
Tarn-et-Garonne	L 2*	(District of Castelsarrasin: missions, Pluviôse II–Year IV)
	L 13	(District of Castelsarrasin: division of commons, Years II–IV)
	L 21*	(District of Castelsarrasin: poor relief, *Livre de la bienfaisance nationale*)
	L 37	(District of Grenade-Beaumont: division of commons, 1791–Year IV)
	L 53	(District of Lauzerte: deliberations, 1792–Year IV)
	L 75*	(District of Montauban: missions, October 1793–Frimaire III)
	L 76	(District of Montauban: resolutions and proclamations, 1793–Year III)
	L 82–5*	(District of Montauban: deliberations, September 1792–Fructidor II)
	L 112	(District of Montauban: education, Years II–IV)
Haute-Vienne	L 106	(Missions of Bordas, Borie, Brival, Cherrier, 1793–Year III)
	L 109	(Missions of Lanot, Pénières, 1793–Year III)
	L 110	(Missions of Romme, Lakanal, Roux-Fazillac, Ingrand, 1793–Year III)
	L 161	(Constitutional referendum of 1793)
	L 181	(Missions of Bordas, Borie, Philippeaux, March–July 1793)

L 195	(Demolition of *châteaux-forts*: resolutions by Borie and Brival, Year II)
L 285	(Tulle and Bergerac arms factories: Roux-Fazillac and Pellissier)
L 382	(Vagrancy in Limoges, 1793–Year II: Brival)
L 384	(Application of the republican calendar, Years II–IV)
L 469	(District of Limoges: small arms, measures by Roux-Fazillac, Lakanal, Legendre)
L 528	(District of Bellac: recruitment, 1793–Year II)
L 534–5	(District of Bellac: primary schools, Years II–III)
L 555	(District of Le Dorat: missions correspondence, Year II)
L 569	(District of Le Dorat: missions of Gay-Vernon, Brival, Cledel, 1793–Year III)
L 750	(District of Saint-Yrieix: missions, Year II)
L 818	(Jacobin club of Limoges; incomplete collection of *Journal du département de la Haute-Vienne*; see municipal archives below)
L 820	(Jacobin club of Limoges, Year II)

MUNICIPAL ARCHIVES [ARCH. MUN.]

Agen	49°/1–3	(Revolutionary taxes, 1793–Brumaire IV)
	124°	(Jacobin club: deliberations 1790–1, subscriptions 1793)
	191°	(Temple of Reason, Year II)
	192°	(Primary schools: lists of teachers)
Bergerac	M 1-U, 42, 44, 48	(Resolutions by Lakanal, Year II)
Limoges	Municipal Library	(Collection of *Journal du département de la Haute-Vienne*, September 1793–Fructidor II)
Périgueux	D/2–4	(Municipal Council register, 26 March 1790–Year III)
	D/5	(Municipal Council register, Ventôse II–Year IV)
Tulle	1D2, IE DEP 272/55	(Council deliberations; July 1792–Ventôse III)
	1R3, 1E DEP 272/236	(Register of school girls, 28 Prairial II–Brumaire IV)

PRINTED SOURCES

OFFICIAL RECORDS, PROCEEDINGS AND COMPENDIA

Note: Abbreviations used given in square brackets.

Archives parlementaires des Chambres françaises: première série, 1787 à 1797, 98 vols., Paris, 1862–1995, vols. X to XCVIII (to 8 October 1794–17 Vendémiaire III), *Constituante, Législative et Convention* [*Arch. parl.*].

F. A. Aulard (ed.), *La Société des Jacobins: recueil de documents pour l'histoire du club des Jacobins de Paris*, 6 vols., Paris, 1889–97 [Aulard, *Jacobins*].

F. A. Aulard, *et al.* (eds.), *Recueil des actes du Comité de salut public, avec la correspondance officielle des représentants en mission et le registre du Conseil exécutif provisoire*, 27 vols., Paris, 1889–1933, and the *Supplément*, ed. by M. Bouloiseau, 2 vols., Paris, 1966–71 [Aulard, *Recueil*].

La Commission des subsistances de l'an II: procès-verbaux et actes, ed. by P. Caron, Paris, 1925.

Les Déclarations des droits de l'homme (du débat de 1789–1793 au préambule de 1946), ed. by L. Jaume, Paris, 1989.

Documents inédits pour servir à l'histoire de l'industrie, du commerce et de l'agriculture en Bas-Limousin à la fin du XVIIIe siècle et au début du XIXe siècle: la manufacture d'armes de Tulle, ed. by G. Mathieu, Paris, 1913.

Documents inédits sur la vie économique de la Révolution française: le Club des Jacobins de Tulle, procès-verbaux (1790 à 1795), ed. by V. Forot, Tulle and Paris, 1912.

Une éducation pour la démocratie: textes et projets de l'époque révolutionnaire, ed. by B. Baczko, Paris, 1982.

Gazette Nationale ou le Moniteur universel, 24 vols., Paris, 1789–Year VIII.

Histoire parlementaire de la Révolution française, ou Journal des Assemblées nationales depuis 1789 jusqu'en 1815, ed. by B.-J. Buchez and P.-C. Roux, 40 vols., Paris, 1834–8.

Notes et documents sur l'instruction publique en Corrèze pendant la Révolution, ed. by G. Mathieu, Paris, 1912.

Papiers inédits trouvés chez Robespierre, Saint-Just, Payan, etc., supprimés ou omis par Courtois, précédés du rapport de ce député à la Convention Nationale, 16 Nivôse an III, 3 vols., Paris, 1828.

Le partage des communaux: documents sur la préparation de la loi du 10 juin 1793, ed. by G. Bourgin, Paris, 1908.

Procès-verbal de la Convention Nationale, imprimé par son ordre, 72 vols. (Paris, 1792–Year IV), I to XLII, and *Table analytique*, ed. by G. Lefebvre, M. Reinhard and M. Bouloiseau, 2 vols., Paris, 1959–61.

Procès-verbaux des Comités d'agriculture et de commerce de la Constituante, de la Législative et de la Convention, ed. by F. Gerbaux and C. Schmidt, 4 vols., Paris, 1906–10.

Procès-verbaux des séances de la société populaire de Rodez, ed. by
B. Combes de Patris, Rodez, 1912.
Procès-verbaux du Comité d'instruction publique de la Convention nationale,
ed. by J. Guillaume, 6 vols., Paris, 1890–1907, vols. I to IV.
Réimpression de l'Ancien Moniteur (May 1789–November 1799), 32 vols.,
Paris, 1863–70.
La société populaire de Beaumont-en-Périgord (1792–1795), ed. by
L. Testut, Bordeaux, 1923.
*La société populaire de Montignac pendant la Révolution: procès-verbaux
des séances*, ed. by E. Le Roy, Bordeaux, 1888.
*La société populaire de Périgueux pendant la Révolution (7 nivôse–8
fructidor an III)*, ed. by E. Poumeau, Périgueux, 1907.

INDIVIDUAL AND COLLECTED WORKS

Note: In the case of printed speeches and pamphlets, the catalogue
reference is to the Bibliothèque Nationale de France [Bibl. Nat.].

Barère, B., *Mémoires*, ed. by H. Carnot and P. J. David d'Angers, 4 vols.,
Paris, 1842–4.
Barnave, A., *Introduction à la Révolution française*, ed. by F. Rude, Paris,
1960.
Baudot, M.-A., *Notes historiques sur la Convention Nationale, le Directoire,
l'Empire et l'exil des votants*, ed. by Veuve E. Quinet, Paris, 1893.
Bernard d'Héry, P., *Rapport sur l'organisation générale des secours publics
et sur la destruction de la mendicité, présenté ... au nom du Comité des
secours publics ... le 13 juin 1792*, Paris, no date, Bibl. Nat., 8° Le^{33}
3 Y (12).
Billaud-Varenne, J. N., *Mémoires inédits et correspondance*, ed. by
A. Bégis, Paris, 1893.
Principes régénérateurs du système social, ed. by Fr. Brunel, Paris,
1992.
Bo, J.-B., *Discours prononcé aux sociétés populaires d'Aurillac, de Mon-
tauban et de Castres*, Castres, Year II, Bibl. Nat., 8° Lb^{40} 2504.
*Rapport sur l'extinction de la mendicité, fait au nom du Comité des secours
publics*, Paris, 21 Vendémiaire II, Bibl. Nat., 8° Le^{38} 499.
Bordas, P. and J. Borie, *Rapport sur le recrutement de 300,000 hommes*,
Paris, 1793, Bibl. Nat., 8° Le^{39} 8.
Brissot, J.-P. (de Warville), *A ses commettans, sur la situation de la
Convention Nationale, sur l'influence des anarchistes*, Paris and
London, 1794.
Mémoires, ed. by M. de Lescure, Paris, 1877.
Théorie des lois criminelles, 2 vols., Berlin, 1781.
Brival, J., *Discours prononcé au temple de la Raison de Tulle*, 10 Nivôse II,
Bibl. Nat., 8° Lb^{41} 3629.
Lettre à la société populaire de Limoges, 20 Germinal II, Bibl. Nat., 8°
Lb^{41} 1049.
Opinion sur la Constitution, Paris, no date, Bibl. Nat., 8° Le^{38} 2338.

Buonarroti, P., *Conspiration pour l'égalité dite de Babeuf*, 2 vols., Brussels, 1828.

Burke, E., 'Reflections on the Revolution in France', in *The Works of the Right Hon. Edmund Burke*, ed. by H. Rogers, 2 vols., London, 1837, vol. I, pp. 382–475.

Buzot, F., *Mémoires sur la Révolution française*, ed. by M. Guadet, Paris, 1823.

Cabarrus, Th., *Discours sur l'éducation, prononcé au temple de la Raison de Bordeaux, 10 nivôse an II*, Bordeaux, Year II, Bibl. Nat., 8° Rés. Lb⁴¹ 3626.

Cavaignac, M. J., *Les mémoires d'une inconnue (Mme Cavaignac), publiés sur le manuscrit original, 1780–1816*, Paris, 1894.

Chabot, Fr., *Projet d'acte constitutif des Français*, Paris, no date, Bibl. Nat., 8° Le³⁸ 2416.

Chaudron-Rousseau, J., *Prière de l'homme libre à l'Eternel*, Toulouse, no date, Bibl. Nat., 8° Lb⁴¹ 3858.

Chauvin, F. A., *Rapport de sa mission et analyse des désordres des départements de la Vienne, de la Haute-Vienne et de la Creuse pendant la 2e année de la République*, Paris, Germinal III, Bibl. Nat., 8° Le³⁹ 245.

Clavière, E., L. Mercier, A. Guy-Kersaint, J.-P. Brissot *et al.*, *La Chronique du mois, ou les Cahiers patriotiques*, Paris, November 1791 to November 1792.

Condorcet, C. de, *Œuvres*, ed. by A. Condorcet O'Connor and M. F. Arago, 12 vols., Paris, 1847–9.

Courtois, E. B., *Papiers inédits trouvés chez Robespierre, Saint-Just, Payan, etc., supprimés ou omis par Courtois, précédés du rapport de ce député à la Convention Nationale,16 Nivôse an III*, 3 vols., Paris, 1828.

Dacier, A., *Les vies des hommes illustres de Plutarque*, trans. A. Dacier, 3rd edn, 10 vols., Amsterdam, 1735.

Danton, G. J., *Œuvres*, ed. by A. Vermorel, Paris, 1866.

Desmoulins, C., *Œuvres*, ed. by A. Soboul, facs. edn, 10 vols., Munich, 1980.

Diderot, D., *Contes*, ed. by H. Dieckman, London, 1963.

Œuvres complètes, ed. by J. Assézat and M. Tourneux, 20 vols., Paris, 1875–7.

Diderot, D. (ed.), *Encyclopédie: ou Dictionnaire raisonné des sciences, des arts et des métiers*, 28 vols., Paris, 1751–72, vols. V and VIII.

Textes choisis de l'Encyclopédie, ed. by A. Soboul, Paris, 1962.

Dupont de Nemours, P. S., *Idées sur les secours à donner aux pauvres malades dans une grande ville*, Philadelphia and Paris, 1786.

Fouché, J., *Mémoires*, ed. by M. Vovelle, Paris, 1993.

Goujon, J. M. C. A., 'Correspondance familiale', in Brunel and Goujon, *Les martyrs de prairial*, pp. 215–363.

Grégoire, H., *Œuvres*, ed. by A. Soboul, facs. edn, 14 vols., Paris and Liechtenstein, 1977.

Harmand, J. B., *Quelques idées sur les premiers éléments du nouveau contrat social des Français*, Paris, 17 April 1793, Bibl. Nat., 8° Le³⁸ 2146.

Hérault de Séchelles, M. J., *Constitution française de 1793*, Paris, 1793, Bibl. Nat., 8° Le^{38} 236.

Rapport sur la Constitution française, Paris, 10 juin 1793, Bibl. Nat., 8° Le^{38} 2227.

Hirzel, H. C., *Le Socrate rustique, ou description de la conduite économique et morale d'un paysan philosophe*, trans. Frey des Landres, Zurich, 1762.

Jaucourt, L. de, 'Impôt', in *Encyclopédie: ou Dictionnaire raisonné des sciences, des arts et des métiers*, 28 vols. (Paris, 1751–72), vol. VIII, pp. 601–4

Jeanbon Saint-André [André Jeanbon], *Opinion sur les bases de l'économie politique*, 26 Floréal III, Bibl. Nat., 8° Le^{38} 1427.

Réflexions sur l'éducation nationale, Paris, 20 December 1792, Bibl. Nat., 8° Le^{38} 2259.

Lakanal, J., *Décret sur le Jardin national des plantes et rapport du 10 juin 1793*, Paris, 1793, Bibl. Nat., 8° Le^{38} 1804.

Exposé sommaire des travaux pour sauver, durant la Révolution, les sciences, les lettres et ceux qui les honoraient, Paris, 1838.

Rapport sur Jean-Jacques Rousseau, Paris, 29 Fructidor II, Bibl. Nat., 8° Le^{38} 945.

Lepeletier de Saint-Fargeau, M., 'Plan d'éducation nationale', in *Œuvres de Maximilien Robespierre*, vol. X, pp. 10–42.

Lequinio, J. M., *Des fêtes nationales*, Paris, Year III, Bibl. Nat., 8° Le^{38} 1131.

Du bonheur: discours prononcé au temple de la Vérité de Rochefort, 20 brumaire an II, Angoulême, 1793, Bibl. Nat., 8° Lb^{41} 3484.

Ecole des laboureurs, Rennes, 30 May 1790, Bibl. Nat., 8° Lb^{39} 11385.

Plan d'éducation nationale, Paris, 2 July 1793, Bibl. Nat., 8° Le^{38} 2546.

Levasseur, R., *Mémoires de René Levasseur (de la Sarthe)*, ed. by A. Roche and F. Levasseur, 2 vols., Paris, 1829–31.

Louvet, J.-B., *Quelques notices pour l'histoire et le récit de mes périls depuis le 31 mai 1793*, Paris, Year III, Bibl. Nat., 8° La^{33} 78.

Mably, G. Bonnot de, *Des droits et des devoirs du citoyen*, ed. by J.-L. Lecercle, Paris, 1972.

Entretiens de Phocion sur le rapport de la morale avec la politique, Paris, 1792.

Observations sur les Grecs, Genève, 1749.

Principes de morale, Paris, 1784.

Sur la théorie du pouvoir politique, ed. by P. Friedmann, Paris, 1975.

Marat, J.-P., *Œuvres politiques, 1789–1793*, ed. by J. de Cock et C. Goëtz, 10 vols., Brussels, 1989–95.

Textes choisis, ed. by M. Vovelle, Paris, 1963.

Mercier, L. S., *L'an deux mille quatre cent quarante, suivi de l'homme de fer*, ed. by R. Trousson, Geneva, 1979.

Monestier, J.-B., *Correspondance*, ed. by U. Jouvet, Riom, 1897.

Montesquieu, Ch.-L. de S., *De l'esprit des lois*, ed. by R. Derathé, 2 vols., Paris, 1973.

Necker, J., *Sur la législation et le commerce des grains*, 2 vols., Paris, 1775.

Paganel, P., *Discours prononcé au temple de la Raison de Toulouse, 20 frimaire an II*, Toulouse, Bibl. Nat., 8° Lb⁴¹ 3577.

Essai historique et critique sur la Révolution française, 3 vols., Paris, 1815.

Rapport au nom du Comité des secours publics, Paris, Year III, Bibl. Nat., 8° Le³⁹ 1004.

Paine, T., *The Rights of Man*, ed. by A. Seldon, London, 1958.

Pétion, J., *Œuvres*, 3 vols., Paris, 1791–2.

Philippeaux, P., *Compte rendu à la Convention Nationale*, Paris, 1793, Bibl. Nat., 8° Le³⁹ 36.

Pinet, J., *Discours prononcé dans la ci-devant église cathédrale de Bayonne, 10 frimaire an II*, Year II, Bibl. Nat., 8° Lb⁴¹ 3553.

Pointe, N., *Des crimes des sociétés populaires, précédés de leur origine*, Paris, no date, Bibl. Nat., 8° Lb⁴¹ 4118.

Discours prononcé au temple de la Raison de Nevers, 30 Germinal an II, Year II, Bibl. Nat., 8° Lb⁴¹ 3820.

Ramel-Nogaret, D., *Rapport et projet de décret faits et présentés au nom du Comité des finances sur l'emprunt forcé d'un milliard, 19 août 1793*, Paris, no date, Bibl. Nat., 8° Le³⁸ 420.

Rétif [Restif] de la Bretonne, N., *La vie de mon père*, ed. by G. Rouger, Paris, 1970.

Robespierre, M., *Œuvres complètes*, or *Œuvres de Maximilien Robespierre*, ed. by M. Bouloiseau, J. Dautry, E. Déprez, G. Laurent, G. Lefebvre, E. Lesueur, G. Michon, and A. Soboul, 10 vols., Paris, Nancy and Gap, 1910–67.

Rœderer, P. L., *Œuvres*, ed. by A. M. Rœderer, 8 vols., Paris, 1853–9.

Roland, J.-M., *Encyclopédie méthodique: manufactures, arts et métiers*, 4 vols., Paris, 1785–90.

Roland, M. P., *Mémoires de Madame Roland* (Paris, 1820), ed. by P. de Roux, Paris, 1986.

Romme, G., *Annuaire du cultivateur*, Paris, Year III, Bibl. Nat., 8° S 20896.

Rapport sur l'ère de la République, 10 septembre 1793, Paris, 1793, Bibl. Nat. 8° Le³⁸ 460.

Rapports sur l'instruction publique, Paris, 1793, Bibl. Nat., 8° Le³⁸ 2127 and R 7251.

Tableau des divers projets de nomenclature du calendrier de la République, 20 septembre 1793, Paris, 1793, Bibl. Nat., Le³⁸ 460 bis.

Rousseau, J.-J., 'Considérations sur le gouvernement de Pologne', in *Œuvres complètes*, vol. III, pp. 527–69.

Discours sur l'origine et les fondements de l'inégalité parmi les hommes, ed. by J.-L. Lecercle, Paris, 1965.

'Du contrat social', in *Œuvres complètes*, vol. II, pp. 518–85.

'Economie politique', in *Œuvres complètes*, vol. II, pp. 276–305.

La Nouvelle Héloïse, ed. R. Pomeau, Paris, 1960.

Œuvres complètes, ed. by J. Fabre and M. Launay, 3 vols., Paris, 1967–71.

'Projet de constitution pour la Corse', in *Œuvres complètes*, vol. III, pp. 492–515.

Rozier, F., *Cours complet d'agriculture théorique, pratique, économique et de médecine rurale et vétérinaire . . . ou Dictionnaire universel d'agriculture*, 12 vols., Paris, 1781–1805, vols. I to VIII, A-Rumination (1781–9).

Saint-Just, L.-A. de, *Discours et rapports*, ed. by A. Soboul, 2nd edn, Paris, 1970.

Frammenti sulle istituzione repubblicane, ed. by A. Soboul, Turin, 1952.

Œuvres complètes, ed. by Ch. Vellay, 2 vols., Paris, 1908.

Théorie politique, ed. by A. Liénard, Paris, 1976.

Sieyès, E. J., *Essai sur les privilèges*, Paris, 1788.

Qu'est-ce que le Tiers Etat?, Paris, 1789.

Smith, A., *An Inquiry into the Nature and Causes of the Wealth of Nations*, ed. by R. H. Campbell, A. S. Skinner and W. B. Todd, 2 vols., Oxford, 1976.

Taillefer, J. G., *Ma réponse aux épisodes de Fréron*, 20 Pluviôse Year III, Bibl. Nat., 8° Lb⁴¹ 1616.

Tallien, J. L., *Discours sur les principes du gouvernement révolutionnaire, 12 fructidor an II*, Bibl. Nat., 8° Le³⁸ 918.

Thibaudeau, A. C., *Mémoires sur la Convention et le Directoire*, 2 vols., Paris, 1824.

Tissot, P.-F., 'Vie de Goujon', in Brunel and Goujon, *Les martyrs de prairial*, pp. 91–214.

Treilhard, J.-B., and Mathieu, J. B., *Compte rendu de leur mission dans les départements de la Gironde, du Lot-et-Garonne et circonvoisins, 30 juillet 1793*, Paris, 1793, Bibl. Nat., 8° Le³⁹ 29.

Turgot, A. R. J., *Ecrits économiques*, ed. by B. Cazes, Paris, 1970.

Œuvres de Turgot, et documents le concernant, ed. by G. Schelle, 3 vols., Paris, 1913–19.

Vergniaud, P. V., *Œuvres de Vergniaud, Guadet, Gensonné*, ed. by A. Vermorel, Paris, 1866.

Vernier, Th., *Impôt sur le luxe et les richesses, établi d'après les principes qui doivent diriger les législateurs républicains*, Paris, 1792, Bibl. Nat., 8° Le³⁸ 2047.

Voltaire, F. M. Arouet, *Dictionnaire philosophique*, ed. by R. Naves and J. Benda, Paris, 1967.

Young, A., *Travels in France and Italy*, ed. by T. Okey, London, 1976.

SECONDARY WORKS

Adher, J., *Département de la Haute-Garonne: le Comité de subsistances de Toulouse (12 août 1793–1er mars 1795)*, Toulouse, 1912.

Ado, A., 'Le mouvement paysan et le problème de l'égalité', in Soboul, *Contributions à l'histoire paysanne*, p. 137.

Paysans en Révolution: terre, pouvoir et jacquerie, 1789–1794, ed. by S. Abadam and M. Dorigny, preface by M. Vovelle, Paris, 1996.

'Les paysans et la Révolution française', *Cahiers historiques de l'Institut M. Thorez* 12 (1978), pp. 39–65.

Aftalion, F., *L'économie de la Révolution française*, Paris, 1987; in Eng. trans., *The French Revolution: An Economic Interpretation*, Cambridge, 1990.

Agulhon, M., *Marianne au combat: l'imagerie ou la symbolique républicaine de 1789 à 1880*, Paris, 1979.

Alhéritière, C., *Les communaux en France, spécialement en Creuse*, Paris, 1912.

Antoine, G., *Liberté, Egalité, Fraternité, ou les fluctuations d'une devise*, Paris, 1981.

Arendt, H., *The Origins of Totalitarianism*, 5th edn, San Diego, 1975.

Arsac, F., 'Une émeute contre-révolutionnaire à Meymac (Corrèze)', *Annales hist. Révol. fr.* 13 (1936), pp. 149–62.

Aulard, F. A., 'La commune de Challignac (Charente): documents inédits, du 21 février 1790 à fin thermidor an II', *La Révol. fr.* 36 (1899), pp. 549–53.

'Le culte de la Raison', *La Révol. fr.* 20 (1891), pp. 97–120, 193–219.

'Le culte de l'Etre Suprême: le culte en province', *La Révol. fr.* 21 (1891), pp. 307–27.

'Les derniers Jacobins', *La Révol. fr.*, 26 (1894), pp. 385–407.

Etudes et leçons sur la Révolution française, 6th series, Paris, 1910.

Histoire politique de la Révolution française: origines et développement de la Démocratie et de la République (1789–1804), Paris, 1901.

'La journée du 4 septembre 1870', *La Révol. fr.* 31 (1896), p. 394.

Review of H. Labroue, *La mission du conventionnel Lakanal dans la Dordogne en l'an II (octobre 1793– août 1794)* (Paris, 1912), *La Révol. fr.* 69 (1916), pp. 225–42.

Baczko, B., *Ending the Terror: The French Revolution After Robespierre*, Cambridge, 1994.

'The Terror Before the Terror? Conditions of Possibility, Logic of Realization', in Baker, *The Terror*, pp. 19–38.

'Thermidoriens', in Furet and M. Ozouf, *Dictionnaire critique*, 1st edn, pp. 425–39.

Badinter, E., and R. Badinter, *Condorcet (1743–1794): un intellectuel en politique*, 2nd edn, Paris, 1988.

Baechler, J., *Démocraties*, Paris, 1985.

Baker, K. M., *Condorcet: From Natural Philosophy to Social Mathematics*, Chicago and London, 1975.

Inventing the French Revolution: Essays on French Political Culture in the Eighteenth Century, Cambridge, 1990.

The Political Culture of the Old Regime, Oxford, 1987.

Baker, K. M. (ed.), *The Terror*, vol. IV, in K. M. Baker, Fr. Furet, C. Lucas and M. Ozouf (eds.), *The French Revolution and the Creation of Modern Political Culture*, 4 vols., Oxford, 1987–94.

Balzac, H. de, *Les paysans*, ed. by P. Barbéris, Paris, 1970.

Bapst, G., 'Inventaire des bibliothèques de quatre condamnés (Louis XVI, Robespierre, Saint-Just, Couthon)', *La Révol. fr.* 21 (1891), pp. 532–8.

Barny, R., 'Robespierre et les Lumières', in Jessenne *et al.*, *Robespierre*, pp. 45–59.

Barry, J., and C. Jones, *Medicine and Charity Before the Welfare State*, London and New York, 1991.

Bart, J., 'Les anticipations de l'an II dans le droit de la famille: l'intégration des "enfants de la nature"', *Annales hist. Révol. fr.* 300 (April–June 1995), pp. 192–3.

'Statut de la propriété, question agraire: usages collectifs et exploitation individuelle', in Jessenne *et al.*, *Robespierre*, pp. 253–61.

Review of J.-L. Halpérin, *L'impossible code civil* (Paris, 1992), *Revue d'hist. mod. et cont.* 41-3 (July–September 1994), pp. 537–9.

Baticle, R., 'Le plébiscite sur la Constitution de 1793: la réunion des assemblées primaires; le vote des armées; le recensement et le résultat; les amendements économiques', *La Révol. fr.* 57 (1909), pp. 496–524 and 58 (1910), pp. 5–30, 117–55, 193–237, 327–41, 385–410.

Becamps, P., 'La question des grains et de la boulangerie à Bordeaux de 1793 à 1796', *Actes du 83e Congrès national des sociétés savantes, Aix-Marseille, 1958*, Paris, 1959, p. 260.

Belloni, G., *Le Comité de sûreté générale de la Convention nationale*, Paris, 1924.

Berlanstein, L. R., Review of J.-L. Halpérin, *L'impossible code civil* (Paris, 1992), *Journal of Modern History* 66 (September 1994), pp. 616–17.

Berriat-Saint-Prix, C., *La justice révolutionnaire: août 1792 à prairial an III, d'après des documents originaux, la plupart inédits*, Paris, 1870.

Bertaud, J.-P., 'An Open File: The Press Under the Terror', in Baker, *The Terror*, pp. 297–308.

'La presse de l'an II: aperçu des recherches en cours', *Annales hist. Révol. fr.* 300 (April–June 1995), pp. 161–72.

La Révolution armée: les soldats-citoyens et la Révolution française, Paris, 1979.

Bianchi, S., 'La déchristianisation de l'an II: essai d'interprétation', *Annales hist. Révol. fr.* 50 (1978), pp. 341–71.

Biard, M., *Jean-Marie Collot-d'Herbois, homme de théâtre et homme de pouvoir (1749–1796)*, Lyons, 1995.

Bloch, C., *L'assistance et l'Etat en France à la veille de la Révolution (généralités de Paris, Rouen, Alençon, Orléans, Soissons, Amiens), 1764–1790*, Paris, 1908.

Bloch, M., *Caractères originaux de l'histoire rurale française*, 2 vols., Paris, 1952.

Bobett, C., and J. Kesti, *European Tax Handbook, 1991*, Amsterdam, 1991.

Bocquet, L., *L'impôt sur le revenu cédulaire et général*, Paris, 1921.

Bornarel, F., *Cambon et la Révolution française*, Paris, 1905.

Bosher, J. F., *French Finances, 1770–1795: From Business to Bureaucracy*, Cambridge, 1970.

Bouloiseau, M., *Le Comité de salut public (1793–1795)*, 2nd edn, Paris, 1968.

Robespierre, Paris, 1965.

Le séquestre et la vente des biens des émigrés dans le district de Rouen, 1792–an X, Paris, 1937.

Bourde, A. J., *Agronomie et agronomes en France au XVIIIe siècle*, Paris, 1967.

The Influence of England on French Agronomes, 1750–1789, Cambridge, 1953.

Bourgin, H., and G. Bourgin, *L'industrie sidérurgique en France au début de la Révolution*, Paris, 1920.

Boutier, J., 'Elie Guadet', in Fr. Furet and M. Ozouf (eds.), *La Gironde et les Girondins*, Paris, 1991, pp. 389–408.

Boutier, J., and Ph. Boutry, 'La diffusion des sociétés politiques en France (1789–an III): une enquête nationale', *Annales hist. Révol. fr.* 266 (September–October 1986), pp. 366–98.

Braudel, F., M. Ferro, A. A. Gouber, A. Z. Manfred and R. Portal (eds.), *Au siècle des lumières*, Paris and Moscow, 1970.

Bredin, J. D., *Sieyès, la clé de la Révolution française*, Paris, 1988.

Brogan, D. W., *The American Political System*, London, 1951.

Broilliard, J.-L., 'Diagoras Boscovir [J.-Fr. de l'Etang]: un homme, un style, un tempérament', in *Pages sostraniennes*, La Souterraine and Guéret, 1982, p. 81.

'Luttes religieuses dans le district de Felletin (Creuse)', *Mémoires de la Société des sciences naturelles et archéologiques de la Creuse* 41 (1982), pp. 331–41.

Brunel, Fr., 'L'acculturation d'un révolutionnaire: l'exemple de Billaud-Varenne (1786–1791)', *Dix-Huitième Siècle* 23 (1991), pp. 261–74.

'Billaud-Varennes', in Soboul, *Dictionnaire historique*, pp. 121–3.

'Bridging the Gulf of the Terror', in Baker, *The Terror*, pp. 327–46.

Brunel, Fr., and S. Goujon (eds.), *Les martyrs de prairial: textes et documents inédits*, Geneva, 1992.

Burstin, H., 'Problems of Work During the Terror', in Baker, *The Terror*, pp. 271–93.

Butel, B. and G. Mandon, 'Alphabétisation et scolarisation en Aquitaine au XVIIIe siècle et au début du XIXe siècle', in Furet and J. Ozouf, *Lire et écrire*, pp. 7–41.

Calvet, H., 'Subsistances et fédéralisme', *Annales hist. Révol. fr.* 8 (1931), p. 229.

Campagnac, E., 'Les débuts de la déchristianisation dans le Cher, septembre 1793–frimaire an II', *Annales révol.* 4 (1911), pp. 626–37, and 5 (1912), pp. 41–9, 206–11.

'Les délégués du représentant Laplanche en mission dans le Cher', *La Révol. fr.* 43 (1902), pp. 300–46, and 44 (1903), pp. 29–54.

'L'impôt sur le revenu dans les statuts d'une société populaire en 1793', *Annales révol.* 3 (1910), pp. 242–4.

Canto, M., Introduction to Plato's *Gorgias*, Paris, 1987, pp. 1–97.

Cardenal, L. de, 'Robespierre et le terrorisme après thermidor', *Annales hist. Révol. fr.* 5 (1928), pp. 314–42.

'Les subsistances dans le département de la Dordogne (1789–an IV)', *La*

Révol. fr. 82 (1929), pp. 217–54, 310–27, and 83 (1930), pp. 18–46, 105–34.

Carlyle, T., 'Chartism' (1839), in *Critical and Miscellaneous Essays*, 4 vols., London, 1899, vol. IV, pp. 118–204.

'Past and Present' (1843), in *The Works of Thomas Carlyle*, 30 vols. (London, 1896–9), vol. X, pp. 7–23.

Caron, P., 'La Commission civile révolutionnaire et de surveillance de l'Aveyron', *La Révol. fr.* 84 (1931), pp. 336–55.

'Recherches biographiques: Foulhioux', *La Révol. fr.* 84 (1931), pp. 225–64.

Certeau, M. de, D. Julia and J. Revel, *Une politique de la langue: la Révolution française et les patois, l'enquête de Grégoire*, Paris, 1975.

Chamboux, M., *Répartition de la propriété foncière et de l'exploitation dans la Creuse*, Paris, 1956.

Chassin, C. L., 'La mission de Lequinio et de Laignelot à Rochefort et en Vendée (1793–1794)', *La Révol. fr.* 28 (1895), pp. 119–40.

Chaumié, J., 'Les Girondins', in A. Soboul (ed.), *Actes du Colloque Girondins et Montagnards, Sorbonne, 14 décembre 1975*, Paris, 1980, pp. 19–60.

Le réseau d'Antraigues, Paris, 1965.

'Saint-Just et le procès des Girondins', in A. Soboul (ed.), *Actes du Colloque Saint-Just, Sorbonne, 25 juin 1967*, Paris, 1968, pp. 23–35.

Chaussinand-Nogaret, G., *La noblesse en France au XVIIIe siècle: de la féodalité aux lumières*, Paris, 1976.

Clamageran, J.-J., *Histoire de l'impôt en France*, 3 vols., Paris, 1867–76.

Clarétie, J., *Camille Desmoulins, Lucille Desmoulins: étude sur les Dantonistes*, Paris, 1875.

Cobb, R. C., *Les armées révolutionnaires, instrument de la Terreur dans les départements, avril 1793–floréal an II*, 2 vols., Paris and The Hague, 1961–3.

'Plaintes des paysans du Cantal, nivôse an III', *Annales hist. Révol. fr.* 33 (1961), pp. 99–102.

The Police and the People: French Popular Protest, 1789–1820, Oxford, 1970.

Cock, J. de, 'Marat prophète de la Terreur?', *Annales hist. Révol. fr.* 300 (April–June 1995), pp. 261–9.

Cocula, A. M., 'Les représentants de la Convention à Bordeaux en juin 1793: une mission impossible', in Fr. Furet and M. Ozouf (eds.), *La Gironde et les Girondins*, Paris, 1991, pp. 207–18.

Coquard, O., *Jean-Paul Marat*, Paris, 1993.

Crépel, P., 'Gilbert Romme et les mathématiques', in Ehrard, 'Gilbert Romme: actes du colloque de Riom', pp. 207–20.

Dard, E., *Un épicurien sous la Terreur: Hérault de Séchelles (1759–1794)*, Paris, 1907.

Darrow, M. H., 'Economic Terror in the City: The General Maximum in Montauban', *French Historical Studies* 17 (1991), pp. 498–525.

Revolution in the House: Family, Class and Inheritance in Southern France, 1775–1825, Princeton, 1989.

Dautry, J., 'Le "bonheur commun" pourrait-il être une formule vide?', *Annales hist. Révol. fr.* 39 (1967), p. 133.
David, M., 'La fraternité au temps du dénigrement (1800–1814)', *Annales hist. Révol. fr.* 295 (January–March 1994), pp. 1–18.
Fraternité et Révolution française, Paris, 1987.
Dayet, M., *Notes sur le conventionnel Vernerey et sur sa famille*, Besançon, 1912.
Delaporte, A., *L'idée d'égalité en France au XVIIIe siècle*, Paris, 1987.
Depors, H., *Recherches sur l'état de l'industrie des cuirs en France pendant le XVIIIe siècle et le début du XIXe siècle*, Paris, 1932.
Derathé, R., 'La place et l'importance de la notion d'égalité dans la doctrine politique de Jean-Jacques Rousseau', in R. A. Leigh (ed.), *Rousseau After Two Hundred Years: Proceedings of the Cambridge Bicentennial Colloquium (1978)*, Cambridge, 1982, pp. 55–63.
Desan, S., 'The Family as Cultural Battleground: Religion vs. Republic Under the Terror', in Baker, *The Terror*, pp. 177–93.
Reclaiming the Sacred: Lay Religion and Popular Politics in Revolutionary France, Ithaca, 1990.
Dommanget, M., 'Les Egaux et la Constitution de 1793', in *Sur Babeuf et la conjuration des Egaux*, Paris, 1970, pp. 174–203.
'Saint-Just et la question agraire', *Annales hist. Révol. fr.* 38 (1966), pp. 33–60.
Donat, J., 'Le maximum et son application dans un district de la Haute-Garonne', *Revue hist. Révol. fr.* 14 (1919–22), pp. 20, 178, 241.
Dorigny, M., 'Les causes de la Révolution selon Rœderer: une interprétation "matérialiste" de la Révolution bourgeoise', *Annales hist. Révol. fr.* 51 (1979), pp. 330–2.
'Conclusions', unpublished research summary, Sorbonne (1992).
'Les Girondins et J.-J. Rousseau', *Annales hist. Révol. fr.* 50 (1978), pp. 569–83.
'Les Girondins et le droit de propriété', *Bulletin d'histoire économique et sociale de la Révolution française*, Paris, 1983, p. 19.
'Recherches sur les idées économiques des Girondins', in A. Soboul (ed.), *Actes du Colloque Girondins et Montagnards, Sorbonne, 14 décembre 1975*, Paris, 1980, pp. 79–102.
'Soutenance de thèse sur travaux', *Annales hist. Révol. fr.* 290 (October–December 1992), pp. 597–613.
'Violence et Révolution: les Girondins et les massacres de septembre', in A. Soboul (ed.), *Actes du Colloque Girondins et Montagnards, Sorbonne, 14 décembre 1975*, Paris, 1980, p. 104.
Duperon, P., 'Etudes sur la société populaire de Castres d'après les procès-verbaux de ses séances (1er avril 1792–14 vendémiaire an II)', *Revue du Tarn* 13 (1896), p. 343, and 14 (1897), pp. 40, 146, 183, 316.
Duprat, C., 'Exposé de thèse [Le temps des philanthropes: la philanthropie parisienne des Lumières à la monarchie de Juillet]', *Annales hist. Révol. fr.* 285 (July–September 1991), pp. 387–93.

Edelstein, M., *La Feuille villageoise: communication et modernisation dans les régions rurales pendant la Révolution*, Paris, 1977.

Ehrard, J., *L'idée de nature en France au XVIIIe siècle*, 2 vols., Paris, 1963.

Ehrard, J. (ed.), 'Gilbert Romme; actes du colloque de Riom (19–20 mai 1995)', in *Annales hist. Révol. fr.* 304 (April–June 1996), pp. 189–464.

Ehrard, J., and A. Soboul (eds.), *Actes du Colloque Gilbert Romme et son temps, Riom et Clermont-Ferrand, 10–11 juin 1965*, Paris, 1966.

Eude, M., 'Le Comité de sûreté générale en 1793–1794', *Annales hist. Révol. fr.* 57 (1985), pp. 295–306.

'La politique sociale de la commune de Paris le neuf thermidor', *Annales hist. Révol. fr.* 13 (1936), pp. 289–316.

Ferry, L., 'Fichte', in Furet and M. Ozouf, *Dictionnaire critique*, 1st edn, pp. 961–5.

Ferry, L., and A. Renaut, *Philosophie politique 3: des droits de l'homme à l'idée républicaine*, Paris, 1985.

Festy, O., *L'agriculture pendant la Révolution: l'utilisation des jachères (1789–1795)*, Paris, 1950.

Forrest, A., 'Bordeaux au temps de la Gironde', in Fr. Furet and M. Ozouf (eds.), *La Gironde et les Girondins*, Paris, 1991, pp. 25–43.

'The Condition of the Poor in Revolutionary Bordeaux', in D. Johnson (ed.), *French Society and the Revolution*, Cambridge, 1976, pp. 217–47.

Conscripts and Deserters: The Army and French Society During the Revolution and Empire, Oxford, 1989.

The French Revolution, Oxford, 1995.

The French Revolution and the Poor, Oxford, 1981.

'Girondins et Montagnards dans une ville de province: l'exemple de Bordeaux', in A. Soboul (ed.), *Actes du Colloque Girondins et Montagnards, Sorbonne, 14 décembre 1975*, Paris, 1980, pp. 149–66.

'The Local Politics of Repression', in Baker, *The Terror*, pp. 81–98.

'The Revolution in Bordeaux: The Significance of the Federalist Movement of 1793', *Colloque Bordeaux et les Iles britanniques, York, 1973* (York, 1975), pp. 99–111.

Society and Politics in Revolutionary Bordeaux, Oxford, 1975.

Forrest, A., and P. M. Jones, *Reshaping France: Town, Country and Region during the French Revolution*, Manchester, 1991.

Forster, R., *The Nobility of Toulouse in the Eighteenth Century*, Baltimore, 1960.

'The Survival of the Nobility During the French Revolution', in D. Johnston (ed.), *French Society and the Revolution*, Cambridge, 1976, pp. 132–47.

Foucault, M., *Histoire de la folie à l'âge classique*, Paris, 1972; 2nd edn, Paris, 1977.

Fray-Fournier, V., *Le département de la Haute-Vienne, sa formation territoriale, son administration, sa situation politique pendant la Révolution*, 2 vols., Limoges, 1909.

Frœschlé, M. 'A propos du calendrier républicain: Romme et l'astronomie', in Ehrard, 'Gilbert Romme: actes du colloque de Riom', pp. 303–25.

Furet, Fr., 'Les Girondins et la guerre: les débuts de l'Assemblée législative', in Fr. Furet and M. Ozouf (eds.), *La Gironde et les Girondins*, Paris, 1991, pp. 189–205.

'Jacobinisme', in Furet and M. Ozouf, *Dictionnaire critique*, vol. IV, *Idées*, pp. 233–51.

Penser la Révolution française, Paris, 1978; 2nd rev. edn, Paris, 1983.

'Terreur', in Furet and M. Ozouf, *Dictionnaire critique*, vol. I, *Evénements*, pp. 293–314.

Furet, Fr., and J. Ozouf (eds.), *Lire et écrire: l'alphabétisation des Français de Calvin à Jules Ferry*, Paris, 1977.

Furet, Fr., and M. Ozouf (eds.), *Dictionnaire critique de la Révolution française*, Paris, 1988; 2nd rev. edn, 4 vols., Paris, 1992.

Gaffarel, P., 'La mission de Maignet dans les Bouches-du-Rhône et en Vaucluse (1794)', *Annales de la Faculté des Lettres d'Aix* 6 (1912), pp. 1–100.

Galante Garrone, A., *Buonarroti e Babeuf*, Turin, 1948.

Gilbert Romme: histoire d'un révolutionnaire (1750–1795), trans. A. Manceron and C. Manceron, pref. by G. Lefebvre, Paris, 1971.

Philippe Buonarroti et les révolutionnaires du XIXe siècle (1828–1837), trans. A. Manceron and C. Manceron, Paris, 1975.

Gallerand, J. 'Quelques lettres de Chabot à Rochejean', *Annales hist. Révol. fr.* 7 (1930), pp. 366–7.

Garnier, S., 'Les conduites politiques en l'an II: compte rendu et récit de vie révolutionnaires', *Annales hist. Révol. fr.* 295 (January–March 1994), pp. 19–38.

Gauthier, Fl., 'De Mably à Robespierre: un programme économique égalitaire, 1775–1793', *Annales hist. Révol. fr.* 57 (July–September 1985), pp. 265–89.

'Robespierre, critique de l'économie politique tyrannique et théoricien de l'économie politique populaire', in Jessenne *et al.*, *Robespierre*, pp. 235–43.

Triomphe et mort du droit naturel en Révolution, 1789–1795–1802, Paris, 1992.

La voie paysanne dans la Révolution française: l'exemple picard, Paris, 1977.

Gauthier, Fl. (ed.), *Colloque Mably: la politique comme science morale, Vizille, 6–8 juin 1991*, 2 vols., Bari, 1995–.

Gauthier, Fl., and G. R. Ikni (eds.), *La guerre du blé au XVIIIe siècle: la critique populaire contre le libéralisme économique*, Montreuil, 1988.

Gérard, P., 'L'armée révolutionnaire de la Haute-Garonne (septembre 1793–nivôse an II', *Annales hist. Révol.fr.* 31 (1959), pp. 1–37.

Gershoy, L., *Bertrand Barère: A Reluctant Terrorist*, Princeton, 1962.

Godechot, J., *Les commissaires aux armées sous le Directoire: contribution à l'étude des rapports entre les pouvoirs civil et militaire*, 2 vols., Paris, 1937.

'L'historiographie française de Robespierre', *Actes du Colloque Robespierre: XIIe Congrès international des sciences historiques (Vienne, 3 septembre 1965)*, Paris, 1967, pp. 191–204.

Les institutions de la France sous la Révolution et l'Empire, Paris, 1951.

Review of C. Petit, 'La terreur à Saint-Geniez d'Olt', thesis, University of Toulouse (1976), *Annales hist. Révol. fr.* 49 (1977), pp. 133–4.

Review of J. Sentou, *Fortunes et groupes sociaux à Toulouse sous la Révolution (1789–1799): essai d'histoire statistique* (Toulouse, 1969), *Annales hist. Révol. fr.* 42 (1970), p. 697.

Godineau, D., *Citoyennes tricoteuses: les femmes du peuple à Paris pendant la Révolution française*, Aix-en-Provence, 1988.

Göhring, M., *Rabaut-Saint-Etienne: ein Kämpfer an der Wende zweier Epochen*, Berlin, 1935.

Gomel, Ch., *Histoire financière de la Législative et de la Convention*, 2 vols., Paris, 1902–5.

Histoire financière de l'Assemblée constituante, 2 vols., Paris, 1896–7.

Gontard, M., *L'enseignement primaire en France de la Révolution à la loi Guizot (1789–1833): des petites écoles de la monarchie d'ancien régime aux écoles primaires de la monarchie bourgeoise*, Paris, 1959.

Gottschalk, L. R., *Jean-Paul Marat: A Study in Radicalism*, New York, 1927.

Goujard, P., 'Egalité', in Soboul, *Dictionnaire historique*, pp. 403–4.

Greer, D., *The Incidence of the Terror During the French Revolution: A Statistical Interpretation*, Cambridge, Mass., 1935.

Gros, J., *Lakanal et l'éducation nationale*, Paris, 1913.

Gross, J.-P., 'L'emprunt forcé du 10 brumaire an II et la politique sociale des Robespierristes', in A. Soboul (ed.), *Actes du Colloque Saint-Just, Sorbonne, 25 juin 1967*, Paris, 1968, pp. 74–5, 81.

'L'idée de pauvreté dans la pensée sociale des Jacobins', *Annales hist. Révol. fr.* 54 (1982), pp. 196–223.

'Note sur la portée des décrets de ventôse dans le centre et le sud-ouest', *Annales hist. Revol. fr.* 275 (January–March 1989), pp. 16–25.

'Progressive Taxation and Social Justice in Eighteenth-Century France', *Past and Present* 140 (August 1993), pp. 79–126.

'Le projet de l'an II: promotion ouvrière et formation professionnelle', *Annales hist. Révol. fr.* 300 (April–June 1995), pp. 209–21.

'La protection sociale en l'an II', in Valette, *Actes du 114e Congrès national des sociétés savantes*, pp. 155–72.

'Robespierre et l'impôt progressif', in Jessenne *et al.*, *Robespierre*, pp. 279–97.

'Saint-Just et la déclaration des droits de 1793', in Vinot, *Actes du Colloque grandes figures de la Révolution française en Picardie*, pp. 171–88.

Saint-Just: sa politique et ses missions, preface by A. Soboul, Paris, 1976.

Gueniffey, P., *Le nombre et la raison: la Révolution française et les élections*, Paris, 1993.

'Robespierre', in Furet and M. Ozouf, *Dictionnaire critique*, 2nd rev. edn, vol. II, *Acteurs*, pp. 247–58.

Guilhaumou, J., *1793: la mort de Marat*, Paris, 1989.

'Fragments of a Discourse of Denunciation (1789–1794)', in Baker, *The Terror*, pp. 139–55.

'Idéologies, discours et conjoncture en 1793: quelques réflexions sur le jacobinisme', *Dialectiques*, Paris, 1978, pp. 10–11, 33–55.

Marseille républicaine, 1791–1793, Paris, 1992.

'Robespierre, la politique, la morale et le sacré: table ronde', in Jessenne *et al.*, *Robespierre*, pp. 427–32.

Guilhaumou, J., and M. Lapied, 'La mission Maignet', *Annales hist. Révol. fr.* 300 (April–June 1995), pp. 283–94.

Guillaume, J., 'La liberté des cultes et le Comité d'instruction publique', *La Révol. fr.* 30 (1896), pp. 481–509, and 31 (1896), pp. 9–53.

Review of A. Crémieux, *Etudes sur l'histoire de l'instruction publique dans le département de l'Indre, Ie partie: l'enquête de 1791–1792* (Châteauroux, 1896), *La Révol. fr.* 32 (1897), pp. 564–7.

Gutwirth, M., 'Sacred Father, Profane Sons: Lynn Hunt's French Revolution', *French Historical Studies* 19 (Fall 1995), pp. 261–76.

Habermas, J., *Strukturwandel der Öffentlichkeit: Untersuchungen zu einer Kategorie der bürgerlichen Gesellschaft*, Neuwied, 1962; in English trans. by T. Burger and F. Lawrence, *The Structural Transformation of the Public Sphere*, Cambridge, 1992.

Theorie und Praxis: sozialphilosophische Studien, Neuwied and Berlin, 1963; in French trans., *Théorie et pratique*, Paris, 1975.

Halpérin, J.-L., *L'impossible code civil*, Paris, 1992.

Hamel, E., 'Euloge Schneider', *La Révol. fr.* 34 (1898), p. 435.

Histoire de Robespierre, 3 vols., Paris, 1865–7.

Hampson, N., 'François Chabot and His Plot', *Transactions of the Royal Historical Society* 5-26 (London, 1976), pp. 1–14.

The Life and Opinions of Maximilien Robespierre, London, 1974.

Saint-Just, Oxford, 1991.

Hanson, P. R., *The Federalist Revolt of 1793: A Comparative Study of Caen and Limoges*, Berkeley, 1981.

Harris, R. D., *Necker, Reform Statesman of the Ancien Régime*, Berkeley, 1979.

Harris, S. E., *The Assignats*, Cambridge, Mass., 1930.

Hayek, F. A., *The Fatal Conceit: The Errors of Socialism*, ed. by W. W. Bartley III, London, 1988.

Herlaut, A. P., *L'éclairage de Paris à l'époque révolutionnaire*, Paris, 1932.

Higonnet, P., '"The Harmonization of the Spheres": Goodness and Dysfunction in the Provincial Clubs', in Baker, *The Terror*, pp. 117–37.

Sister Republics: The Origins of French and American Republicanism, Cambridge, Mass., 1988.

Hill, C., *The World Turned Upside Down: Radical Ideas During the English Revolution*, London, 1972.

Hincker, Fr., 'Extinctions des impôts d'ancien régime', in Soboul, *Dictionnaire historique*, pp. 561–2.

Les Français devant l'impôt sous l'Ancien Régime, Paris, 1971.

Hirsch, J.-P., 'Terror and Property', in Baker, *The Terror*, pp. 211–22.

Hufton, O. H., *The Poor of Eighteenth-Century France, 1750–1789*, Oxford, 1974.

Women and the Limits of Citizenship in the French Revolution, Toronto, 1992.

Hunt L., *The Family Romance of the French Revolution*, Berkeley, 1992; in French translation, *Le roman familial de la Révolution française*, Paris, 1995.

'Male Virtue and Republican Motherhood', in Baker, *The Terror*, pp. 195–208.

Politics, Culture and Class in the French Revolution, Berkeley, 1984.

'Reading the French Revolution: a Reply', *French Historical Studies* 19-2 (Fall 1995), pp. 289–98.

Ikni, G. R., 'Crise agraire et révolution paysanne: le mouvement populaire dans les campagnes de l'Oise, de la décennie physiocratique à l'an II', thesis, 6 vols., Sorbonne (1993).

'Jacques-Marie Coupé, curé jacobin (1737–1809)', *Annales hist. Révol. fr.* 56 (1984), pp. 339–65; and in Gauthier and Ikni, *La guerre du blé*, pp. 159–63.

'Sur les biens communaux', *Annales hist. Révol. fr.* 54 (1982), pp. 71–94.

Jacob, L., *Hébert, le père Duchesne, chef des sans-culottes*, Paris, 1960.

Les suspects pendant la Révolution, 1789–1794, Paris, 1952.

Jaume, L., *Le discours jacobin et la démocratie*, Paris, 1989.

'Robespierre, la politique, la morale et le sacré: table ronde', in Jessenne *et al.*, *Robespierre*, pp. 427–32.

Jaume, L. (ed.), *1789 et l'invention de la constitution: Actes du Colloque de Paris, 2–4 mars 1989*, Brussels and Paris, 1994.

Jaurès, J., *Histoire socialiste de la Révolution française*, ed. by E. Labrousse and A. Soboul, 7 vols., Paris, 1969–86.

Jessenne, J.-P., *Histoire de la France: Révolution et Empire, 1783–1815*, Paris, 1993.

'The Land: Redefinition of the Rural Community', in Baker, *The Terror*, pp. 223–47.

Pouvoir au village et Révolution: Artois, 1760–1848, Lille, 1987.

Jessenne, J.-P., G. Deregnaucourt, J.-P. Hirsch and H. Leuwers (eds.), *Robespierre: de la Nation artésienne à la République et aux Nations; Actes du Colloque d'Arras, 1–2–3 avril 1993*, Villeneuve d'Ascq, 1994.

Jones, C., *The Charitable Imperative: Hospitals and Nursing in the Ancien Régime and Revolutionary France*, London, 1989.

Charity and Bienfaisance: The Treatment of the Poor in the Montpellier Region, 1740–1815, Cambridge, 1982.

'A Fine Romance with No Sisters', *French Historical Studies* 19 (Fall 1995), pp. 277–87.

Jones, P. M., 'The "Agrarian Law": Schemes for Land Redistribution During the French Revolution', *Past and Present* 133 (November 1991), pp. 96–133.

The Peasantry in the French Revolution, Cambridge, 1988.

Jorland, G., 'Le problème Adam Smith', *Annales ESC* 39 (1984), pp. 831–48.

Jouanel, A., 'La démolition du château de La Force', *Bulletin de la Société historique et archéologique du Périgord* 86 (1959), p. 183.

Kaplan, S. L., *Bread, Politics and Political Economy in the Reign of Louis XV*, 2 vols., The Hague, 1976.

The Famine Plot Persuasion in Eighteenth-Century France, Philadelphia, 1982.

Farewell Revolution: The Historians' Feud, France, 1789/1989, Ithaca, 1995.

Kates, G., *The 'Cercle Social', the Girondins and the French Revolution*, Princeton, 1985.

Kawa, C., 'Le fonctionnement d'une administration en l'an II: la Commission des subsistances', thesis, Institut d'histoire de la Révolution française, Paris (1984).

Keane, J., *Tom Paine: A Political Life*, London, 1995.

Kuscinski, A., *Dictionnaire des conventionnels*, Paris, 1916; facs. edn, Brueil-en-Vexin, 1973.

La Rochefoucauld, J. D. de, C. Wolikow and G. R. Ikni, *Le duc de La Rochefoucauld-Liancourt, 1747–1827, de Louis XV à Charles X, un grand seigneur patriote et le mouvement populaire*, Paris, 1980.

Labroue, H., *La mission du conventionnel Lakanal dans la Dordogne en l'an II (octobre 1793– août 1794)*, Paris, 1912.

La société populaire de Bergerac pendant la Révolution, Paris, 1915.

Lacape, H., *Le conventionnel Lequinio*, Bordeaux, 1955.

Laffon, R., 'La commune de Pazayac (Dordogne) pendant la Révolution', *La Révol. fr.* 66 (1914), pp. 321–47.

Laurent, G., 'La Faculté de droit de Reims et les hommes de la Révolution', *Annales hist. Révol. fr.* 6 (1929), pp. 329–58.

Le Cour Grandmaison, O., *Les citoyennetés en Révolution (1789–1794)*, Paris, 1992.

Le Roy Ladurie, E., *Le carnaval de Romans: de la Chandeleur au mercredi des Cendres, 1579–1580*, Paris, 1979.

Lefebvre, G., *Les paysans du Nord pendant la Révolution*, Paris, 1924.

Questions agraires au temps de la Terreur, Strasbourg, 1932; 2nd edn, Paris, 1954.

'Répartition de la propriété et de l'exploitation foncières à la fin de l'Ancien Régime', in *Etudes sur la Révolution française*, Paris, 1954, pp. 201–22.

La Révolution française, Paris, 1930; 3rd rev. edn, Paris, 1963.

Les Thermidoriens, Paris, 1937.

Preface to Galante Garrone, *Gilbert Romme*.

Review of A. Galante Garrone, *Buonarroti e Babeuf* (Turin, 1948), *Annales hist. Révol. fr.* 22 (1950), pp. 78–82.

Review of D. Guérin, *La lutte des classes sous la première République: bourgeois et 'bras-nus' (1793–1797)*, 2 vols. (Paris, 1946), *Annales hist. Révol. fr.* 19 (1947), pp. 173–9.

Lemay, E. H. (ed.), *Dictionnaire des Constituants, 1789–1791*, 2 vols., Oxford, 1991.

Leroy-Beaulieu, P., *Essai sur la répartition des richesses et sur la tendance à une moindre inégalité des conditions*, Paris, 1897.

Lévy-Schneider, L., *Le conventionnel Jeanbon Saint-André, membre du Comité de salut public, organisateur de la marine de la Terreur, 1749–1813*, 2 vols., Paris, 1901.

'Quelques recherches sur Jeanbon Saint-André', *La Révol. fr.* 24 (1893), pp. 415–30, and 29 (1895), pp. 64–76.

'Le socialisme et la Révolution française (à propos du livre de ce titre de A. Lichtenberger, Paris, 1898)', *La Révol. fr.* 36 (1899), pp. 116–32.

Lewis, G., *The Second Vendée: the Continuity of Counter-Revolution in the Department of the Gard, 1789–1815*, Oxford, 1978.

Lewis, G., and C. Lucas (eds.), *Beyond the Terror: Essays in French Regional and Social History, 1794–1815*, Cambridge, 1983.

Lichtenberger, A., *Le socialisme au XVIIIe siècle: étude sur les idées sociales dans les écrivains français du XVIIIe siècle avant la Révolution*, Paris, 1895.

Ligou, D., 'L'épuration des administrations montalbanaises par Baudot', *Annales hist. Révol. fr.* 26 (1954), pp. 58–62.

'Jeanbon Saint-André et la journée du 10 mai 1790 à Montauban', *Annales hist. Révol. fr.* 21 (1949), pp. 229–40.

Montauban à la fin de l'Ancien Régime at aux débuts de la Révolution française (1787–1794), Paris, 1958.

Liris, E., 'On rougit ici d'être riche', *Annales hist. Révol. fr.* 300 (April–June 1995), pp. 295–301.

Lods, A., 'Lettre à Jean Filsac, 18 juin 1793', *La Révol. fr.* 24 (1893), p. 156.

Loutchisky, J., *La propriété paysanne en France à la veille de la Révolution (principalement en Limousin)*, Paris, 1912.

Lucas, C., 'Nobles, Bourgeois and the French Revolution' (*Past and Present*, 1973), in D. Johnson (ed.), *French Society and the Revolution*, Cambridge, 1976, pp. 88–131.

'Revolutionary Violence, the People and the Terror', in Baker, *The Terror*, pp. 57–79.

'Robespierre: homme politique et culture politique', in Jessenne *et al.*, *Robespierre*, pp. 13–17.

The Structure of the Terror: The Example of Javogues and the Loire, Oxford, 1973.

Lucas, C. (ed.), *Rewriting the French Revolution* (Oxford, 1991).

Lyons, M., 'The Jacobin Elite of Toulouse', *European Studies Review* 7 (1977), pp. 259–84.

Revolution in Toulouse: An Essay on Provincial Terrorism, Bern, 1978.

Mackenzie, C. B., *The Political Theory of Possessive Individualism*, Oxford, 1962.

Property: Mainstream and Critical Positions, Oxford, 1978.

Madelin, L., *Danton*, Paris, 1914.

Fouché, 1759–1820, Paris, 1900.

Marion, M., *Histoire financière de la France depuis 1715*, 6 vols., Paris, 1914–31.

Les impôts directs sous l'Ancien Régime, principalement au XVIIIe siècle, Paris, 1910.

Marion, M., J. Benzacer and H. Caudriller, *Département de la Gironde: la vente des biens nationaux*, 2 vols., Paris, 1912.

Martin, G., *Carrier et sa mission à Nantes*, Paris, 1924.

Martin, H. (ed.), *Documents relatifs à la vente des biens nationaux dans la Haute-Garonne: district de Toulouse*, Toulouse, 1916.

Marx, K., and F. Engels, 'The Communist Manifesto' (1848), in D. J. Struik (ed.), *Birth of the Communist Manifesto*, New York, 1971.

Marx, R., *La Révolution et les classes sociales en Basse-Alsace*, Paris, 1974.

Massé, P., 'Baux à cheptel dans la Vienne sous la Révolution', in Soboul, *Contributions à l'histoire paysanne*, pp. 210–13.

Matharan, J. L., 'Suspects', in Soboul, *Dictionnaire historique*, pp. 1004–8.

'Suspects et suspicion, 1792–1794', thesis, 3 vols., Sorbonne (1985).

Mathiez, A., *Autour de Robespierre*, collected articles, 2nd edn, Paris, 1957.

'Le carnet de Robespierre: essai d'édition critique', *Annales révol.* 10 (1918), pp. 1–21.

'La Constitution de 1793', *Annales hist. Révol. fr.* 5 (1928), pp. 497–521.

La corruption parlementaire sous la Terreur, Paris, 1927.

Le Directoire, du 11 brumaire an IV au 18 fructidor an V, ed. by J. Godechot, Paris, 1934.

Etudes sur Robespierre (1758–1794), ed. by G. Lefebvre, Paris, 1973.

Girondins et Montagnards, Paris, 1930; reprint, Paris, 1973; 2nd edn, Paris, 1988.

'Lettre de Rochejean à Chabot', *Annales hist. Révol. fr.* 7 (1930), pp. 73–5.

'Le manifeste des Enragés du 23 juin 1793', *Annales révol.* 7 (1914), pp. 547–60.

'Notice sur l'article de G. Bourgin, "Synthèse bibliographique des études sur l'agriculture, la classe paysanne et la Révolution française"', *Annales révol.* 5 (1912), p. 423.

Un procès de corruption sous la Terreur: l'affaire de la Compagnie des Indes, Paris, 1920.

'La Révolution et les subsistances: l'application du premier maximum', *Annales révol.* 11 (1919), pp. 294–321 and 500–1.

'La Révolution française et les prolétaires: la loi du 13 septembre 1793, ses antécédents et son application', *Annales hist. Révol. fr.* 8 (1931), pp. 479–95.

'Robespierre et la déchristianisation', *Annales révol.* 2 (1909), p. 327.

La vie chère et le mouvement social sous la Terreur, Paris, 1927; 2nd edn, 2 vols., Paris, 1973.

Review of L. R. Gottschalk, *The Era of the French Revolution, 1715–1815* (New York, 1929), *Annales hist. Révol. fr.* 7 (1930), pp. 194–6.

Review of L. R. Gottschalk, *Jean-Paul Marat: A Study in Radicalism* (New York, 1927), *Annales hist. Révol. fr.* 4 (1927), pp. 599–602.

Review of H. Labroue, *La mission du conventionnel Lakanal dans la Dordogne en l'an II (octobre 1793–août 1794)* (Paris, 1912), *Annales révol.* 8 (1916), 438–41.

Mautouchet, P., *Le conventionnel Philippeaux*, Paris, 1901.

Mauzi, R., *L'idée du bonheur au XVIIIe siècle*, Paris, 1969.

Mazauric, C., 'Le Jacobinisme sous la Révolution', *Annales hist. Révol. fr.* 52 (1980), pp. 462–72.

Mazauric, C. (ed.), *Robespierre, écrits*, Paris, 1989.

Mazet, F. de, *La Révolution à Villeneuve-sur-Lot*, Villeneuve, 1894.

Meysonnier, S., *La balance et l'horloge: genèse de la pensée libérale en France au XVIIIe siècle*, Paris, 1989.

Michelet, J., *Histoire de la Révolution française*, ed. by G. Walter, 2 vols., Paris, 1939.

Mill, J. S., *Principles of Political Economy, with Some of Their Applications to Social Philosophy*, 2nd edn, 2 vols., London, 1849.

Miller, J. A., 'Politics and Urban Provisioning Crises: Bakers, Police and Parlements in France, 1750–1793', *Journal of Modern History* 64 (1992), pp. 227–62.

Minzes, B., *Die Nationalgüterverausserung während der französischen Revolution mit besonderer Berücksichtigung des Department Seine und Oise*, Jena, 1892.

Mollat, M., *Les pauvres au Moyen-Age: étude sociale*, Paris, 1978.

Moriceau, J.-M., 'Au rendez-vous de la "révolution agricole" dans la France du XVIIIe siècle: à propos des régions de grande culture', *Annales HSS* 1 (January–February 1994), pp. 27–63.

Nicolet, C., *L'idée républicaine en France: essai d'histoire critique*, Paris, 1982.

Noiriel, G., 'Foucault and History: The Lessons of a Disillusion' (review article), *Journal of Modern History* 66 (September 1994), pp. 547–68.

Ozouf, M., 'Egalité', in Furet and M. Ozouf, *Dictionnaire critique*, 2nd rev. edn, vol. IV, *Idées*, pp. 139–63.

La fête révolutionnaire, 1789–1799, Paris, 1976.

'Madame Roland', in Fr. Furet and M. Ozouf (eds.), *La Gironde et les Girondins*, Paris, 1991, pp. 307–27.

'La Révolution française et l'idée de fraternité', in *L'homme régénéré: essais sur la Révolution française*, Paris, 1989, pp. 158–82.

'Symboles et fonctions des âges dans les fêtes de l'époque révolutionnaire', *Annales hist. Révol. fr.* 42 (1970), pp. 569–93.

'The Terror After the Terror: An Immediate History', in Baker, *The Terror*, pp. 3–18.

Palmer, R. R., *Twelve Who Ruled: The Committee of Public Safety During the Terror*, Princeton, 1941.

Parieu, E. de, *Histoire des impôts généraux sur la propriété et le revenu*, Paris, 1856.

Pastre, M., *Le district de Grenade-Beaumont de 1790 à 1795*, Toulouse, 1948.

Patrick, A., *The Men of the First French Republic: Political Alignments in the National Convention of 1792*, Baltimore, 1972.

'Montagnards', in S. E. Scott and B. Rothaus (eds.), *Historical Dictionary of the French Revolution, 1789–1799*, 2 vols., Westport, Conn., 1985, vol. II, pp. 669–74.

Payne, H. C., '*Pauvreté, Misère*, and Enlightened Economics', *Studies on Voltaire and the Eighteenth Century* 154 (1976), p. 1581.

Perroud, C., 'Le Père Duchêne à Bergerac', *La Révol. fr.* 41 (1904), pp. 288, 459.

Petit, C., 'La terreur à Saint-Geniez d'Olt', thesis, University of Toulouse (1976).

'Le triomphe du pauvre: les pauvres contre les riches à l'époque révolutionnaire à travers une fête rouergate', *Annales du Midi* 90 (1978), pp. 141–54.

Portal, C., 'Un village pendant la Révolution: Cordes, chef-lieu de canton du Tarn', *La Révol. fr.* 26 (1894), pp. 522–47.

Poussou, J.-P., 'Recherches sur l'alphabétisation de l'Aquitaine au XVIIIe siècle', in Furet and J. Ozouf, *Lire et écrire*, Paris, 1977, pp. 294–351.

Ratineau, F., 'Les livres de Robespierre au 9 thermidor', *Annales hist. Révol. fr.* 287 (January–March 1992), pp. 131–5.

Rawls, J., 'Justice as Fairness', *Philosophical Review* 67 (April 1958), pp. 164–94.

Political Liberalism, New York, 1993.

A Theory of Justice, Oxford, 1972.

Rebérioux, M., 'Jaurès et Robespierre', *Actes du Colloque Robespierre: XIIe Congrès international des sciences historiques (Vienne, 3 septembre 1965)*, Paris, 1967, pp. 191–204.

Reinhard, M., *Le Grand Carnot*, 2 vols., Paris, 1950–2.

Revel, J., 'Robespierre, la politique, la morale et le sacré: table ronde', in Jessenne *et al.*, *Robespierre*, p. 429.

Preface to L. Hunt, *Le roman familial de la Révolution française*, Paris, 1995, pp. i–xv.

Richard, C., *Le Comité de salut public et les fabrications de guerre sous la Terreur*, Paris, 1921.

Richert, G., 'Biens communaux et droits d'usage en Haute-Garonne pendant la réaction thermidorienne', *Annales hist. Révol. fr.* 23 (1951), pp. 274–84.

Rist, Ch., 'Les rapports du Comité de mendicité de l'Assemblée constituante', *La Révol. fr.* 29 (1895), pp. 265–81.

Rose, R. B., *Gracchus Babeuf, the First Revolutionary Communist*, Stanford, 1978.

The Making of the Sans-Culottes: Democratic Ideas and Institutions in Revolutionary Paris, 1789–1792, Manchester, 1983.

'The "Red Scare" of the 1790s: The French Revolution and the "Agrarian Law"', *Past and Present* 103 (1984), pp. 113–30.

Sagnac, Ph., *La législation civile de la Révolution française (1789–1804): essai d'histoire sociale*, Paris, 1898.

Schnerb, R., 'L'application des décrets de ventôse dans le district de Thiers (Puy-de-Dôme)', *Annales hist. Révol. fr.* 6 (1929), pp. 24–33, 287–8.

Les contributions directes à l'époque de la Révolution dans le département du Puy-de-Dôme, Paris, 1933.

'Les hommes de 1848 et l'impôt', *1848 et les révolutions du XIXe siècle* 176 (1947), pp. 5–51.

'Les lois de ventôse et leur application dans le département du Puy-de-Dôme', *Annales hist. Révol. fr.* 11 (1934), pp. 403–34.

'Notes sur les débuts politiques de Couthon et des Monestier dans le département du Puy-de-Dôme', *Annales hist. Révol. fr.* 7 (1930), pp. 323–8.

Schwab, R. N., W. E. Rex and J. Lough, 'Inventory of Diderot's *Encyclopédie*', *Studies on Voltaire and the Eighteenth Century* 80 (1971), pp. 62–74; 83 (1971), p. 12; 85 (1972), p. 537.

Scott, W., *Terror and Repression in Revolutionary Marseille*, London, 1973.

Secondat, M., 'L'affermage des terres en Périgord au XVIIIe siècle (bassin de la Vézère et ses affluents)', *Actes du 82e Congrès national des sociétés savantes, Bordeaux, 1957*, Paris, 1958, p. 253.

Sedillot, R., *La maison de Wendel de 1704 à nos jours*, Paris, 1958.

Sée, H. 'Les conceptions économiques et sociales du Comité de mendicité de la Constituante', *Annales hist. Révol. fr.* 3 (1926), pp. 330–7.

Sen, A., *Inequality Reexamined*, New York and Oxford, 1992.

On Ethics and Economics, Oxford, 1987.

Poverty and Famines: An Essay on Entitlement and Deprivation, Oxford, 1982.

Sen, A., and B. Williams (eds.), *Utilitarianism and Beyond*, Cambridge, 1982.

Sentou, J., *Fortunes et groupes sociaux à Toulouse sous la Révolution (1789–1799): essai d'histoire statistique*, Toulouse, 1969.

Sewell, W. H. Jr, 'The Sans-Culotte Rhetoric of Subsistence', in Baker, *The Terror*, pp. 249–69.

Work and Revolution in France: The Language of Labor from the Old Regime to 1848, Cambridge, 1980.

Shackleton, R., *Montesquieu: une biographie critique*, trans. J. Loiseau, Grenoble, 1977.

Soboul, A., 'A propos d'une thèse récente sur le mouvement paysan dans la Révolution française (A. Ado)', *Annales hist. Révol. fr.* 45 (1973), pp. 85–101.

'Egalité: du pouvoir et des dangers des mots', *Annales hist. Révol. fr.* 46 (1974), pp. 371–9.

Problèmes paysans de la Révolution française, 1789–1848, Paris, 1976.

Les sans-culottes parisiens en l'an II, Paris, 1958.

Soboul, A. (writing as P. Derocles), *Saint-Just*, Paris, 1938.

Soboul, A. (ed.), *Contributions à l'histoire paysanne de la Révolution française*, Paris, 1977.

Dictionnaire historique de la Révolution française, ed. by J.-R. Suratteau and Fr. Gendron, Paris, 1989.

Sol, E., *Eglise constitutionnelle et église réfractaire*, Paris, 1930.

La Révolution en Quercy, 4 vols., Paris, 1926–32.

Sonenscher, M., 'A Limitless Love of Self: Marat's Grim View of Human Nature', *The Times Literary Supplement* 4827 (6 October 1995), p. 3.

'Les sans-culottes de l'an II: repenser le langage de travail dans la France révolutionnaire', *Annales ESC* 40 (1985), pp. 1087–1108.

Work and Wages: Natural Law, Politics and the Eighteenth-Century French Trades, Cambridge, 1989.

Spurlock, J., 'Essays in Reform on the Eve of Revolution: The Public Essay Contests of the Academy of Châlons-sur-Marne', *Studies on Voltaire and the Eighteenth Century* 191 (1980), p. 885.

Suratteau, J.-R., 'Fouché', in Soboul, *Dictionnaire historique*, pp. 462–7.

Sutherland, D., 'The Vendée: Unique or Emblematic?', in Baker, *The Terror*, pp. 99–114.

Sydenham, M. J., *The First French Republic, 1792–1804*, London, 1974.

The Girondins, London, 1961.

'The Republican Revolt of 1793: a Plea for less Localized Local Studies', *French Historical Studies* 12 (1981), pp. 120–38.

Tackett, T., 'The Constituent Assembly and the Terror', in Baker, *The Terror*, pp. 39–54.

Talmon, J. L., *The Origins of Totalitarian Democracy*, London, 1952.

Theuriot, F., 'La conception robespierriste du bonheur', *Annales hist. Révol. fr.* 40 (1968), pp. 207–26.

Thompson, E. P., 'L'économie morale de la foule dans l'Angleterre du XVIIIe siècle', in Gauthier and Ikni, *La guerre du blé*, pp. 31–92.

'The Moral Economy of the English Crowd in the Eighteenth Century', *Past and Present* 50 (February 1971), pp. 76–136.

Thuillier, G., 'Les secours aux parents des défenseurs de la patrie (1792–1796): orientation de recherche', in *Actes du 113e Congrès national des sociétés savantes, Strasbourg, 1988: Colloque sur l'histoire de la sécurité sociale*, Paris, 1989, pp. 459–89.

Tocqueville, A. de, *L'Ancien Régime et la Révolution*, ed. Fr. Melonio, Paris, 1988.

Trénard, L., 'Pour une histoire sociale de l'idée de bonheur au XVIIIe siècle', *Annales hist. Révol. fr.* 35 (1963), pp. 309–30, 428–52.

Troux, A., *La vie politique dans le département de la Meurthe*, 3 vols., Nancy, 1936.

Valette, J. (ed.), *Actes du 114e Congrès national des sociétés savantes, Paris, 1989: Colloque sur l'histoire de la sécurité sociale*, Paris, 1990.

Vauthier, G., 'Lettres inédites de Lakanal', *Annales révol.* 5 (1912), pp. 71–8, 250–1, and 7 (1914), pp. 109–11.

Viguier, J., 'Les émeutes populaires dans le Quercy en 1789 et 1790', *La Révol. fr.* 21 (1891), pp. 36–50.

Vinot, B., *Saint-Just*, Paris, 1985.

Vinot, B. (ed.), *Actes du Colloque Grandes figures de la Révolution française en Picardie, Blérancourt, 17–18 juin 1989*, Chauny, 1990.

Vissac, M. de, *Camboules*, Riom, 1893.

Vovelle, M., 'Une approche marxiste de la Révolution française', *Pensée* 220 (1981), pp. 121–9.

    Combats pour la Révolution Française, Paris, 1993.

    'De la biographie à l'étude de cas: Théodore Désorgues', in Vovelle (ed.), *Problèmes et méthodes de la biographie: actes du colloque, Sorbonne, 3–4 mai 1985*, Paris, 1985, pp. 191–8.

    Les métamorphoses de la fête en Provence de 1750 à 1820, Paris, 1976.

    Religion et Révolution: la déchristianisation de l'an II (dans le Sud-Est), Paris, 1976.

    La Révolution contre l'Eglise: de la Raison à l'Etre Suprême, Brussels, 1988.

Wallon, H., *Les représentants du peuple en mission et la justice révolutionnaire dans les départements en l'an II (1793–1794)*, 5 vols., Paris, 1889–90.

    La Révolution du 31 mai et le fédéralisme en 1793, ou la France vaincue par la Commune de Paris, 2 vols., Paris, 1886.

Walter, G., *Robespierre: la vie, l'œuvre*, 2 vols., Paris, 1961.

Weiner, D. *The Citizen-Patient in Revolutionary and Imperial Paris*, Baltimore, 1993.

Werhane, P., *Adam Smith and His Legacy for Modern Capitalism*, New York and Oxford, 1995.

Woloch, I., 'The Contraction and Expansion of Democratic Space During the Period of the Terror', in Baker, *The Terror*, pp. 309–25.

    Jacobin Legacy: The Democratic Movement Under the Directory, Princeton, 1970.

    The New Regime: Transformations of the French Civic Order, 1789–1820s, New York, 1994.

    'On the Latent Illiberalism of the French Revolution', *American Historical Review*, 95 (December 1990), pp. 1452–70.

Woronoff, D., *L'industrie sidérurgique en France pendant la Révolution et l'Empire*, Paris, 1984.

Index

Condorcet, Marie-Jean-Antoine Nicolas
de Caritat, marquis de 5, 11, 20, 43,
45, 68, 124, 125, 147, 148, 179, 180,
193
confiscation, *see* sequestration
Confolens 82
Constituent Assembly, *see under*
assemblies
constitution, republican 43, 46, 99, 120,
152, 188, 201
contract, social 9, 200
Convention, *see under* assemblies
Coquard, Olivier 15, 28
Cordeliers, *see under* clubs
corn trade 5, 37, 48, 68–71
corporations 154, 155, 156, 157, 161
Corrèze 21, 34, 60, 83, 87, 95, 117, 120,
129, 158–60, 169, 171, 177, 182,
184, 192
Corsica 150
corvée 150
Côtes-du-Nord 129
Coulanges-sur-Yonne 75
Coulommiers 57
counter-revolutionaries 57, 90, 96,
115–17
Coupé, Jacques-Michel (de l'Oise) 96,
182
Courrier de l'Europe 187
Couthon, Georges-Auguste 21, 22, 44,
57, 69
crafts 137, 186
craft unions, *see* corporations
craftsmen 154
apprentices 158, 160–1
journeymen 158, 160–1
master 157, 161
Creuse 18, 21, 58, 61, 74, 118, 133, 134,
138, 160, 170–2
Creuzé-Latouche, Jacques-Antoine 70
Cromwell, Oliver 20
crops
barley 85, 88, 105
buckwheat 85, 191
carry-over, *see soudure*
cash 12
chestnuts 81
chicory 191

forage 190, 191
millet 85
oats 85
pears 105
potatoes 81, 191
pulses 191
protection 190–1
roots and tubers 191
rye 78, 85, 88, 191
tobacco 138
turnips 191
vetch 192
wheat 78, 85, 88

Dacier, André 179
dancing 48, 66, 197, 198–9, 200
Danton, Georges-Jacques 14, 22, 30, 93,
127, 179, 180, 181
Darrow, Margaret 98
Dartigoeyte, Pierre Arnaud 21, 33, 85,
96, 109, 111, 115, 197
Daubenton, Louis Jean-Marie
d'Aubenton 192
Dauphiné 17
David, Marcel 47, 52, 204
dearth 75, 77, 80, 85, 165
artificial 77, 145
death
penalty 70, 93, 125
sentence 30, 93
debt, public 130
décadi 111, 187, 190, 196
declaration, *see under* independence;
rights of man
dechristianisation 23, 175, 176, 193,
197
deism 23, 35
Supreme Being 23–4, 35, 193
see also under festivals
Delaporte, André 11
democracy 1, 8, 11, 17, 24, 27, 28, 33,
45, 47, 56, 60, 62, 74, 96, 101, 115,
117, 121, 123, 143, 185, 189, 200,
201–2
dependence 145
dépôts de mendicité, see under welfare,
relief agencies
dérapages 25, 193, 197

Past and Present Publications

General Editor: JOANNA INNES, *Somerville College, Oxford*

Family and Inheritance: Rural Society in Western Europe 1200–1800, edited by Jack Goody, Joan Thirsk and E. P. Thompson*

French Society and the Revolution, edited by Douglas Johnson

Peasants, Knights and Heretics: Studies in Medieval English Social History, edited by R. H. Hilton*

Towns in Societies: Essays in Economic History and Historical Sociology, edited by Philip Abrams and E. A. Wrigley*

Desolation of a City: Coventry and the Urban Crisis of the Late Middle Ages, Charles Phythian-Adams

Puritanism and Theatre: Thomas Middleton and Opposition Drama under the Early Stuarts, Margot Heinemann*

Lords and Peasants in a Changing Society: The Estates of the Bishopric of Worcester 680–1540, Christopher Dyer

Life, Marriage and Death in a Medieval Parish: Economy, Society and Demography in Halesowen 1270–1400, Zvi Ravi

Biology, Medicine and Society 1840–1940, edited by Charles Webster

The Invention of Tradition, edited by Eric Hobsbawm and Terence Ranger*

Industrialization before Industrialization: Rural Industry and the Genesis of Capitalism, Peter Kriedte, Hans Medick and Jürgen Schlumbohm*

The Republic in the Village: The People of the Var from the French Revolution to the Second Republic, Maurice Agulhon†

Social Relations and Ideas: Essays in Honour of R. H. Hilton, edited by T. H. Aston, P. R. Coss, Christopher Dyer and Joan Thirsk

A Medieval Society: The West Midlands at the End of the Thirteenth Century, R. H. Hilton

Winstanley: 'The Law of Freedom' and Other Writings, edited by Christopher Hill

Crime in Seventeenth-Century England: A County Study, J. A. Sharpe†

The Crisis of Feudalism: Economy and Society in Eastern Normandy, c. 1300–1500, Guy Bois†

The Development of the Family and Marriage in Europe, Jack Goody*

Disputes and Settlements: Law and Human Relations in the West, edited by John Bossy

Rebellion, Popular Protest and Social Order in Early Modern England, edited by Paul Slack

English and French Towns in Feudal Society: A Comparative Study, R. H. Hilton*

An Island for Itself: Economic Development and Social Change in Late Medieval Sicily, Stephan R. Epstein

Epidemics and Ideas: Essays on the Historical Perception of Pestilence, edited by Terence Ranger and Paul Slack*

The Political Economy of Shopkeeping in Milan, 1886–1922, Jonathan Morris

After Chartism: Class and Nation in English Radical Politics, 1848–1874, Margot C. Finn

Commoners: Common Right, Enclosure and Social Change in England, 1700–1820, J. M. Neeson*

Land and Popular Politics in Ireland: County Mayo from the Plantation to the Land War, Donald E. Jordan Jr*

The Castilian Crisis of the Seventeenth Century: New Perspectives on the Economic and Social History of Seventeenth-Century Spain, edited by I. A. A. Thompson and Bartolomé Yun Casalilla

The Culture of Clothing: Dress and Fashion in the Ancien Regime, Daniel Roche*

The Sense of the People: Politics, Culture and Imperialism in England, 1715–1785, Kathleen Wilson

God Speed the Plough: The Representation of Agrarian England, 1500–1660, Andrew McRae

Fair Shares for All: Jacobin Egalitarianism in Practice, Jean-Pierre Gross

The Wild and the Sown: Botany and Agrriculture in Western Europe, 1350–1850, Mauro Ambrosoli

* Published as a paperback

† Co-published with the Maison des Sciences de L'Homme, Paris